SEA STORIES

OF

A

U.S. MARINE

BOOK 2

ROTORHEADS

BY
W.R. SPICER

DEDICATED

TO FAMILY
TO FRIENDS
TO FALLEN COMRADES
TO ALL MARINES

AND

ALL ROTORHEADS

PREFACE

DEFINITION: ROTORHEAD, n. A helicopter pilot or member of a helicopter crew. (Military. A term of address.)

The United States Marine Corps is one of the most unique military organizations in the World. It is unique because it possesses its own air power. The Marine Corps identifies the organization as the "Air Ground Team" and as such has fully integrated the use of air power, both rotary and fixed wing, into its entire scheme of maneuver.

Helicopter assets provide exceptional battlefield mobility from both land and ship, while fixed wing assets provide "Close Air Support" able to bomb targets in a very timely manner also from both land and ship bases. Many people are surprised to learn that all the aircraft are manned and piloted by Marines. They were all trained as Marines first and then go on to training as pilots or aircrew. It's "Air for Marines by Marines".

After becoming Marines, the officers volunteering for flight duty are sent to the U.S. Naval Flight School in Pensacola and are trained as "Naval Aviators". Here they earn their "Wings of Gold" designation as pilots or aircrew before returning to the Fleet Marine Forces. It is also here at Pensacola the officers under training make a basic decision: Rotary or Fixed wing.

They are all trained initially to fly fixed wing but the decision to specialize in helicopters sets the pilot trainees on a different course and if they have chosen helicopters, they will eventually be affectionately referred to by their fellow Marines as "Rotorheads".

4

PROLOGUE

I'd quit college, just walked away from a full football scholarship. I was in that purgatory of youth searching for myself and a direction for my life. Joining the service seemed the logical thing to do. The Military draft was breathing down my neck, I didn't like college, I didn't have a job that meant anything more to me than a paycheck and certainly didn't provide for any type of future. Sooner or later the military obligation would have to be fulfilled, so why not go ahead and get it over with.

The three and a half years I served as an enlisted man after joining the Marine Corps had literally been my "Trial by Fire". I'd seen over half of the world, served in combat and found myself. When the Marine Corps offered me a chance to get a commission and I'd obtained it, I'd found my direction. Along the way I'd found the perfect person to share my direction, as well as the love of my life.

TABLE OF CONTENTS

CHAPTER ONE

PENSACOLA HERE WE COME

Marine Officers Basic School
Class 3-66
Marine Corps Base Quantico, Virginia
April 1966

We'd already been told that our class was the crest of a huge build up in preparation for expanding the war in Vietnam. So when we graduated in May most of us would be on our way to Vietnam very shortly. "They" had even sent a Lieutenant Colonel down from headquarters to talk about our futures.

Normally an officer would be a 2nd Lieutenant for 18 months, a 1st Lieutenant for about 3 ½ years, then, receive promotion to Captain with about 5 years total service. The Lieutenant Colonel told us "to learn our lessons well because those of us who could stand and muster would all be Captains within 36 months." We were amused and there was a slight ripple of laughter then but he wasn't laughing. The Basic School Staff that were in attendance didn't laugh either. Their silence provided a definite sobering effect. It was the "Stand and Muster" part that was difficult to believe.

The Basic School here at Quantico was the next step in the commissioning process. You received a commission after ten weeks of Officers Candidate School but you kept it by successfully completing the Basic School. It was the Marine Corps version of "War College" for 2nd Lieutenants. You learned your trade and in the process were able to decide what specialty you wanted to pursue. That specialty was known as your MOS or Military Occupational Specialty. This process was a little like medical school. Here at the Basic School you were exposed to it all. You fired every weapon, drove every piece of equipment, blew up anything that would explode; the only thing we didn't get to try was flying a plane. We got to ride in planes and helicopters and worked with them on exercises to learn their capabilities but that was the extent of our exposure.

Just like medical school where students are rotated through all the various departments and then allowed to pick a specialty: surgery, dermatology, general practice and so on. For us it was things like infantry, artillery, tanks and lots of other fields. It was competitive as hell. The higher your class standing, the greater chance you had of getting the MOS you wanted. Once all the fields were filled, you were assigned what was left over," according to the needs of the service". The only exception to that rule was aviation. If you volunteered and could qualify mentally and physically, you went to flight school.

Our syllabus had been shortened by several weeks. Normally Basic School was six months but we were doing it in 21 weeks. "They" didn't want to drop anything from the syllabus so we worked six days a week and were prepared to work seven should the need arise. Having started in January and progressed to April we were well past half way and had reached that point in school when it was time to submit your "dream sheet," which was your first three choices for an MOS.

Since starting in January, working our way through snow storms and other bad weather, there hadn't been much mention of Vietnam. Our training hadn't reflected any lessons learned from over there because not very many Marines had served there, yet. So as we were approaching the end of our training, the realities of what was in our immediate future suddenly came to the forefront. The forthcoming MOS selection would have a lot to do with determining your fate in more ways than one.

22 April, 1966, Friday

The mechanism that Basic School used to aid in the process of MOS selection was an "MOS Party". The MOS Party was held in a huge hall at the Basic School Bachelor Officers Quarters (BOQ). Essentially it was a "Beer Bust" with "small groceries". The school staff invited officers who were stationed at Quantico to represent their particular MOS. There were signs posted on the huge columns indicating the field, 03 Infantry, 08 Artillery, 7500 Aviation, and so on. The guest officers took up station under the sign for their field. Their job was to answer all the Lieutenants questions about the field and even try and "recruit" any good prospects into that particular MOS. The MOS party created an informal and relaxed atmosphere which was certainly welcomed by the Lieutenants.

My brand new bride, Marguerite, had found a position at the First National Bank of Quantico and before I left our apartment this morning I told her today was the MOS party and I would be late getting home. The bank was open late on Friday's so she told me it wasn't a problem but I would have to treat her to dinner when I got home.

Our apartment complex was brand new and all twelve units were occupied by brand new 2nd Lieutenants and their brand new wives. All of them were my classmates so it was really hard to keep secrets. I told her we might have some guests that would want to go out for dinner with us.

The party started at 16:30 (4:30pm) and I'd planned to meet my buddy Rusthoven and go with him. We were starting to get quite a history. We'd known each other since Sea School; served on the same aircraft carrier occasionally, gone to OCS on the same commissioning program and he'd been the best man at my wedding. His enlisted MOS had been in the 01 Field, administration and mine had been 03 Infantry. Russ and I had given aviation

9

some serious thought but weren't sure we'd qualify. We'd agreed that 03, Infantry was where we wanted to be.

I met up with Russ outside the BOQ (Bachelor Officers Quarters) and we went straight over to the party. Just inside the doors to the big hall we took a couple seconds to get our bearings and finally saw the big 03, Infantry sign on one of the posts. The crowd there was pretty large.

We decided to make a stop by the beer and "small groceries" station on our way. As we were heading in that direction we had to pass the column that had the 7500, Aviation sign adorned with a huge set of gold navy pilot and flight officer wings. Standing there was the only officer on the basic school staff that was an aviator: Capt Chuck "Buddha" McLennan.

Capt McLennan was a little shorter than most of the officers on the staff, a little stocky, a hell of an athlete and just plain "Cool". Based on all the other Naval Aviators I'd been around while on Sea Duty, he fit the mold. He was always sharp as a tack; he always knew the answer, never got excited and considered nothing too difficult. He was my favorite officer here; I had a lot of respect and admiration for him and not just because he was a pilot, which made things even better.

All Navy and Marine pilots are trained at the Naval Air Training Command in Pensacola. The selection process is very rigid and demanding. I'd heard that the men who qualified for the Navy Flight training program were in the top three percent mentally and physically of all males in the age group 19 to 26. Navy Flight School was eighteen months of intensive training and the government investment in a pilot was well over a million dollars. If you made it and were awarded your "Wings of Gold," you were the best of the best. You weren't just a pilot you were a "Naval Aviator". The one thing that separated you from all the other pilots in the United States Military was you could take an aircraft and land it on a ship, in daylight or dark.

It was with this knowledge that Rusthoven and I really hadn't given much thought to the 7500, Aviation field. For a couple of years as "Sea Going Marines" both of us had watched Naval Aviators, both Navy and Marine, land on aircraft carriers in daylight, dark, good weather , really bad weather and some with battle damage coming back from missions over North Vietnam.   We'd seen some crash and die as well.   We both thought these guys were some of the bravest, coolest guys in the world. I couldn't speak for Russ but being a pilot had always been one of my dreams but I didn't think there was any way in hell I would ever qualify or be good enough.

We'd grabbed a beer, a handful of "small groceries" and were almost past the 7500 Aviation column when we heard this voice saying, "And just where do you two think you're going?"

We turned and both saw Capt McLennan at the same time and said, "Good Afternoon Sir."

Russ said, "Well Captain, Spice and I are on our way over to sign up for the Grunts, you know, Infantry, 03.

"Yeah, I know what a grunt is and anybody can be a damn grunt but not everybody can be a Naval Aviator, so come on over here and sign up for Aviation, pilot training. You're gonna be a hell of a lot more valuable to the Corps as a pilot than as a grunt."

I said, "Well I can understand that sir but I don't think I can pass test. When I went through Boot Camp I was told I qualified for the Marine Aviation Cadet Program but then "They" said my eyes weren't good enough."

"What the hell do 'They' know, when you were in Boot Camp 'They' probably got you up at 4 in the morning, kicked your ass and then sent you over to sick bay to have your eyes checked by some disinterested Corpsman.   I know neither one of you is stupid, I've seen your class standings so here's a thought, 'Take the damn test, it's free'."

Russ and I looked at each other; the good Captain had a point. Without saying a word to one another we turned toward the Captain and said, "Ok sir, where do we sign?"

Capt McLennan produced a clip board with a signup sheet and it was all over in a matter of seconds. He told us we would be notified fairly quickly about the aptitude test and flight physical. After we'd signed up there wasn't much left to do.

Russ and I hung around with the Captain, he said we would be good advertising and we did get some of our classmates stopping by with some interest. Two more guys we knew signed up and then Russ and I slowly drifted off on our own.

During the time we were hanging around I mentioned to Capt. McLennan that I was worried about passing the eye test. He told me to check out a book store in D.C., and look for a book called "Sight Without Glasses" by Harold M. Peppard. He said to get the book as soon as I could and follow the instructions to the letter doing the exercises every day until the flight physical and to keep doing them until I passed the flight physical in Pensacola.

Before we left the party Russ and I agreed that our choices on the dream sheet would be Aviation, Infantry and Artillery. I also asked Russ if he had any concerns about the eye test or any part of the flight physical and he didn't. He had a dinner date with some gal from D.C. and wasn't interested in hanging around much longer. I was anxious to get home and tell Marguerite the news so we left the party.

Marguerite's only question about flight school was "Where is Pensacola?" When I told her Florida I didn't get much reaction at all. After a minute or so she said, "You mean we're going to live in Florida for a while?

"That's right my dear. Sunshine, beautiful white sand beaches, palm trees; the whole works."
I got no other response other than, "Hmmm."

Over the weekend we got up to DC, found the book store and acquired a copy of "Sight Without Glasses". I spent the rest of the weekend reading it from cover to cover and during the self- test with the enclosed eye chart discovered that my suspicions were correct, my left eye was just borderline 20/20. For flight school your eyes had to be 20/20 or better and you also had to pass several additional eye tests.

I set up a program of exercises following the instructions to the letter. I decided that if once a day was good then twice a day would be even better. Marguerite thought I was going over the top a little but if it made the difference between going to flight school or not, then I was going over the top.

I did my eye exercises every morning and evening without fail and took the aviation aptitude test the following week. The results were posted on Friday. Russ and I went over to the administration bulletin board to look together. Guys were milling around, going up and having a look and then walking away without saying a word. When we saw the list of course the first thing we looked for were our names.

Rusthoven, B.R., Naval Flight Officer, (NFO)
Spicer, W.R., Naval Aviator (Pilot/NA)

When I read my name I could feel my pulse quicken; I was half way there, only the flight physical stood between me and a dream I thought was impossible. I didn't want to say a thing. Russ appeared disappointed by not qualifying for pilot training. Naval Flight Officer was a new thing especially for the Marine Corps, a completely new field so no one really knew what the career possibilities were going to be. An NFO would fly in aircraft that needed two crewmen, like an F-4 Phantom or an A-6 Intruder. They operated the weapons systems which was extremely important.   Although disappointed, he was undeterred and we both still had the flight physical hurdle to get over. We felt pretty damn good because less than half the names on the list even passed the test.   There was a note at the bottom of the list telling us to be at the Airfield Dispensary on Monday morning, 0700 for flight physicals and not to eat or drink anything before showing up.

Russ wasn't worried about the eye exam at all.   The vision requirements for NFO weren't quite as stringent as for pilot training, besides he'd already used my eye chart for a test and he had eyes like a damn eagle.   I think he read at 20/15.   When I'd started my exercises, I'd read at 20/30 sometimes in the left eye and 20/20 in the right eye. Sometimes the left eye would be a shaky 20/20. The exercises were working because I was now reading the chart with a solid 20/20 score, but that was on my chart in my apartment.

I tried not to think about the physical over the weekend but didn't do a very good job. Marguerite did her best to try and take my mind off of it but this could be a dream come true.   I might not make it through flight school, but just to have the chance meant so much to me.

The Flight Physical
The air station at Quantico is like a small base within a base and sits well away from the main gate and right on the Potomac River. It's pretty much self-contained and its medical facility is the only place on the base set up for aviation medicine, complete with flight surgeons.

I arrived at 0645 along with a classmate, friend and neighbor, Rod Bell.   Rod and I had been in the same platoon in OCS and he was one of the many Lieutenants, like me, who'd been married between OCS and Basic School and now lived in the same new apartments in the little town of Triangle.

14

I'm not sure Rod had any intention of going to flight school when he signed up for Marine OCS and probably thought it sounded interesting and might be fun to do. He had a Master's Degree in Mathematics from California Polytechnic Institute. He was really smart, never seemed to study, but always got one of the top grades in the class. He could never find his wallet, he would occasionally forget his rifle or some other piece of equipment, and when chastised about his forgetfulness seemed unaware that anything could possibly be wrong. He was an exceptional athlete and most things came very easily to him except for those pesky little details.

This morning he was not the least concerned about our flight physical and I wasn't surprised when he nodded off for a quick nap while we were seated in the Dispensary hallway outside the first testing station for the flight physical, the initial eye check. The procedure was used as a screening. If you didn't pass the initial eye check you would be dismissed and sent back to Basic School; there was no point in continuing the examination.

We were told to be here at 0700 but the only person here when we arrived had been the Duty Corpsman. Apparently the Navy didn't start work until 0800. So we sat and watched as the corpsman slowly filtered into their work stations, got their morning coffee and prepared for work. It was 0800 and we hadn't seen an officer appear.

The waiting didn't help my nervousness one bit but Rod helped to break up the tension. After about a twenty minute nap, he decided to have a look around. He went into the eye screening room and was having a look at the equipment and spent some extra time looking at the large eye chart that was hanging on the far wall. When he returned I asked him if he found anything particularly interesting. He told me he didn't and, except for the eye chart, didn't have a clue as to the purpose for the rest of the equipment.

15

Finally at 0815 the corpsman for the eye screening station called in the first man. I didn't know the guy because his name must have started with A and I was too far down the alphabet in our class to have known him other than by sight. Rod Bell was called next, and as the first man came out, we all wanted to know what was taking place.

"You read the eye chart on the wall, do a depth perception test, they put a thing like a ruler on your nose and slide a little square thing with letters down the stick and as soon as you can read it they stop and take a measurement. The last thing they do is put drops in your eyes to dilate your pupils. We will all have to go back and the flight surgeon will put a light in our eyes checking something, that's all I know. It's a piece of cake, no sweat."

I moved to a seat across the passageway so I could see into the room and also hear the corpsman's instructions and Rod's responses.

"All right, Lt Bell is it"?

"Yes, that's correct."

"Ok Lt, with this patch stick please cover your left eye and read the lowest line on the big chart at the end of the room."

I watched Rod cover his eye and then pause for a moment.

"American Optical Company, Bedford, New York."

"I meant the lowest line of letters but where in the hell did you see that?"

"It's at the bottom of the chart, down there at the very bottom."

I watched the corpsman walk the length of the room to the big eye chart and lift it up so he could get a better look at the bottom of the chart.

"Shit, it does say American Optical Company, Bedford, New York."

"I already told you it did."

"Ok Sir, well humor me and read the lowest line of letters you can read."

Rod read off the very bottom line of letters in rapid fashion.

"Now Sir, please cover your right eye and do the same for me."

"You want me to read the American Optical Company or the letters?"

"Just the letters please sir that will be good enough."

Rod rattled off the bottom line of letters and I quit watching to keep from bursting out laughing.

When my turn finally came I think I could have passed the test without even looking at the chart but I was still very nervous when I sat down in the chair. I was elated when the twenty/twenty line appeared crystal clear with both eyes. I could feel my entire body relax and I really didn't pay much attention to the other tests or the drops being put in my eyes. What really got my attention was when I heard the corpsman say, "Next Officer, please."

I drifted through the rest of the physical and was a little bit nervous when I came in to see the Flight Surgeon. I'd already seen another one for the "touchy feely" part but this was the final check of the eyes.

The Flight Surgeon had me put my head in this device so I had to look straight ahead and then began shining a very bright light into my eyes, one at a time. Curiosity got the best of me and I finally asked him what he was looking for.

"Any abnormalities at the back of your eyes. I'm also taking a measurement, or refraction, of light. We measure the refraction of light on a cylindrical meridian and this measurement allows us to determine how well your eyes are constructed."

"Oh, I wish I knew what that meant."

"You will some day. You're finished; send in the next man please."

"You mean I passed, everything is ok?"

17

"You passed with flying colors Lt, you've got great eyes."

I did tell the next guy to go in but after that I think I floated out of the place. Rod was waiting for me at the car. He was smoking a cigarette and drinking a coke. He held up the coke and said, "I didn't know if you wanted breakfast or not."

We were required to finish the day at the Basic School so I headed the car in that direction.

"Ok Rod, you gonna tell me what that was you had going on with the corpsman at the eye screening?"

"Well, I was getting pretty annoyed with them letting us sit on our asses for an hour plus so I decided to screw with them a little. I went in and memorized the bottom five lines of the chart, including the American Optical line. Just thought I'd pull their chain a little for the inconvenience."

When we arrived back at The Basic School I used the phone in the student administration office to make a very important phone call. I called Marguerite at the bank where she was working. Her boss was a very nice lady that had worked at that bank for years. She liked Marguerite very much and I'd met her a couple of times.

"Well she can't come to the phone right now Bill but I'll be glad to take a message. What would you like for me to tell her?"

"Miss Cloe, message is as follows; Pensacola here we come."

CHAPTER TWO

PREFLIGHT AND THE MYSTERY HOUR

Naval Air Basic Training Command
Naval Air Station, Pensacola, Florida
Duty: Student Naval Aviator
July 1966

As usual, the graduation from the Basic School was anticlimactic. The majority of my classmates were given
thirty days leave enroute to their assignments in Vietnam.
The Lt's selected for NFO (Naval Flight Officer) training
were given leave enroute to Naval Air Basic Training
Command, NAS Pensacola and for those of us selected for
Naval Pilot Training, we were held on the base at Quantico
until a "slot" opened up in the pilot training "pipeline"
down in Pensacola.

Since graduating in May, those of us waiting for orders
to Pensacola were immediate candidates for all sorts of
"keep busy" jobs and mine had been as executive officer of
a schools demonstration troops company. It was one of the
better jobs. When the Captain that was the Commanding
Officer of the company saw that I was ex-enlisted with
some combat ribbons on my shirt, he immediately put in
for two weeks leave; making me the acting commanding
officer. It wasn't all that bad, my contemporaries were
scattered all over the base doing all manner of things and
were referred to as SLJO's (Shitty Little Jobs Officers).

Although it had only been a few days over a month, the
wait for orders seemed much longer. We had moved out
of our little apartment in Triangle and moved into base
housing. Marguerite had given her notice at the bank, but
her boss Miss Cloe told her she could stay right up until the
day she left. We'd shipped what little household effects

we had and were basically living out of our suitcases so it was great news when the Captain told me I had orders for Pensacola and could detach Friday, 1 July. We'd be on our way in 48 hours.

As thousands had done before us, we left Quantico heading for the unknown and I think both of us felt a great sense of adventure. Marguerite had never been to Florida and I had only been once, a brief trip to Fort Lauderdale when I was in high school and that was it.

It was to be about a 1000 mile drive with both cars pretty well packed. Since I was driving my 1955 Volkswagen bug I led and Marguerite would follow in our 1963 Thunderbird. She said she was worried about keeping up but I really didn't see there could be a problem.

The trip went well for the most part. Marguerite kept telling me I was going too fast and she was having trouble keeping up but all I could do about that was laugh. To say I was "driven" to get there might have been a fair statement but I was pretty sure my '55 VW wasn't ever gonna press that T-Bird for speed.

We both knew we were traveling on a holiday weekend but really didn't give it all that much thought. We cut down through Georgia and across the northern tip of the Okefenokee Swamp. For a couple of kids from the north these scenes were really something. We dropped out of Georgia and the first big town we came to in Florida was Tallahassee.

It had been a rough couple of days and while we were refueling Marguerite suggested we find a motel for the night and quit. I looked at the map and Pensacola was only about 200 more miles and I told her I was just too anxious about getting there to quit, so we pressed on to Pensacola.

Neither of us had any idea about what a popular beach attraction Pensacola was for tourists. We were just thinking Navy Flight School. We arrived well after dark and very tired. It came as a great surprise that there wasn't a motel room to be had anywhere, the motel clerks gave us funny looks and told us that it was Fourth of July weekend and they'd been booked for months. One clerk told us we might be allowed to sleep on the beach but couldn't give us any idea of how to get there.

We'd come into town on a road called Scenic Highway which ran along high bluffs overlooking what I thought was probably a bay. There had been plenty of places to pull off the road and park so we back tracked out Scenic Highway and finally found a parking place that had just enough room left for two cars. Evidently we weren't the only people without a motel reservation.

After thinking it over for a few minutes we decided that it would be easier to take the seats out of the VW and make beds in there rather than unload and try to sleep in the T-Bird. It didn't take long for me to realize that my anxiousness to arrive in Pensacola had completely clouded any good judgment and we were in for a very hot, sticky, uncomfortable, mosquito-filled night. To make matters worse, I really didn't have to check into the base until Friday. I think Marguerite realized that for me this had been a dream and she was willing to overlook my bad judgment and humor me even if she was miserable. We were both very relieved to see the sun rise.

After putting the VW back together we found a place for breakfast and bought a local paper. Even though it was a major holiday weekend we decided to house hunt. By late afternoon on the Fourth we'd found a modest two bedroom house on Winehurst Street in Pensacola. Our landlord was a local fellow with a very southern accent and manner. He introduced himself as "Red" and didn't seem to think our house hunting on the Fourth of July was strange at all, he'd "Hepped a lot of service boys over the years". He also told us if we wanted to "Do any painting or fixen up we was more than welcome to do it."

21

I was all set to check in on Tuesday morning but Marguerite decided to help me stop the nonsense and wisely suggested a much better plan. She convinced me to use the next few days to get our household effects delivered, clean the place up and get settled in so that when I did check in I could turn my full attention to my new duties. She also told me she was pregnant.

MARDET NABTC PENSACOLA (MARINE AVIATION DETACHMENT NAVAL AIR BASIC TRAINING COMMAND)

Checking in with the MARDET was the easy part. The admin guys were all ready for us so that part didn't take long at all. It was obvious right from the start that things would come at you fast and furious. If you didn't keep up you were gone and as I was checking in there were three or four guys checking out because they didn't make it through some phase of training.

We all didn't check in at exactly the same time but by lunch time there were ten new Marine flight students sitting in the snack bar comparing notes. We'd been issued book bags full of all sorts of texts, a complete schedule for the next six weeks. Our Preflight Class would consist of 30 officers, ten Marine and twenty Navy.

Our first four weeks would be all academics. The Navy guys had some physical training to keep up with but for the Marines it was optional. Our classes would start on Monday. First there was a welcome aboard followed by a math and physics inventory exam. The "word" was that if you didn't pass the math and physics inventory exam, you would be held back one week for review and tested again. If you failed that time you were gone. After the math and physics inventory, classes would start in earnest with aircraft engines, hydraulics and aerodynamics.

Tom Presley had a buddy that was a couple months ahead of us and was getting the "Word" on preflight. Tom also told us that this business of being held back for a review was called "Stupid Study". If you bilged (failed) a subject, you were given a week of instruction, one on one, with an expert. If you'd qualified mentally and physically "They" really didn't want to let you go unless you just couldn't get the material. I breathed a sigh of relief when I heard that because I was never a whiz in math, had been out of school for four years, had never taken calculus and really wasn't sure how you spelled aerodynamics.

We were all finished for the day so after lunch I was going to have a look around the main side base and then go home. I was really curious about when we actually got our hands on an airplane and was disappointed to learn from Presley that the airplane part wouldn't come for at least six weeks and we would be sent out to Saufley Field, a small airfield north of town for Primary Flight.

As I was heading out to the parking lot my pal Rod Bell caught up with me and wanted to know if I could handle a couple of house guests for the weekend or maybe longer. Seems Rod and his wife Nancy, had taken off on a long trip up to New York before coming south to Florida. Rod had drawn 3 months advance pay, (called a Dead Horse) to pay for seeing the sights of New York, purchasing a brand new Ford Mustang for the trip and wound up so broke they were borrowing money from gas station attendants, with a promise to send it back, just to get to Pensacola. He remarked that being a Marine Officer went a long way with people trusting you.

"Jesus Christ Rod, what the hell were you thinking? Do you have any idea how long it will take you to pay off your Dead Horse?"

"Well not really, that's why I came to see you, you've been around."

"I guess you better follow me home then."

"Hey great, but I need a small immediate loan for some gas."

"Here's 5 bucks, where's your car?"

He proudly pointed to a new 1966 Mustang, sitting about ten cars away in the parking lot. Nancy waved when she saw me looking.

"You left her sitting in the car all this time?"

"Well you know Nancy, she's a little pissed that we ran out of money."

On the way home I thought about Rod and those "Pesky little details" that he so often over looked. Marguerite took it in stride that we would have a couple of house guests until they could get their feet on the ground. Any one of us would have done the same for each other, that's just the way it was, an unwritten code, if you ever needed help all you had to do was ask.

I spent the weekend going through the materials in my book bag while Rod and Nancy tried to find a place to live. By Monday, they were still going to be house guests and Rod wanted to leave the car for Nancy to continue the hunt, hopefully with Marguerite's help. So once again it would be Rod and I driving to work in my old VW.

On Monday, in the big auditorium on the base, we met the Navy officers that would be our Preflight class mates. I believe all but a very few had just graduated from the United States Naval Academy. They carried their slide rules in a leather case on their belts. They were all very self-assured, some might have said cocky. All the names of our class were called out and once everyone had been identified we were seated as a group.

A Navy Lieutenant walked out on the stage, didn't bother to introduce himself but did introduce a Navy Captain. The Captain was wearing wings and lots of ribbons. He paused for a very long time and finally congratulated us for making it to flight school and told us we were about to enter a period of training that would be the most challenging thing we'd ever done in our "young lives".

The Captain said, "Gentlemen I want you to look at the person sitting to your left and right. If you stay in Naval Aviation for a twenty year career, one of you won't be there at the end. Naval Aviation or the type of flying you will be doing is inherently dangerous and has no respect for inattentiveness, it has no respect for rank or position, its penalties for poor performance are severe and the dangers exist whether someone is shooting at you or not. Learn your lessons well. Welcome aboard, and Good Luck".

Most of my fellow classmates took the sobering welcome aboard rather lightly I thought. In any case it was on to the biggy of the day for me, the math and physics inventory exam. Not far from the auditorium was the classroom building for Pre-Flight. A big bulletin board in the main hall indicated where we were to report for our test. For our class it was a room on the second deck and even though I would be a good twenty minutes early I went straight up to the room.

I wanted to take a few minutes and think about the task at hand. I hadn't had any math or physics for four years. My math skills had always been suspect and I had struggled through Algebra, Geometry, both solid and plane. The last math I'd taken was trigonometry. Calculus was the next math course offered after Trig and when I found out it wasn't a requirement for my course of study I drew the line at Trig. I'd always liked physics and did well in that course, would have done even better except for my poor math skills. So this test which was coming at me right up front was going to be a big hurdle.

Everyone was in their seats five minutes before the appointed time, except for one Lt R. Bell who managed to arrive just as the Navy LT who was giving us the exams walked in the door. Lt. Anderson introduced himself and told us that we would now begin the Math and Physics inventory exam. Each test would be the standard Navy 40 question exam. We would finish our exams at noon and then we were to come back and check in at the office window on the first floor for our results at 1300. If you passed, our first class would be tomorrow commencing at 0800, in this building, second deck, aircraft engines. If you didn't, there would be instructions for remedial study and your fate would be determined at a later date. He actually asked if anyone had any questions before he passed out the test and surprisingly no one did. As he was passing out the tests I noticed the Naval Academy guys pulling their slide rules out of the leather cases and placing them on their desks. This made me just a little nervous.

It was just a few minutes after 0900 and we had until 1200 to turn in our exams. I thought the best thing for me to do was have a close look through the whole damn thing right away. There were forty questions combined on Algebra, Geometry and Trig, forty questions on Calculus and the same for physics. They were all multiple choice, which was a real break for someone like me. There was still one hell of a lot of questions to be answered in 180 minutes.

I was very surprised at how quickly a lot of information came back to me once I started on the test. As I went through the first forty questions of Algebra, Geometry and Trig I was very confident in my answers. The test was hard enough to make sure you had a good grasp of the subject but I was pretty sure you didn't have to be a straight A math student to pass. I finished the first part in good time and turned to the Calculus section. Since I had never taken a minute of Calculus the words on the paper might as well have been Greek; I didn't have a clue. I decided not to panic and moved on to the last part, physics.

Here I found much more comfortable territory. I was very confident in most of my answers, and remembered a lot more of the formulas than I thought I would have. If I didn't blow the math part of working the formula I thought

I would do pretty well here. I finished this section quickly and turned back to the Calculus.

I read over several of the questions and thought I would just make a logical, educated, calculated guess at each answer and hope for the best. After reading the fourth question I knew that idea was simply "Bullshit"! I didn't understand a word of the question so how the hell was I going to make a "Logical, Educated, Calculated Guess?" I still had bags of time, but no matter how long I sat here wouldn't make a bit of difference. I had a good look around the room. Everyone had his head down in deep concentration and the Navy guys were about to burn up their slide rules sliding them back and forth. I thought what the hell, rolled my answer sheet over to the calculus test answer section, took my no.2 pencil and went straight down the page marking "C" for all forty questions. I folded up my test booklet, got up and turned it in to Lt. Anderson. I was the first officer to do this.

"You've still got plenty of time to double check all your answers Lieutenant."

"I know sir, but I doubt it's going to make much difference."

"Ok, we will see you down at the office window at 1300."

"Please tell Lt Bell I'll be in the snack bar at the PX across the street." I said it loud enough so Rod and the other Marines would hear me and saw Rod give a slight nod. Lt Anderson gave me a funny look and I didn't expect him to do it but my ploy to get Rod that message without speaking directly to him had worked.

I sat in the snack bar for over an hour before Rod and a couple of the other Marines came in and joined me. Over lunch there was a lot of discussion but the one thing that stuck in my mind was Rod's comments about the Calculus part of the test. Here was a guy with a Master's Degree in mathematics from Cal Poly University.

27

"Damn, I thought that Calculus section was really hard, how about you guys? I think in order to score well on that you would have had to just finish a Calculus course. I'd almost bet that if you got one or two right you would probably pass."

Lt's Mel Gibbs and Bob Reedhill both shrugged their shoulders and both said they hadn't had any calculus since high school. They both agreed that they couldn't see a connection between flying an aircraft and calculus. I decided to remain silent and hoped like hell they were all right.

At 1300 we all went back to the academic building and out of habit lined up at the office window in alphabetical order. Lt Anderson had a clipboard list with all the names. Rod talked to him for quite a while, I think he was having a detailed discussion about the difficulty of the Calculus section. After what seemed like way too much time Lt Anderson called for the next man. Mel and Bob weren't at the window very long at all and as they turned away each gave me the thumbs up signal.

I stepped up to the window and gave my name. Lt Anderson picked up his clipboard and found my name. He glanced at me and then said, "Spicer, let's see, ok, nice score in physics, ok algebra, geometry and trig, and just barely ok in Calculus. Looks like you're a little shaky there you might want to get some of the program texts and brush up."

"Does that mean I pass sir?"

"Yeah, you passed; you're just a little shaky in Calculus, next man." I didn't hear anything he said after "you passed."

Our classes started in earnest the next morning. There were three primary subjects we had to deal with in the next three weeks: Aircraft engines, Hydraulics, and Aerodynamics. It seemed that the Navy theory was to put it to you fast and furious, like trying to drink out of a fire hose. They knew you couldn't possibly get it all but you'd get enough not to be thirsty and get very damp in the process.

The aircraft engines and hydraulic classes were great and I knew I would not only like them but would pass them with no problem. A little hard study and I might even do real well. They consumed the morning and at 1300 we were on the second deck of the academic building for our first class in Aerodynamics.

A Navy Lt named Kelly introduced himself as our instructor for the next three weeks and then proceeded to the black board and wrote a formula. He started by drawing a large square root radical and then inside the radical symbol he wrote ½ Rho V^2.

He said, "Can anyone tell me what this stands for?"

No one made a sound, not even the Naval Academy grads.

"Gentleman, the square root of ½ Rho Velocity squared is what makes an aircraft fly. It's the lift equation and within the next three weeks you will know how this works both backwards and forwards. Are there any questions before I begin?"

An Ensign named Terrell asked what Rho was and the Lt explained it was the Greek letter Rho and from that point on I was lost. We had two hours of Aero with a ten minute break after the first hour. I listened intently all afternoon and could only make out a word or two occasionally. My first stop after class before going home was the training aids room to pick up every programmed text available on Aerodynamics.

The next several days in the Aero classes were a blur. I found out I wasn't the only guy in there that was struggling. By Friday we all started calling Aerodynamics class, "THE MYSTERY HOUR". Terms like anhedral, dihedral, mean aerodynamic cord, and camber were bouncing around in our heads. During breaks you could see guys actually

29

using their hands to simulate an aircraft and you would see them talking to themselves. The scariest thing we heard on Friday however was that we had our first test on Monday, followed by, "Enjoy your weekend Gentlemen."

I'd been a pretty miserable companion all week. Marguerite was handling the first few months of her pregnancy well but I had been so absorbed in my academic work I wasn't much of a partner. She was one hundred percent supportive and never complained. We went out for dinner Friday night just to get out of the house and when we went to bed that night I was pretty restless in my sleep. I guess I was flopping around, and at some point I rolled over and my knee caught her flush in the stomach. We both awoke with a start. I know it hurt her very much and scared hell out of me for fear I had injured her or the baby.

The house we rented from "Red" was furnished. Our bed was a very old and tired regular double bed that was probably very nice twenty years ago but it had really seen its better days. On Saturday morning I said to Marguerite, "How about we go and do a little shopping?"

"What do you want to shop for?"

"I want to shop for the biggest damn bed we can find, cause I don't ever want what happened last night to happen again."

"Good idea, I'm ready if you are and how about breakfast while we are out?"

We stopped at a diner for breakfast, bought a local newspaper and went through the ads for the weekend. Our search for a furniture store led us to a place on the north side of Pensacola. We found something called a California King-sized bed. There were King-sized beds but the California King was the biggest. I also spotted a color TV. Marguerite was a much more skillful negotiator than me and in a very short time had negotiated a much lower price for both and an agreement to have them delivered and setup today, for cash.

We established a time for delivery of our first ever furniture purchase and left in search of sheets for a California King. It took a couple of tries before we found a place that sold that size sheets. During our travels we came across a new store called K-Mart. We'd never seen a store like this; it had everything. While strolling up and down the aisles I managed to stroll down the toy aisle. About midway down the aisle I saw several different types of molded plastic airplanes. For some reason my eyes settled on a molded model of a P-40 Tomahawk. It was red plastic but the mold was quite detailed. It was small with a wingspan of about four inches. I picked it up and looked it over very closely; I could even detect a slight anhedral to the wings. Something told me to buy it and I did. I got a wry smile from Marguerite at the checkout counter but she never said a word.

By bed time that evening we were lying on our brand new King-sized bed on freshly laundered sheets, watching our brand new color TV. Marguerite was playing instructor and using the Aero Text book and the program texts. She was putting me through my paces and asked a particular question that caused me to stop and try to work out the answer about a lift vector. I got out of bed, went into the living room and found the bag with my little red P-40. I took it back to the bedroom and told her to ask me that question again. She did and I used the airplane to visually put the airfoil in the position described in the question and BINGO!!! It suddenly all made sense. I couldn't believe it. What I was unable to intellectualize I was able to visualize. Marguerite went back over all the material again and we both finally drifted off to sleep on our huge bed.

MONDAY

After two terrific night's sleep on our new bed along with a complete Aero drilling by Marguerite I felt I was better prepared for any exam I had taken thus far. As soon as I entered the classroom I showed Lt Kelly my little model aircraft and asked if I could keep it on my desk and use it during the tests. He gave me a funny look followed by a wry smile and said it was ok.

It wasn't until question number eight that I picked up the model and held in a position to illustrate the question. The answer certainly didn't come automatically but the little aircraft went a long way in solving the "Mystery". I finished the test well ahead of most of my classmates, double checked all my answers and turned in my test.

Our grades were posted the following morning and I was ecstatic to see that I'd only missed three questions. As the week progressed in Aero class I noticed more and more small aircraft models appearing on the desks of my classmates. If Lt Kelly noticed the increase he never said a word. Although it remained "The Mystery Hour," I somehow felt if I could ever get my hands on a real airplane to see how this stuff really worked it would make things a lot easier.

Our academic section of Pre-flight seemed over very quickly. We dropped one Marine and a couple Navy officers but for the most part the original group was intact. Academics were followed by a week each of Sea and Land survival courses. For the college boys it was a revelation, but I just considered it fun. My buddy Rod had some serious trouble with the swimming part of Water Survival. Swimming a mile in a flight suit in under an hour was just not his cup of tea and he spent two weeks in remedial swim, better known as "Stupid Swim," but managed to finally pass.

Word was that we wouldn't be moving along to the next phase of training, Primary Flight at Saufley Field as soon as we completed Pre-Flight, but would be held up in a student "Pool" until there were openings at the next phase of training. There were only so many instructors and so many aircraft. The word was only partially correct. Most of our Navy class members went into the personnel pool, but all Marine Student Naval Aviators were to be sent directly to Saufley Field to begin Primary Flight. Airplanes at last.

CHAPTER THREE

SAUFLEY FIELD AND THE MAYTAG
MESSERSCHMIDTT

Naval Air Training Command
Primary Flight, NAS Saufley Field
Training Squadron One (VT-1), Flight 18
Pensacola, Florida
October 1966

Flight 18 at Saufley Field was the all Marine Flight. If you were a Marine Student Naval Aviator (SNA) you were automatically assigned there. If you were a Navy Student Naval Aviator (SNA) and got assigned there, all your fellow Navy Officers felt sorry for you. For some reason they were all terrified of Flight 18 and wouldn't even come in the ready room unless required to do so. For the moment there were now twenty Marine and two Naval SNA's, in Flight 18.

Of course all the instructors were Marine pilots, most were the rank of Captain, same as a Navy Lt. Most of them were helo pilots but there were a few F-8 Fighter, A-4 Attack and even KC-130 tanker pilots; the majority of them just back from Vietnam. Whatever their backgrounds, they were the task masters that would take us into the heavens and teach us how to fly. They were task masters with a little bit of an edge to them. A little like a Drill Instructor in boot camp or a Sergeant Instructor in OCS. They weren't about to grant you entrance into their exclusive club unless you could prove beyond any doubt that you belonged. They came in two varieties: "Screamers and Chippers", nasty and somewhat nice. Nobody wanted to draw a screamer for their first flight instructor but a Chipper wasn't much better; they didn't get in your face or scream in the intercom system but their little remarks and chips cut just as deep. They didn't want to be your buddy or pal, they didn't want to call you by your first name, they wanted you to do it right the first time, every time. If you got a well done from them, you had by god earned it.

The drill here would be ground school for half a day, flying the other half. One week you would fly in the mornings and have ground school in the afternoons and then the schedule would be just the opposite for the next week. From pre-flight you brought a numerical grade score. Here you would have a numerical grade score for both ground school and flying. These added up to points, and point accumulation was the name of the game. At the end of primary flight, those guys with the most points got to pick the direction they wanted to specialize in flight school. For the Navy it was either the Jet pipeline which would send you on to Basic Jet Training in Meridian, Mississippi and eventually to a jet with a tail hook and a carrier somewhere in the South China Sea. The other option was the prop or multiengine pipeline which would send you to NAS Whiting Field and Basic prop training in the T-28 and then on to either P-2's or P-3's or Helicopter training at Ellyson Field. To go to jet training the Navy guys would need at least 140 points.

For the Marines, the need for helo drivers was critical. They didn't need a lot of jet pilots so competition for a seat in Basic Jet Training was very keen and a Marine SNA would need at least 200 points to qualify and then there may be only one or two spots open. More often than not there were none. This selection was done on a weekly basis as the various groups of SNA's completed Primary Flight. Most Marines went straight to NAS Whiting Field and the T-28 as soon as Primary Flight was completed.

Everyone knew the rules now so the game was definitely on and the key was going to be memorization. Although we had ground school subjects like meteorology, more engineering, and a little more aerodynamics, we now had to learn all about a real aircraft, the T-34C Mentor. Not only did we have to know all the particulars about this machine but something completely new, Flight Procedures. A step by step list of exactly how you did everything in this aircraft. It all had to be committed to memory along with all sorts of other facts like engine temperatures, hydraulic pressures, engine oil, cylinder heads, etc. It became apparent right from the get go that if you didn't have all this stuff committed to memory you didn't have a chance in hell of getting through primary flight.

We were given an initial issue of flight gear, suit, helmet, gloves, boots and a locker. We were introduced to something called a "Procedures Trainer". In a huge room at the end of the building there were a dozen of these things. They were exact duplicates of a T-34 cockpit. The Trainers didn't actually do anything they just had all the knobs, dials, and levers that were in the aircraft. You got in and pretended you were flying. First you memorized the procedures for various maneuvers and then moved the controls or levers into the correct position for the maneuvers. These things may not have been very sophisticated but it was exciting for me to think I was getting that close to flying a real airplane.

I was very nervous the day the instructor assignments were made. There was a huge plastic flight schedule board that covered one whole wall of the Flight 18 ready room. You had to locate your name on the board, and then look to see what instructor's name you were listed under. Each instructor would have three or four students and they were listed in order. The new guys were last; the guys that were further along in training or about to finish were listed first. The instructor had the latitude to decide who had priority in scheduling.

My name was listed last under Captain Slowey and there were three guys above me. I located one of the other guys and asked about our instructor. I was relieved when the guy told me he wasn't a screamer or a chipper.

Rod seemed indifferent to the instructor he drew, but Rod was always that way. Mel Gibbs had a grim look on his face. He told me his instructor was a Captain McAdams better known as Captain McNasty. He'd already met him and the first thing he asked Mel to do was recite the procedures for the first flight not only forwards but backwards. It wasn't a good start according to Mel. Lt John Mills and Bob Reedhill were already scheduled for their first flights and were really excited. I managed to meet Captain Slowey and he told me he wanted to finish up the two men ahead of me. That way we could fly almost every day once we started. There wasn't much I could say about it but "Yes Sir" and he did seem like a pretty reasonable fellow.

Rod, Mel, John Mills and Bob Reedhill had their first flights and they all had different stories. The accounts went from Rod's "No big deal" to Mel's "I puked all over the place and then they made me go out and clean the cockpit and I puked some more." I was getting more anxious by the day for my chance to get into a real aircraft.

The week of the 24th of October we were to fly in the morning and attend ground school in the afternoon. When I checked the schedules board for Monday the 24th I watched as the scheduler put my name up for my first hop. It was to be a 0700 brief for a 0800 takeoff and I felt my heart beat just a little faster for a few moments.

I was thirty minutes early for my brief and didn't think 0700 would ever come. At exactly 0700 Captain Slowey walked in the door, saw me and motioned for me to join him in the briefing room. I wasn't responsible for doing a lot of flying on this hop, it would be more or less an aircraft ride and he would be watching me closely to see how I handled the whole thing. He went over all the emergency procedures very thoroughly and quizzed me extensively on those and my responsibilities in case it all went wrong. It suddenly hit me that although this might be very exciting and a lot of fun, it was also dangerous. Much like the sea, flying or aircraft don't tolerate incompetence or inattention.

We headed for the flight line at 0730 and were assigned an aircraft, bureau number 140891. It was parked on the very far end of the line. Captain Slowey let me do the preflight and asked me several questions as we checked various sections of the aircraft. The engine start and taxi were just as I expected but I had a fair amount of difficulty understanding the radio. I later learned I didn't have the ear pieces in my helmet correctly installed and that I had to turn up the volume switch on the UHF radio. This also made it difficult for me to understand Captain Slowey on the aircraft's intercom system.

The takeoff was simply a thrill for me. I couldn't believe the rate of acceleration of the aircraft or the roar of the engine. It was a sensation that penetrated clear into my bones. The takeoff roll went by very fast and the next thing I knew we were airborne and I could hear the hydraulic system functioning as the landing gear came up. I never noticed Captain Slowey raise the landing gear lever.

I dropped my left hand down to the aircraft trim tabs. These had always remained a mystery to me in school but as the aircraft changed configuration and accelerated I could feel the tabs moving very quickly and knew Captain Slowey was trimming the aircraft throughout the process.

For the first fifteen minutes he told me to just relax, sit back and enjoy the view as we flew out to the operating areas. Out here, over mostly open farm land or water, was where everyone practiced the various maneuvers and acrobatics. For the moment I was a long way from any of that. As we entered the operating area Captain Slowey began to demonstrate and describe one of everything. First he performed an aerobatic checklist and then started with a Wing Over, followed by a Barrel Roll, next a Loop, an

Immelman and finally something called a Split S. Last but not least he deliberately stalled the aircraft and induced a Spin, allowing the aircraft to make two and one half revolutions before applying the anti-spin controls and returning the aircraft to normal flight. All the while he kept up a running narrative of exactly what he was doing during each maneuver, what he was using for visual references and how he was moving the controls.

Captain Slowey referred to this demonstration as a "Squirrel Cage". It was during this series of aerobatic maneuvers that I was introduced to a powerful, and yet unknown to me, force called a "G". The G stood for Gravity. It's gravity that holds you on the earth, it was gravity that made the apple fall from the tree and hit Sir Isaac Newton on the head. One G is not noticeable; it's what you experience all the time. At a fair on certain rides like the Tilt-A-Whirl you might have noticed 1 and 1/2 G's, maybe a little more, but 2 G's or more are definitely noticeable. At 2 G's you weigh double your body weight. So does the flight helmet sitting on top of your head. You feel like you are being squashed down into your seat and it's difficult to keep your head up and see what's going on. As you go to three or five G's it gets much worse. If you weigh 200 lbs with your flight gear on, at five G's you weigh 1000 lbs. The squashing is so severe it's difficult to concentrate on what you're trying to do and see. You can't raise your arms or lift your feet. You start to feel hot and a little sweaty. There's a funny feeling in the pit of your stomach and you think that if this giant force doesn't stop squishing the hell out of you the slight nausea you're feeling may develop into a full blown puke all over your brand new flight suit.

Captain Slowey had leveled the aircraft and was now demonstrating a maneuver called a steep turn. He was at 2000 feet of altitude and on a heading of 270. He smartly rolled the aircraft into 45 degrees angle of bank to the left and commenced a 360 degree turn to arrive back on the heading of 270 and the same altitude of 2000 feet, smoothly reversing the turn by rolling the aircraft into a 45 degree banked turn to the right for another 360 degrees arriving back on the heading of 270 and the altitude of 2000 feet. During the turn he demonstrated that by increasing back pressure on the stick he could increase his rate of turn and also decrease the radius of the turn and in doing so he would be progressively increasing the G forces on the aircraft as well as the two of us. When the aircraft G meter read 5 he asked me if I felt OK. I tried to raise my hand from my thigh to the top of the throttle to press the intercom button to answer him but couldn't raise my arm.

"If you can't raise your arm to respond just nod your head if you are ok and not sick."

I tried to nod my head but found it extremely difficult so my nod was more like a barely noticeable bob but it sufficed.

Once we leveled off from the last steep turn we flew directly to one of the outlying fields where he demonstrated the entry into the flight pattern and the touch and go landings I would be doing in the next few hops. Once the aircraft was in the landing configuration, gear and flaps down, he told me to open my canopy. The rush of fresh air was more than welcome and helped get rid of that horrible squashed G feeling.

From memorizing the procedures for landing the aircraft I thought it would be more of a mechanical type thing but it was a combination of both strict adherence to the procedures and the feel of the aircraft. He executed a couple touch and goes and we departed the landing pattern for our return flight back to Saufley.

He suddenly said, "You have the aircraft."

In the brief I was told that when passing control of the aircraft from one pilot to another I should respond by replying, "I have the aircraft" and lightly shake the stick from side to side. I responded as briefed.

Here I was on a beautiful fall morning in Florida on the edge of Perdido Bay heading back to Saufley Field in a Navy Aircraft. In control of a Navy aircraft. I had no idea what the hell to do. After watching all the war movies as a kid, the carriers in the Victory at Sea programs, watching the aircraft "peel off" and dive at the targets, all that cool stuff and here I was now getting ready to try and join that elite club and I had no damn clue what to do with these controls.

My first movements of any of the controls were more than a little tentative and finally Captain Slowey said, "Why don't you try a set of steep turns, move the controls, get the feel of the damn thing. You have to make it do what you want it to do; these Maytag Messerschmitt's won't fly themselves."

I turned the aircraft to a heading of 090 and noted that I was level at 2000 feet. I rolled the aircraft fairly smoothly into 45 degrees of bank to the left and started my steep turn. The thing I noticed immediately was I started to lose altitude, then I noticed that I was out of balanced flight, I had lessened my angle of bank so I was barely turning, I applied more bank and now tried a little back pressure on the stick but forgot to add power or step on the rudder to put the aircraft into balanced flight and now I lost even more altitude. I'd lost 200 feet of altitude in less than 90 degrees of turn and still had 270 degrees to go. There were just so many things to watch and coordinate I didn't know what to look at next and when I did notice something wrong I really didn't know how to quickly correct it. I was squeezing hell out of the stick and throttle and without noticing it I was pressing so hard on the rudder pedals that I was actually applying the brakes.

Captain Slowey noticed the brake pressure gauge fluctuating and wanted to know why I was pressing on the brakes. I didn't know and didn't know I was. I was beginning to wish he would retake control of the aircraft before we fell out of the sky but he didn't so I continued to struggle. By the time I'd made the first complete turn and was back around to a heading of 090 I'd lost 300 feet of altitude and when I attempted to roll the aircraft back in the opposite direction and commence the turn to the right I over banked to about 60 degrees angle of bank and lost more altitude. I applied too much power which increased my airspeed which increased my G force and also made me gain altitude. With the gain of altitude I was losing airspeed now and had to rectify that or I knew I would stall the aircraft and I certainly didn't want to do that this close to the ground. I turned right through my 090 heading and managed to get the wings level on a heading of 120 at an altitude of 1700 feet when I heard, "I have control of the aircraft." It was immediate relief. I gave the required answer, "You have control of the aircraft" and raised both my hands. I felt exhausted.

Captain Slowey headed directly for Saufley Field and entered the landing pattern. He executed what appeared to be a perfect landing and we taxied to the flight line and were directed to a parking spot. The shut down and post flight were a nonevent and exactly one hour and eighteen minutes after we took off it was all over.

As we were walking back to the ready room, Captain Slowey said, "I really don't have much to say as far as a debrief. This was more of an aircraft ride for you and a test to check for airsickness. You seemed to handle everything just fine. You might think those were the worst set of steep turns ever attempted by an SNA but they weren't; at least you completed the maneuver and you'll get better. Do you have any questions?"

"No Sir, not at the moment."

"Ok, then I'll see you on Thursday for Fam 2; you're finished with me for now."

When I got back to my locker to change back into my uniform I simply sat there for several minutes. I had sweat dripping off my chin, the back of my flight suite was damp and I felt drained. I never thought this would be easy, but I really had no idea.

FAM flights 2, 3, 4, 5, and 6 were fine. With each hop I was doing better and better and actually felt comfortable. I was getting used to the G's and really didn't even notice three G's any more. I could do all the maneuvers satisfactorily except the damn steep turns. Captain Slowey was always on my ass about them. He told me he couldn't understand how I could do all the other stuff so well and screw up something as simple as a set of steep turns. Fam 8 would be a progress check with a different instructor. I would have to do one of everything and hopefully the instructor would not have to take the aircraft during the entire hop. If he did, you'd done something wrong. Either I couldn't do it correctly or Captain Slowey didn't teach it correctly so it was a reflection on both of us. Today was Fam 7 and it was a rehearsal for Fam 8 so Captain Slowey should not have to take the aircraft for the entire hop.

I could tell the next two flights were very important. The "Eight Check" was a make it or break it flight. If you got a "Down" on that hop, most likely you would be out of flight school and on your way to training for a different MOS. Two guys had already departed for Artillery school. Lt Tom Priestly couldn't get over being airsick and was dismissed after four flights. Lt Allen Bakeman couldn't handle the pressure and performed so poorly on his "Eight Check" the instructor simply took control of the aircraft and came back to base. He gave Bakeman a down for the hop and when Bakeman went in front of the Flight Performance Board he told them he'd had enough.

Rod had already passed his "Eight Check" and thought it was no big deal; it probably wasn't for Rod. Mel and I were up for FAM 7&8 at the same time. In fact Captain Slowey was to be his "Eight Check" instructor. Our briefs were scheduled for 0900 with a 1000 takeoff.

"Hey Spice, you know if I get by this hop today that I'll have my "Eight Check" with your guy Slowey; how's he to get along with?"

"He's not a screamer at all; I really like him. He doesn't give you any slack and he will chip at you constantly but for your "Eight Check" as long as you aren't being radical I don't think you'll hear a word until you get back for the debrief."

"I feel better already. Captain McNasty has been giving me fits, makes me memorize procedures backwards. I keep throwing up in the aircraft but he told me as long as I could keep flying and performing up to standard he didn't care. So I bring back a bag of puke just about every day. At least I'm getting it in the bag now."

"Well Mel, that's an improvement. I was feeling sorry for you every time I'd see you heading back out to an aircraft with a bucket and brushes."

"Did you hear what happened on my last hop with him?"

"No, nothing serious I hope."

"He told me to do a Squirrel Cage and I keep forgetting to do the acrobatic check list so I wrote the damn check list down on my pilot's knee board. (a black metal note pad that pilots strapped to their right leg, used for copying instructions from air traffic control, or notes about the flight, issued to all pilot trainees) I naturally looked down to make sure I was getting it done correctly before starting into the maneuvers and he saw me duck my head. He wanted to know if I was getting airsick and when I told him no, he wanted to know if I had written procedures down on my knee board. I knew you weren't supposed to do this, but I didn't want to lie so I told him yes. When I did that he told me to open the canopy and throw out my knee board. It was a good thing we weren't over a populated area."

"Did he say anything else?"

"No, but now instead of resting my right arm on the knee board while holding onto the stick it's resting on my thigh and I haven't got used to that yet, it's messing me up a little."

"Can't you get another knee board?"

"I went to supply and tried but they just told me it was 'Tough Shit'."

"Well just hunker down and get on with it Mel, you can do it. Good luck today on the Fam 7, I'll see you when we get back on the ground."

Captain Slowey had me head in the direction of Perdido Bay. In the brief he went over everything he wanted me to do and went through each maneuver with me in detail. He told me he wasn't going to say much unless I really needed correcting.

I climbed the aircraft up to the pre-briefed altitude and started through the sequence of maneuvers. When I finished all the aerobatics, I headed for one of the outlying fields for touch and goes. I heard Mel broadcasting on the radio that he was entering the pattern at Fairdale, so I headed for another outlying field called Silverhill. I entered the pattern and did six touch and go's departing the pattern just as briefed.

Last on my list of maneuvers was the dreaded steep turns. I leveled the aircraft at 2000 feet of altitude and aligned the nose of the aircraft on a heading of 360, due north. I started the turn to my left and for the first 180 degrees of turn was doing fairly well, I'd only lost about 50 feet of altitude and then, as usual, it all went to hell. I didn't maintain my 45 degrees angle of bank so my turn shallowed. I wasn't holding enough back pressure on the stick, I let the aircraft get out of balanced flight, and when I corrected my bank angle I didn't add enough power. I started falling out of the sky again. By the time I got around to North for my turn reversal I'd lost 200 feet again. Try as I might, I couldn't seem to get it back so I just held what I had and tried not to lose any more altitude.

When I rolled wings level Captain Slowey said, "Goddamnit Spicer, what the hell's the matter with you? You do all the hard stuff to near perfection and something as simple as a set of steep turns you're all over the Goddamn sky. Your 'Eight Check' is gonna be with Captain Landry, he's an F-8 Fighter Pilot. You pull that sorry shit with him he'll give you a Goddamn down. I have control of the aircraft."

Captain Slowey immediately pulled the nose of the aircraft up slightly and slammed the stick smartly to the left allowing the aircraft to roll almost to the inverted position. He kept the G on the aircraft pulling the nose down till we were in about a thirty degree dive. We were just about dead center of Perdido Bay and the water was starting to look very close. I could feel my eyes getting bigger. About the time I thought impact with the water was going to be imminent he smartly rolled the aircraft upright pulling back on the stick and leveled off at exactly 200 feet above the surface of the water. I'd never been this fast this close to ground or water.

"You have the aircraft. Now do another set of steep turns and lose 200 feet you Sonofabitch."

"I have control of the aircraft." I was scared shitless. Had he lost his damn mind? I had never heard him raise his voice or use any profanity. I sat there for a couple of seconds and it was too damn long.

"Do it Goddamnit and quit fucking around. I don't care what heading do it on this one and do it right Goddamn NOW!!!"

I just knew that if I rolled into a steep turn this close to the water we would be dead. Before I realized what I was doing I pushed the stick to the left, rolled exactly to 45 degrees angle of bank, put some back pressure on the stick, added just a little power, stepped on the bottom rudder to stay in balanced flight, and was half way through the first turn before I realized I hadn't lost a foot of altitude. Out of the corner of my eye all I could see was water and it looked as if my wing tip was only inches from being wet. I hit my turn reversal dead on the heading and brought the aircraft back around to the right all the way to the entry heading again. I smoothly rolled out on the original heading and at exactly the original altitude.

Captain Slowey said, "Now was that so Goddamn hard? Take me home."

After landing at Saufley the only thing he said to me was, "Good Job, make sure you got your head and ass wired together tomorrow; Landry is a tough customer. Good luck."

The dreaded "Eight Check" was a nonevent. Captain Landry was one of the shortest Marine Officers I'd ever met. He wasn't a lot older than me. He handed me a written brief sheet, something he'd made up himself. His only instructions were for me to do exactly what was on the sheet and he wanted to know if I had any questions; I didn't. Those were the last words he said to me until we were walking back to the ready room after the flight.

"Spicer you flew a good hop, everything was more than satisfactory and that may have been the most perfect set of steep turns I've ever seen on an "Eight Check."

29 November, 1966
Tuesday
Today was Solo day, it was my thirteenth hop. The U.S. Navy was going to allow me to fly a T34-C Mentor, bureau number 144115 all by myself. The flight eighteen duty officer gave me my solo brief and off I went. I think I was moving automatically until I'd leveled the aircraft at 2000 feet of altitude on my way to the Solo area. It was a

glorious Florida day; chilly but clear with perfect visibility. I could see myself in the reflection of the canopy and all sorts of thoughts came rushing into my head. I thought of all the hard work and luck it took to get here. I thought about my uncle who told me the only way I'd ever be a pilot was when somebody told me to pile it here or pile it there. I thought of my father who was killed in World War II in a B-24 and how badly he'd wanted to be a pilot. I thought of Marguerite and wondered what she was doing at this moment and wished I could share this moment directly with her and I found myself looking at my reflection in the canopy and suddenly beating my hands against the inside of the canopy and screaming, "You did it, You dumb Sonofabitch, You Did It!!!!" And then, reality set in. I was in this aircraft all by myself, there was nobody in the back seat that would say, "I have control of the aircraft" if everything turned to shit. I was alone in this aircraft and I alone would be responsible for getting it back on the ground. That thought broke my reverie and I realized it was time to get down to business.

I did all the maneuvers at altitude that I was supposed to do and found out very quickly that I was a much more demanding task master on myself than the flight instructors. I made myself redo a couple of things I knew I didn't get perfect and once satisfied with all the upper air work was most anxious to head for an outlying field and get in a few touch and goes before returning to base and my final landing. I headed for Silverhill and entered the touch and go pattern.

My first approach was so bad that I executed a waved off and went around again. My second approach was even worse so I waved off again and exited the landing pattern. I flew about 10 miles from the field and put myself in an orbit around a very smooth looking farmer's field. I couldn't figure out why my approaches were so awful. The first I was too close abeam the landing area and the second just didn't feel right from the beginning. I told myself that what goes up must come down and right now I'm the only person that could put this aircraft back on the earth in one piece. I have to make this thing do exactly what I want it to do no matter what.

I re-entered the Silverhill pattern and made four satisfactory touch and goes then exited and headed back for Saufley Field. I had to transit across Perdido Bay so I let down to 500 feet over the water and did a set of steep turns just for good measure. I was back on the deck and in the chocks at the appointed time. My flight was only one hour and eighteen minutes and I was elated but tried to act as if it was no big deal.

On Friday the 28th there was the weekly Solo Party at the Officers Club. Tradition required you to present whatever bottle of booze your instructor requested and it required him to cut off your uniform neck tie and present it to you as a souvenir. It always seemed to me that the ceremony was always anticlimactic compared to the actual deed or accomplishment and this party proved no exception.

The 1st of December would be our last week. During this week we had to put in for what we wanted to do for the next phase. I had 210 points, was the Marine with the highest total for this week and if I put in for jets and there was an opening, I'd be on my way to Meridian, Mississippi for Basic Jet Training. There was a friend of mine, Dee Habermacher, who had about five points less than me and desperately wanted to fly jets. When he saw my name on the list for the helicopter pipeline he almost jumped straight up in the air. He wanted to know why I wanted to go helos instead of jets and I told him I wanted to make sure I would go where the action was. He didn't have a response.

During this last week I got to fly three more solos, had a final check ride and on Friday the 9th was told to report on Monday to NAS Whiting Field, Training Squadron Two for

49

Basic Prop Training in the T-28.   No more Maytag
Messerschmitt.

CHAPTER FOUR

THE TANGO 28 and the KINGS OF STUPID STUDY

NAS WHITING FIELD, NORTH
TRAINING SQUADRON TWO (VT-2)
MILTON, FLORIDA
December/January 1966/67

Basic Flight Training in the T-28 was conducted at NAS
Whiting Field, which was located about twenty miles east
of Pensacola in the small town of Milton, Fla. There were
actually two airfields on the base, North and South
Whiting. North field was the home of Training Squadron
Two (VT-2) and South Field was the home of Training
Squadron Three (VT-3). I would have to complete the
training here at Whiting before going on to helicopter
training at Ellyson Field.

Along with several other Marines, my buddy Rod and I
had all been assigned to North Whiting and VT-2, which by
accident or design seemed to have more Marine students
and instructors than VT-3. The CO and XO were naval
officers but the operations/training officer was a Marine
Major.

Even though we'd all been anxious to get started in
ground school and our first flights (hops) in the T-28, all
we could do was draw our ground school books, course
rules for the airfields, flight procedures and NATOPS
Manuals for the T-28. (Naval Aviation Training and
Operational Procedures) Nothing was going to happen
until after the Christmas leave period.

Marguerite and I prepared for Christmas in our little
house in Pensacola but were planning a move just after
Christmas. She was entering her third trimester of
pregnancy and neither one of us was interested in trying to

visit either set of parents over the holidays. Besides it was cold up north and after all, we were in sunny Florida.

There were other factors involved in making a move. By doing so Marguerite would go under civilian medical treatment for the birth of our child. The Santa Rosa County hospital was small but very nice and certainly beat hell out of driving all the way to mainside for prenatal care along with 200 other expectant ladies. The second part was I would be very close to Whiting Field and not have to make the daily commute from Pensacola out there. If I had a hop with a real early brief time I would have to get up very early to make it.

We found a great house for rent, much nicer than our current residence and made the move a couple days after Christmas. We thought it would be good to celebrate our first anniversary with a household move. We didn't have much so we were all set up to celebrate New Years in our new home.

I was anxious to get a jump on things so I went to the base and checked in at the squadron, drew my books and found out that I could go ahead and complete some of the academic preliminaries at the squadron during the leave period. There wouldn't be any formal classroom presentations but I could self- study and get the course rules out of the way, which was actually a very involved test. By getting course rules out of the way I'd be one week closer to crawling into a T-28.

While I was checking into all this I met a fellow Marine that I hadn't seen before. His name was Lt Don Wiley. He was a brand new Second Lieutenant and had been one of the many officers that went to Marine OCS in Quantico and then came straight down to flight school. He'd started preflight in the group behind mine but had somehow managed to catch up and was now assigned to VT-2 here at Whiting.

Wiley was from El Paso, Texas, and I liked him the minute we met. He was trying to do the same thing so we decided to come out to the squadron every day and study course rules together in the squadron ready room. Over the next week we met every day and studied hard, but the course rules were voluminous.

There were two sets of course rules, one for each field, North and South. Although they were similar, the differences were considerable because each field had several different entry points depending on which runway was in use. The entry points were geographic features on the ground that were supposed to be readily identifiable from the air. We had to know them all in case an emergency at one of the airfields closed down the duty runway.

At the end of the week we thought we had everything down pat and decided to take the test and get it out of the way because the leave period would be ending and we would be starting ground school on the T-28 and other things. It would be the same routine as Saufley Field, ground school half a day and flying the other half.

We told the Petty Officer in charge of giving the course rules test that we were ready and wanted to take the test on Friday morning. At 0800 the Petty Officer in charge administered our test. It took well over an hour to go through all the questions and about half way through I knew I wasn't doing too well. Some of the questions on the test didn't even sound familiar. Just like Aerodynamics, if I'd had a familiarization flight and actually seen the course rules in use I think I would have been fine, but this wasn't going to be the case. I waited until Don was finished and we turned our test into the Petty Officer who immediately broke out the key to the answer sheet and started grading our papers. I could tell by the red x's he was making that we were both in trouble.

When he finished grading both papers he looked up and said, "I'm very sorry but you both failed. I have to report your scores to the training officer Major Moriarity and he will assign you to remedial course rules study starting Monday evening at 1900 in the classroom here. It will take three days of remedial study and then a retest."

Wiley said, "So Monday night we have to be in the classroom up here for course rules stupid study, is that what you're telling us?"

"Yes Sir, but we aren't allowed to call it that."

We left the squadron and headed for the snack bar. Neither one of us said a word to each other. Don got a hot dog and I got a cup of coffee. Don put mustard on the hot dog and then reached across the small table and got the bottle of Texas Pete vinegar pepper hot sauce. It had little green peppers in it. He very carefully unscrewed the lid and took out several of the little green peppers and began lining them up along both sides of his hot dog in the bun.

"Damn Wiley, what the hell are you doing to that hot dog?"

Don would often use a comic accent of a Mexican speaking English; it was his "On" persona. He would sometimes identify himself as a character named Chuey who was a Mexican bandito in some movie about a horse.

In the accent he said, "Well, I'm jus putting dese lil cactus grapes on my tortas (Mexican term for a sandwich) to gib it a lil flavor."

"Cactus grapes?"

"Jyes, you see back home dese lil grapes grow on de cactus and we harvest them. Jyou should try them on a sandwich like dis one."

"I think I will."

I went back to the counter, got a hot dog and doctored it up just like Don's. After the third bite I knew this was a serious mistake. I'd learned to like hot food, both Mexican and Chinese, but this was way over the top. Maybe one

54

pepper would have been ok, even two but I'd put three down each side of my hot dog just like he did.

"Jesus Christ Wiley, I think you've killed me."

Don was laughing very loudly. "Well you stupid shit nobody told you to do that. I've been eating this type of stuff since I was in diapers. You think this is bad, give it a couple of hours."

We sat in silence for a few minutes. Don was watching me and I was trying to recover from the peppers. He finally said, "That's goddamned embarrassing to fail that damn test, damned embarrassing."

"Yes it is."

He shook his head in a shameful fashion, got up and said, "I'll see you Monday."

I went home to share the bad news with Marguerite. I hadn't flunked any test since I was in college and Don was right, it was very embarrassing. About two hours after I got home I started experiencing some gastrointestinal distress I had never experienced before in my life. Marguerite wanted to know what was wrong and I told her about the hot dog, cactus grapes and Wiley. I couldn't manage to get off the toilet for about thirty minutes. I was experiencing spastic contractions in the lower part of my anatomy and they wouldn't stop. Marguerite was totally unsympathetic and told me I most likely was getting what I deserved for being so stupid. She also let me know that if I hadn't been in such a damn hurry to try and get ahead in flight school and had waited for the regular course rules stuff I wouldn't be in this mess in the first place. I knew she was right.

STUPID STUDY

Monday night Don and I were the only two people in the classroom. Our instructor was a Navy Lt, who was also a flight instructor and the squadron duty officer for the day, so he had to be here no matter what. He wasn't too thrilled about having to spend two hours with a couple of dumbass Marine Second Lieutenants teaching course rules for the airfield. He never bothered to introduce himself but started right in with the basics.

After three nights of instruction with a different instructor each night we marched into the testing office and told the Petty Officer in charge we were now ready to take the test. We both finished the test just a couple of minutes apart and the Petty Officer set in grading them. He seemed very embarrassed, almost apologetic, when he told us that we had once again failed the test, only this time just barely.

We were assigned to another session of stupid study for the course rules and managed to flunk that test as well. By now our fellow flight students were back from the Christmas leave period and we not only went to stupid study but also to the course rules classes with the regular instructor.

Word got out that Wiley and I had managed to bilge the course rules exam three times so we were taking a fair amount of ribbing from several of our buddies, of course Rod Bell and Mel Gibbs. Another classmate, Lt Doug Delair, who was a few weeks ahead of us and already flying, told us that the course rules were really hard and most guys flunked it the first time around. He'd flunked it four times before finally getting it right. He said that he had all the answers to every test memorized and he'd be glad to share them with us just so we could get on with ground school. He was sure that once we started flying the course rules would fall right into place and make sense.

Don and I figured we had nothing to lose. Our plan was to get the answers from Delair for the fourth test, look them up in the material and make sure we knew them. We told Delair that we were desperate at this point and were ready to try anything. We told him we were up for the fourth test. He proceeded to provide the answers to a 40 question multiple choice test and we sat there writing down the a, b, c or d's.

We attended stupid study that night and the next morning we met in the snack bar an hour before our test with the Petty Officer. We spent an hour memorizing the damn answers and then went off to take the test.

I thought the answer to the first question corresponded with the answer Delair had given us so I was pretty sure the information was correct. I checked a couple further down the page and they seemed to check out so I went right down the page and filled in the answer sheet with the answers Delair had given us. Wiley appeared to be taking his time, going over the questions one at a time.

I turned my answers into the Petty Officer who broke out his test key for the answer sheet. He was making a lot of red x's and I thought he must be marking the answers as correct but I was wrong and so were all my answers. He looked up at me with a very painful expression and said, "Sir, I'm sorry but the curve doesn't go that low." I could hear the pencil Wiley was using snap in half. When we caught up with Delair, he was having a great laugh and after thinking about it, we did too. Delair spread that story around and it only added fuel to the Stupid Study status.

By the time we finished the next session of stupid study we knew all the course rules by heart. There were other guys that flunked the test as well; Delair was right, it was very hard. We were now being sought out for advice on what to study.

With course rules finally behind us and the Christmas leave period over we started ground school in earnest. It was similar to Saufley; we studied the aircraft in great detail but now there were several other subjects. It was obvious that at each level of training the ante would go up considerably. Our additional subjects for the moment included Navigation, Instrument Flight Rules and Morse code.

Since our shitty performance with course rules, Wiley and I were doing pretty well in ground school passing all our tests with excellent grades. It was fun watching some of the other guys struggle for a change. And then along came Morse code.

The class was taught by a very salty old Chief Petty Officer who'd been a signalman in the Navy for well over twenty years. He could do it all, semaphore, code, flashing light, daylight or dark, good weather or bad it didn't matter. He'd been teaching this class here for several years and had seen them come and go.

First we had to learn the code itself, each letter. Then we had to listen to the code until we could understand and turn the dots and dashes into words and lastly we had to send the code, one letter at a time. The object was to be able to send or receive ten words a minute or better.

I had no trouble memorizing the code and I could tap out the dots and dashes but when it came to receiving and understanding the code I had no clue. The Naval Academy guys had no trouble with this stuff. The Marines for the most part weren't familiar with any of this but most of the guys were catching on pretty fast, except for Wiley and me. The Chief noticed the ribbons on my shirt and knew I was one of the very few students that were combat vets so he seemed sympathetic to my struggle and tried his best to help me. It was all to no avail; Wiley and I bilged the final exam and were immediately given a week of stupid study.

Being assigned to code stupid study was also a punishment of sorts for the Chief because he was also the instructor at night. Wiley and I met in the code lab every night for the next week and it didn't seem to get any better. The Chief said we should be able to hear the words, to recognize the dots and dashes in groups that would instantly signal the word in our brains, but it didn't happen for either of us. We failed again and got an additional week of stupid study.

We were flying now. Going to ground school in the mornings and flying in the afternoon and then going to stupid study at night; it was making for some very long days.

It was Thursday of the last week of code stupid study. I was beginning to understand the code if it was transmitted at a rate of about 5 words a minute but at the required ten it was just noise. We had about a half an hour to go and Wiley took off his head phones and stood up. The Chief stopped the tape and looked straight at Wiley.

"Chief, we need to talk about this shit for a minute."

"What do you mean Lieutenant?"

"Look, I'm from El Paso, Texas, I never heard of Morse code. Spicer ain't no eagle scout and he's never heard of Morse code either. We are Marines, hell he even volunteered for helos. We get our wings; we are heading straight to Vietnam and probably get our asses shot off in some helicopter. Helicopters got two pilots, not one, two. I can't think of a single situation that I'm ever gonna have to send or especially receive ten damn Morse code words a minute and if I do there will be another guy with me and hopefully he will be alive. So here's the deal, I know you're as sick of looking at us as we are of looking at you, so why don't you give us the test. Let one guy write down the damn dots and dashes and the other guy fill in the letters for the dots and dashes and we should be able to pass the damn test and get the hell out of your hair."

The Chief sat in complete silence for a good minute and finally said, "You know Lieutenant, you might just have a good point. I could be at the club tossing down a few cold ones or home watching the tube but I'm here with a couple of Marine Lt's that I'm pretty sure will only ever use the code to send an SOS. I checked on you two guys and found out you nearly broke the record for bilging the course rules test. I also know that you both have very high flight grade averages, so I know damn well you can fly. The rest

59

of your ground school grades are excellent so on a one time basis I'll take your deal but I promise you both if you screw this up or ever tell anybody I'll somehow get you both drawn and quartered. Now decide which one is going to listen and which one is going to fill in the letters, put on your damn head phones and let's begin because I really am tired of looking at you guys. You're definitely the Kings of Stupid Study."

Don made the decision, he'd listen and put down the dots and dashes and I would fill in the letters. The test went by in a flash; we got 100% and the Chief's best wishes for a safe journey.

CHAPTER FIVE

MEL

TRAINING SQUADRON TWO, BASIC FLIGHT
TRAINING
NAS WHITING FIELD
MILTON, FLORIDA
January/February 1966

Lieutenant Walter Melvin Gibbs and I had known each other since his first day in the Marine Corps. He was in my OCS and Basic School classes at Quantico. Although we were in the same classes, I hadn't come to know him real well until we were both assigned to Flight 18 at Saufley Field and soloed the same week. We'd made it through Saufley without too much trouble. Although Mel had some serious problems with air sickness, he managed to hang in there and finish with a very high flight grade. A Navy 4.0 was perfect but nobody got that, but anything over 3.5 was considered pretty damn good.

Mel was a native Floridian, born and raised in Jacksonville; a true "Southern Gentleman" in every sense. At Saufley, he'd helped me immensely with memorizing flight procedures and was always good at passing along the "word" on how certain maneuvers were completed.

The first phase of flight in the T-28 was called TPA (Transition, Precision and Acrobatics).
There were seven dual hops and then a check ride to ensure you were safe for solo on the eighth hop. After the "eight check" you were considered NATOPS qualified in model and moved on to the next phase of training in the T-28.

Just like Saufley Field, most of our flight instructors were Marine Helicopter pilots who had flown UH-34 helos in Vietnam and had only been back a very short time. My instructor was named Kingston and Mel's instructor was named Lucci. The two instructors were very good friends and we all thought they were squadron mates in Vietnam.

We were all getting pretty close to our "eight check" hop which would be flown with a different instructor than our regular one. Not only was it a flight check but there was a pretty extensive oral exam conducted during the flight. I wondered who my check ride instructor would be and hoped I would get a "good guy" and not a screamer.

I hadn't seen Mel in a couple of days and noticed he wasn't on the flight schedule either, so I was surprised when I saw him in the pilots ready room talking to my instructor, Capt Kingston. I waited till the conversation was over and as soon as Mel saw me he came straight over.

"Hey Mel, where ya been, haven't seen you in a couple days?"

"Been down at Main side Pensacola messing with a damn shrink."

"A shrink? What the hell do you mean a shrink?"

"I mean a damn shrink, a nut doctor."

"What the hell for?"

"You remember that airsickness shit I had back at Saufley? Well my instructor, Captain McAdams never reported me because, although I was throwing up in the airplane during the flight, it never stopped me from flying the aircraft. Of course I always had to clean up the damn plane when we got back, which made me throw up even more, but McNasty (Students name for Capt. McAdams) never wrote me up for it. It didn't happen on the first few hops out here but on the last couple it's happened every time and the instructors are supposed to report any incident like that. Capt Lucci reported it; I got temporarily grounded and sent to Main side for another flight physical. There wasn't anything physically wrong with me so they sent me to this damn Navy shrink."

"Wow, what the hell did he have to say?"

"He said that as far as he was concerned, all this throwing up in an airplane was all in my head, and I had two ET's (Extra Times) and a recheck flight with a different instructor. If I threw up on any one of those flights, I was out."

"Out, what do you mean out?"

"I mean O-U- **FUCKING**- T, out of the flight program and most likely on my way to Vietnam as an infantry officer!"

"Holy shit, when is this supposed to happen?"

"I get my two ET's today and tomorrow with my regular instructor and then I get my check ride with your instructor. That's why I was talking to him because I don't want to wait."

I didn't see Mel for the next couple of days, but saw his name on the flight schedule with Capt Lucci. When I checked the flight schedule for the next day, Friday, I saw that I was scheduled for an "Eight Check" with Capt Lucci and Mel was schedule to fly with my instructor, Capt Kingston. The hops were scheduled for mid- morning so it would be all over one way or another by noon.

Friday morning we were seated at the same briefing table in the ready room with Capt's Lucci and Kingston. Capt Lucci didn't have much to say so our brief didn't take very long and we took off a good fifteen minutes before Mel and Kingston.

It was one of those chilly but crystal clear days in the Pensacola area and the ceiling and visibility were unlimited. Initially the air might be a little bumpy but it would be a great day for flying. I liked Capt Lucci from the first time he spoke to me and was really ready for this hop. So far in my very short flying career, I'd had days when I really had to work at making the aircraft do exactly what it was supposed to do; and then there were days when it felt like the aircraft was part of me and I could make the aircraft slip seamlessly from one maneuver to the next.

Shortly after takeoff I knew it was going to be one of those days. I did every maneuver Capt Lucci had briefed me to do in exactly that order and he never said a word until after my last touch and go at the outlying airfield up in Brewton, Alabama when he said, "Good hop, take me home."

We were back on deck in the flight line shack signing off the aircraft maintenance report (called the yellow sheet) when we saw Mel and Capt Kingston taxi into a parking place. When they got out of the aircraft, Capt Kingston headed straight for the line shack and Mel headed for the squadron ready room. I really didn't know what this meant but hoped it wasn't bad. I could tell Capt Lucci was taking his time because I was pretty sure he wanted to know how the hop went. As Capt Kingston entered the line shack and started signing off his yellow sheet I decided to step outside but stay close enough that I could eavesdrop on any conversation. As soon as I stepped outside I could hear Capt Lucci start speaking to Capt Kingston.

"Well Bill, how did Gibbs do?"

"Mike, it was one of the damnedest things I've ever seen."

"What do you mean by that, did he pass or not?"

"Before I give you my answer I want you to just listen. Take off, climb out, and all the high work were fine. He did the spins, stalls, and acrobatics no problem. Performed well on the High and Low altitude emergencies I gave him. I told him to take us into the landing pattern at Brewton and put a couple approaches in the carrier box. His pattern entry and break in the overhead were perfect, downwind perfect. As he came off the 180 (abeam position for landing) I thought I saw him retching. I said 'Gibbs, are you getting sick?' He simply shook his head. I kept watching him very closely and I could clearly see him retching. I said 'Gibbs, are you getting airsick?' and again he shook his head. I said 'Goddamnit don't lie to me I can see puke running out the left side of your mouth.' He shook his head again. I said, 'You better put em all in the damn carrier box or you're finished.' That kid did 5 perfect touch and goes into the carrier box and I told him to exit the landing pattern and head back here. As soon as he got us out of the pattern and leveled off for the trip home I took the aircraft. Now get this Mike, I said 'Lt Gibbs, I just want to know how a guy with a mouthful of puke can fly 5 perfect approaches?' After a slight pause he says, 'Well Sir, I just kept swallowing the juice and put the big pieces off to the side.' So Mike, no matter what the rules are, I can't turn somebody in that wants to fly that bad. As far as I'm concerned, he passed with flying colors."

I never told Mel that I overheard that conversation and to my knowledge, he was never airsick again during flight school.

CHAPTER SIX

FATHERHOOD AND THE STUDENT NAVAL
AVIATOR

NAS WHITING FIELD, NORTH
Training Squadron TWO (VT-2)
March 1966

Marguerite was getting very close to her due date and I had
finished TPA and was entering Basic Instrument Flight.
I'd really loved TPA and I loved everything about the T-28.
I loved the sound of that big old nine cylinder radial engine
as it cranked through eight blades before turning on the
magnetos and hitting the engine primer button. I loved the
sound that the engine made when it caught and came up to
idle speed. I loved the smell of the exhaust fumes and I
really loved the dulcet tones of the engine as the aircraft
passed by overhead smoothly cruising along.
   As much as I had enjoyed it all, there were two things
getting ready to happen that made me very nervous now.
After the joys of feeling like a real pilot in TPA, I now had
to start all over again and learn to fly the aircraft using
basic instruments. This was a whole new ball game.
They had something called a "Link Trainer" which was a
simulator for instrument flight. You flew your first hops in
that and then you got into the back seat of the aircraft and
snapped closed a canvas cover that encompassed the entire
rear cockpit; it was called the "Bag". All your instrument
hops in the actual aircraft from now on would be "Under
the Bag". It wasn't going to be fun; just one hell of a lot of
hard work. Up to this point we had learned to fly visually,
using visual flight rules, or VFR. Now we had to learn to
fly the aircraft under instrument conditions using
Instrument Flight Rules, or IFR. The weather wouldn't

always be good so we had to learn not only to fly by instruments, but to navigate from place to place without ever seeing outside the cockpit.

The second thing that was going to happen was the impending birth of our child. As a military wife, she had been nothing but supportive and I'd made her a promise before we got married that when we had children I would find a way, no matter what, to be right by her side during the birth of our children.

My concern for the impending birth of our child was showing in my work. My primary thoughts were for the safety and well- being of Marguerite and the baby. I was trying very hard to think about instrument scan, the different patterns flown on basic instruments, but I wasn't thinking hard enough. I'd struggled through the first two hops and knew if I didn't do better I would most likely get a down. I told my instructor about the impending birth and he suggested that I take myself off the schedule for a couple days. He said it wasn't a good idea to fly with something like that hanging over your head and told me to see Major Moriarity.

When the Major heard what I had to say he told me this was a very common problem for young officers. Besides learning to fly, the next thing they did was start a family.

"If you don't have your head and ass wired together you have no business in a cockpit. I'm taking you off the flight schedule but you check in at the squadron every day and once that kid is born, I'm gonna fly your ass off to make up for lost time."

Friday, 17 March 1967

My mother and little sister flew into town to "Help Out" if the baby was born in the next few days. It was my little sister's spring break so it was a good deal for her. Marguerite and I weren't too sure how much help they

67

would be because now that they were in Florida, their main interest was going to the beaches.

Saturday, 18 March 1967
   The visit was coming along about like you would expect when your mother or mother-in-law comes to town.   We toured around the airfields and took some pictures near the aircraft.

Sunday, 19 March 1967
   We took our guests to the beach.   It was windy, very cool and a real crappy day for the beach.   The road down to the beach was very bumpy and I could tell Marguerite was not comfortable.

Monday, 20 March 1967
   We ventured out in the morning but I could tell that Marguerite would be much better off at home and that's where I made sure we went.

Tuesday, 21 March 1967
   I woke up at 0630 and looked over at Marguerite.   She was lying on her back of course but being very still.   I could clearly see a tear running down her right cheek.   I said, "Are you all right?"
   "I think it's time we head for the hospital."
   To a guy experiencing this for the first time this is like sounding "General Quarters".   I came straight out of bed and got dressed.   Marguerite already had an outfit laid out just in case and she'd packed a bag several days before.   I went in and woke my mom to tell her we were leaving and of course she got up and immediately started asking questions.   I was doing my best to quickly answer her questions without being rude but she was slowing us down.
   Marguerite said, "Would you please come on, NOW!"

I grabbed the suitcase and left my mom standing there. I yelled over my shoulder that I would call her later. Marguerite had been experiencing labor pains for most of the night but didn't want to wake me until she was sure it was really time to go.

We got to the hospital very quickly and since it was a small place they had Marguerite back into the delivery area and started prepping her right away. She'd told the doctors several times that I wanted to be with her during the birth so a nurse came out, put a gown on me, and took me back to Marguerite. She was in a bed- like thing that had metal rails on the sides. She was partially sitting up and had her feet in those stirrup things. There were a couple of nurses nearby and a man that I assumed was her doctor.

He said, "Your wife is pretty well dilated so I don't think it will be very long before you're a father. Are you going to be all right watching this happen?"

"I think I'll be just fine, doctor."

I was standing on Marguerite's right side and I reached over the railing of her bed and offered her my left hand. When she took it I gave her hand a gentle squeeze and looked directly into her eyes and gave her a wink. She seemed to relax a little but didn't turn loose of my hand. The doctor made another check of the dilatation progress, stepped back and sat down on a stool that had wheels. I allowed myself to relax a little seeing as how the doctor didn't seem to be too concerned at the moment and all of a sudden Marguerite experienced a major contraction. She stiffened up a bit, let out a small animal-like noise and with a force not of this world, squeezed my hand so hard that I could not only feel the bones breaking, I could hear them.

I felt my face go flush and for a second, thought I might pass out but got control of myself. The doctor must have known exactly what happened because he asked me, not Marguerite, if I was ok. As soon as the contraction subsided, Marguerite relaxed her grip and with the best forced smile, I extracted my hand from hers and said, "Honey, why don't you just hang onto these metal railings for a while" and eased my hand down to my side. That wasn't very comfortable so I managed to slip my hand inside my left trouser pocket, which seemed to help with the pain.

There was one more contraction and I was damn glad she didn't have a hold of me. I thought she was going to bend those aluminum rails in half. Minutes later, we were the proud parents of a beautiful baby girl. The delivery room crew was very nice and allowed us to have a good look at our baby and know all the fingers, toes and everything else was as it should be, then they were whisked away.

As I was standing there watching my family roll away, the doctor came over and wanted to see my hand.

"Lt Spicer, you might want to go by your sick bay when you're finished here, and have them take a good look at this because I'm pretty sure you may have at least one broken bone." He smiled, showed me to the door and walked away.

Shortly before noon I got back out to the base and went to the sickbay. The Corpsman on duty took a look and then an x-ray of my left hand. While we were waiting for the film to develop he asked me how this happened. I told him and he said, "Sir, you let a pregnant woman get a hold of you while having contractions. That's a dangerous thing to do." I had to agree.

Without waiting for a flight surgeon, he looked at the film. I had a crack in the bone on the left edge of my hand and my little finger had a more impressive crack.

The last thing I wanted was a grounding chit from a flight surgeon, so I told the Corpsman that I was going on leave and to wrap it up as best he could and I would check back with them when I came off leave. I think he knew I was bullshitting him from the start, but I also was pretty sure he knew why. I wasn't the only Student Naval Aviator that wanted no part of flight surgeons or grounding chits.

The Corpsman did a terrific job of wrapping up my hand and immobilizing my finger; I think it was far better than a cast. I knew he was taking a chance for me and told him so. He didn't say a word. He provided some extra wraps and told me once the swelling went down to rewrap my hand but keep the wrap on for at least three weeks. I thanked him and went on my way.

I'd called my mom and given her the news and then went to the squadron to check in with the Major. When I reported to him in his office I made sure to try and keep my left hand either behind me or at least out of sight.

He said, "You bringing your family home from the hospital tomorrow?"

"Yes Sir."

"Well you get that baby home. Nobody is gonna get a wink of sleep the first couple of days, and you won't be worth a shit for flying. You take tomorrow off, get them home and settled in and come in just for ground school the rest of the week. I'll put you back in the hopper for Monday and you better show up ready with your 'Head and Ass wired together', you read me?"

"Yes Sir, I read you loud and clear." I knew better than to say thank you.

It was a little tricky working the engine fuel mixture lever, the propeller lever, and the throttle with a bandaged hand. Every once in a while I would bang it up against something that really hurt. But by the time I'd finished Basic Instruments, and our daughter finally slept all night, both Marguerite and my left hand were as good as new.

CHAPTER SEVEN

ELLYSON FIELD, WINGS OF GOLD

HELICOPTER TRAINING SQUADRON 8, (HT-8)
NAVAL AIR TRAINING COMMAND
PENSACOLA, FLORIDA
August, 1967

Ellyson Field was the last stop on a journey I never
believed possible and there was just one more hurdle to
clear: learning to fly a helicopter. I was a fully trained
fixed wing pilot. I could make the T-28 do just about
anything and fly it in all kinds of weather, both daylight
and dark. As far as my friends and I were concerned, we
were pilots and had come here just to check out in helos
and get our wings. We discovered very quickly it wasn't
going to be that easy.

Here at Ellyson they currently had two different types of
helicopters. The basic trainer was the TH-13M Bell. It
was a little bubble canopy thing with a metal frame work
for a fuselage, a rotor head with two blades and a very
under powered motor. It looked like a toy. They also had
a real no shit helicopter, the type I'd seen over in Vietnam:
the Sikorsky UH-34 Sea Horse. It was considered a
medium transport helicopter. Oddly enough it had exactly
the same engine, the R-1820, that was in the T-28 but it
was mounted backwards in the airframe for reasons
currently unknown to most of us.

The training format here would be the same. We would
start off with ground school half a day and scheduled
flights the other half. Due to the war in Vietnam, Marine
students were being hustled along. Since Saufley Field we
would be scheduled for multiple hops as soon as we
completed ground school.

Our first flights would be in the TH-13M and we would actually be allowed to solo it a few times, but the priority was to get us into the UH-34 because that's what a lot of us would be flying after graduation.

GROUND SCHOOL

The first class would be Aerodynamics of the Rotating Foil, or what makes a helicopter fly. Our instructor was a Navy Lt. Commander Allen. When LCDR Allen introduced himself he stated that he was a Naval Academy graduate and that he also had a Master's degree in Aerodynamics.

"Gentlemen, we are about to embark on a master's level course on the Aerodynamics of the rotating foil. You will be given a year of intensive instruction at this level in just six weeks. It will be like trying to drink from a fire hose. Do the best you can. At the end of these six weeks, some of you will know exactly what it is that makes a helicopter fly and some of you will swear that it's all Bullshit and Black Magic! I've been teaching this course for almost two years and personally I'm a Bullshit and Black Magic man myself."

He didn't waste any time and started right in with our first lesson. I listened intently, made some notes and on my way home that night went by K-Mart and picked up a small plastic helicopter that had four blades on the Rotorhead. My premise was still holding true for me: what I couldn't intellectualize I could visualize and I certainly wasn't going to get started behind the eight ball here.

There wasn't going to be too much else to ground school. Of course we had to learn the systems of the TH-13M and the UH-34 but it was the Aerodynamics of the rotating foil that would make or break you.

Lt Allen wasn't kidding; the information was coming at us very fast. We were learning about articulated Rotorheads, Semi-rigid Underslung Rotorheads, and Rigid

Rotorheads. We learned about lead and lag, hunt and drag, power settling or vortex ring, and last but not least, the deadly Retreating Blade Tip Stall. Throw in a couple calculations on the HIGE/ HOGE Charts (Hover In Ground Effect, Hover Out of Ground Effect), a complete understanding of Density Altitude, and the mysteries of the rotating foil started to make sense.

This time I was ready, I was getting it. Besides my little plastic helo, we were also flying at the same time; therefore I could visualize, actually see the different aerodynamic phenomena he was talking about, all except the Retreating Blade Tip Stall. But after one flight I could picture what that would be like. I was getting it good enough that my buddy Rod even asked me for help and I had to pinch myself to believe it.

FLYING THE TH-13M BELL

On the 25th of August I had my first flight in the Bell. I would have flown sooner but I had to wait for a very small instructor. Heat affects helicopter performance. In Aerodynamics, we'd learned about Density Altitude and the HIGE and HOGE calculations. The Bell was pretty underpowered so if you were a big guy like me or Rod Bell, both six foot and over two hundred pounds with our flight gear on, you needed to have a very small instructor to keep the weight down, otherwise on very hot days you didn't have enough power to lift the helo off the ground. Mel, Wiley and some of the other guys were a good forty pounds lighter than Rod and I, so their options for instructors were far greater. The hot sticky August afternoons created a very High Density Altitude, which greatly reduced the TH-13M's performance and was the reason for the forced pairings on the flight schedule.

I was finally scheduled with a Navy Lt named Prunell. He was about five foot seven inches; tall and whippet like. If he weighed 140 lbs with his flight gear on, I would have been surprised. The first hop was simply a helo ride. He told me to sit back, relax and enjoy the ride which is exactly what I did. This was really great. You could see all sorts of things going on below; it was a real bird's eye view. The visual sensations were radically different from anything I'd experienced thus far. We left the airfield proper and headed out to what he called site 4, which was a huge empty field that had lots of the Bells buzzing around. He made an approach to a spot on the field, hovered briefly, then took off and climbed back up to altitude. He then demonstrated an autorotation, which is what would have to be done if the engine should quit. Unlike an airplane, there was no bailout from a helo. Once you strapped in, you were there until the helo was back on the ground one way or another.

Autorotation occurred when the rotor system was no longer being driven by the engine. Under engine power as the blades rotated, air is pulled down through the rotor system. Without engine power the air flow is reversed and it goes up through the rotor system providing the force necessary to drive the rotors and allow the pilot to bring the aircraft down under control.

Other than the helicopter coming down very quickly, it all seemed to work out just fine and Mr. Prunell made a very soft touchdown right on the spot he'd selected. Next, he picked up the helo into a hover and "Air Taxied" over to a square that was marked out on the ground. Since this model of helo had skids and not wheels, it had to be lifted into the hover and then maneuvered over the ground, hence "Air Taxi". Unlike an aircraft with wheels that you could taxi on the ground, you had to fly this helo before you ever officially took off.

He proceeded to demonstrate the hover and control movements required to hover around the square. He told me these would be the maneuvers I would be learning to master in the next 12 hops. He lifted the helo out of the hover and climbed back up to altitude heading back for the base. It was generally a very pleasant experience and I thought this helo flying was going to be pure fun.

My first impression was just a little hasty because the very next day I met my regular instructor and it was going to be all business. Navy Lt Redman was shorter than Lt Prunell; he must have been the minimum height for the flight program and an officer. I have no idea what he would have weighed, his flight suit hung on him like a large bag. He gave me a once over glance, a quick brief on the contents of the hop and said, "Let's go."

Like yesterday, he headed the aircraft straight for Site 4 and shot an approach into the big field. He then air taxied or "translated" the helo to a position near the far northwest corner and brought it to a steady hover facing the fence about 30 feet from the third fence post from the corner. We were facing Highway 90 and could see cars passing by.

"Ok Spicer, we are going to sit here in the hover and I am going to turn the controls over to you one at a time. As we do this I want you to maintain the same position this aircraft is currently holding. You know what the controls are and what they do, so let's start with the rudder pedals. Place your feet on the rudder pedals and get the feel of them, keep the nose of the aircraft pointed right at that fence post."

I put my feet on the rudder pedals and was amazed at the sensitivity. Just putting them on the pedals I caused the aircraft to yaw. I readjusted my feet and got another pronounced yaw. I thought I would try a little pressure in each direction just too get a little more feel. What I got was a very rapid yaw, almost snappy and a little bit scary.

"As you can see, the rudder is very sensitive in this aircraft. Don't think about consciously pushing on the pedal like you did in a T-28, it's enough to think about adding a little rudder and that will most likely be enough."

He was right and things got better. Next he told me to put my hand on the cyclic, which was the name for the control stick in between my legs, just like the stick in a regular aircraft. The cyclic controls the tilt of the rotor disc. That's the way the blades appear as they are rotating around, as if they form a disc. It was a term unique to helicopter flying. To go forward, backward, left or right you pushed the cyclic in the corresponding direction.

I placed my right hand on the cyclic and he waved his right hand in the air to show me I now had that control. It felt strange, there was vibration and the slightest movement resulted in a rapid movement of the helo. I felt like I was sitting on a top that was about to go completely out of balance.

"Try and hold the cyclic very lightly, like you hold an egg."

I could feel my hand gripping hell out of the cyclic and tried to relax it a little and even as I did so the aircraft started moving in a direction I didn't want it to go. I was starting to work very hard at keeping this whirling dervish 30 feet from the post.

"When I came through training here there was a Royal Navy helo pilot on exchange instructor duty. He was my instructor during this phase of training. When it came to how tightly to grip the cyclic he described it to me as, 'About the amount of pressure that the Queen would use in holding a Tramps penis.'"

It broke up my efforts a little but he let me struggle on. I was beginning to work up a little perspiration and my hand started to hurt.

"Ok, now we are going to try the collective. I want you to put your left hand down on your collective and get the feel of that. I'll keep my hand on my collective for the moment."

The collective is the control that is completely different from a fixed wing aircraft and the most difficult to operate.

It's to the left of the pilot's seat. While seated in the cockpit, if you drop your arm down the left side of the seat it will be the first thing you feel with your hand. The pilot pulls the collective up or pushes it down and the rotor blades move correspondingly. Pulling up increases the pitch on the blades and would cause the helo to climb. Pushing down reduces the pitch of the blades and the helo will descend. However, pushing down or pulling up must be coordinated with an increase or decrease of the engine throttle. At the end of the collective is a throttle grip, much like one on a motorcycle. If pulling up on the collective, you must add throttle by twisting the throttle grip to the left and if pushing down, reduce the throttle by twisting to the right. Just the opposite directions of a motorcycle. We were told to avoid riding motorcycles during helicopter training.

I dropped my left hand down and easily found the collective. I could feel Lt Redman making very small and subtle movements both up and down as well as adjusting the throttle. It didn't seem too bad at the moment. As I'm sitting there with both feet and both hands on the controls of a helicopter for the first time it suddenly dawned on me that in order to fly this thing you would have to have both feet and both hands moving all the time. Unlike a fixed wing aircraft that you could trim up and actually take your hands off the controls, this thing was going to be like an out of control top anytime you didn't have your hands and feet on the controls. There would be no sitting back and relaxing. It was going to be a little like standing up, alternately stomping your feet very lightly while using your right hand to rub your stomach in a circular motion and your left hand to pat the top or your head. If you couldn't walk and chew gum at the same time you better stay the hell out of helos.

"Anytime you're ready just nod your head and I will give you complete control."

I had the helo about 30 feet from the post and pointed right at it, was holding this position pretty well and gave the nod.

"You have complete control of the aircraft."

Nothing happened for a full 5 seconds and then I started drifting backwards and going up. I pushed forward on the cyclic and the fence post started getting bigger immediately and I was still going up. I pulled back on the cyclic and reduced too much power; the aircraft was going backwards, sinking toward the ground and yawing to the left. The crash was imminent, and just about the time I was feeling an adrenalin spurt expecting to crash, I heard those lovely words, "I have the aircraft."

Lt Redman took control and without me being able to even perceive the movement of the controls put the aircraft right back into a perfect hover about 30 feet from the post. I was dazzled and discouraged to say the least.

"You have the aircraft. Try and relax."

It might have been a full ten seconds before everything went to hell. I was all over the place. I couldn't figure out what to do next and just taking care of one axis wasn't going to get it; there had to be simultaneous corrections in all three axes to get the damn thing under control.

"I have the aircraft."

He took control again and turned the helo around and from the hover pushed the nose down to start forward and climbed away to the traffic pattern altitude of 300 feet.

"We will take it around the pattern one time and give you a chance to relax for a minute or two."

We repeated this cycle for the next forty some minutes until it was time to head back to the main field at Ellyson. Each time I tried to hover I got a little better and the last time I tried I held the damn thing in position for almost one minute. Of course I was all over the place and if Lt Redman hadn't been there I seriously doubt I could have kept the helicopter within the confines of that 80 acre field.

He let me fly the aircraft about half way back to
Ellyson. Straight and level wasn't too bad and it actually
gave me a chance to play with the collective and throttle a
little bit. This part I would get very quickly but the
hovering and the air taxiing was gonna take a lot of work.

During the debrief Lt Redman told me that I had
performed well above average for the first hop and not to
be discouraged. He said most guys on their first hovers
don't last more than 30 seconds before the instructor had to
take it. The comments didn't help. I was completely
discouraged, my right hand ached from squeezing the
cyclic, my calf muscles hurt from trying to hold my feet
just so on the rudder pedals. I thought I could fly and now
this; it was a humbling experience.

The next several hops were pure frustration. I was a
pilot but this little toy-looking sonofabitch was kicking my
ass as well as all of my buddies'. One of the guys scared
his instructor so badly he made him get out and ride back to
base with the duty crash crew that was stationed at site 4.

It wasn't until hop six that it all started coming together
for me. It was a little like learning to ride a bicycle. At
first you wobble all over the place. You are going forward
but almost out of control, your mom or dad are running
alongside to steady you up and one day you just ride away
from them; you got it. You don't think about how to do
something, you just do it. That's what happened for me.
When we started, Lt Redman hadn't said a word. I got the
engine started and the rotor head engaged, lifted into the
hover and taxied out to the take- off point. Once away
from the airfield I headed straight for site 4 and upon
entering the pattern he told me to shoot an approach to one
of the boxes marked on the field. I just did it; I didn't
think about doing it, I just did it. I came to the hover right
in the middle of the box and he told me to translate over to
our favorite spot by the post in the northwest corner of the
field. It was the same thing, I just made sure we were clear

of any traffic and taxied right over, putting the aircraft into a nice steady hover pointing at the post. I sat there in the hover for a good three, or four minutes before he told me to do something else. He was right, the less pressure you used on the stick the easier it was to fly this thing. I could feel the gyroscopic effect of the rotor blades going around and by lightly holding the cyclic you could actually use the effect to keep the aircraft steady. For the rest of the hop it seemed as if all I had to do was think about the maneuver and the helicopter did it. Lt Redman didn't say a word but I would catch an occasional look of satisfaction on his face.

We finished our ground school and our flying pace picked up quite a bit. From the 11th of September until the 18th I flew two hops a day, three of which were solos. The 18th was my last hop in the TH-13M, I was just another step closer to those Wings of Gold.

UH-34 SIKORSKY SEA HORSE

During the last phase of training, the run for the wings would be in a real no kidding tactical machine. I'd seen and flown in these things in Vietnam and it was hard to believe I was now going to get a chance to fly one. The differences were enormous. The Bells maximum gross weight was 2952 pounds, just over a ton, and the engine was only 260 horsepower. The H-34 empty weight was 8,000 pounds with a maximum gross weight of 14,000 pounds. The engine put out 1475 shaft horse power, the fuselage was 56 feet long and the rotors had a diameter of 56 feet as well; talk about a difference. It was over 15 feet tall and the cockpit was damn near 10 feet off the ground, just climbing up to get in was a chore. On a nice hot afternoon you could work up a full sweat during the pre-flight.

My first hop in the H-34 was with the officer that would be my regular instructor for the final phase of training, Navy Lt Bill Bailes. There were no more free rides, you were expected to jump right in and fly the damn thing from day one. Lt Bailes did the first start, got the rotors going and showed you how to taxi; this time on the ground because the H-34 had wheels, but from there on you were "Hands On". He talked you through things but you were expected to do it. Compared to the sensitivity of the Bell, this thing felt like you were flying a freight train, and if you needed to apply some rudder, it took a boot full compared to the Bell.

H-34's practiced at Site 8; it wasn't a good idea to mix up the Bells with the H-34's. Before I even got to site 8 my right hand was starting to ache. We would do exactly the same maneuvers with the H-34 as we did in the Bell, but it felt so big. My first approach to a hover was a little erratic but I got it into a hover of sorts. Lt Bailes did not appear to be the excitable type which for the moment was a good thing.

Once you got the thing in the hover it wasn't too bad, but going from flight into a hover you passed through something called "translational lift". It was very recognizable in the H-34 and as the aircraft passed through this phase of flight it made a distinct shudder. When taking off, once you felt the shudder, you knew you were flying, not hovering. Upon landing approach, the shudder was a good signal to make sure you were coming up on the power to cushion your landing.

The aircraft also had something called an ASE (Automatic Stabilization Equipment). It was an electro-hydraulic system that made the aircraft more stable, especially in the hover. It wasn't an autopilot by any sense but if you didn't think it helped much just turn it off and watch what happens. The ASE was used by the instructors as a punishment or attention getter. If you weren't doing well or had "Your Head Up Your ASS" they would have you turn off the ASE. The aircraft was flyable but that's when the "Whirling Dervish" came back, it was like trying to hover a TH-13 that was on steroids. The ASE had a test that had to be performed on the ground after start to make sure it was going to function properly. I could never get the sequence right and it annoyed Lt Bailes. Mel and Wiley could do the test in their sleep and I finally got both of them to take me out to an empty aircraft and get me straightened out.

Although this was my first hop Lt Bailes had me turn off the ASE for about half the hop. It wasn't fun but he told me not to completely rely on something like that. In combat, I couldn't abort a mission for something that simple.

We started on the 19th of September and flew almost every day. "They" had given Lt Bailes two Marine students and the priority was to get us finished in the shortest possible time. My flying partner was Lt John Mills. He and Lt Bailes were both from the Greenville Spartanburg area of South Carolina. We flew almost every day until the 31st of October. Our last phase of training was instrument flying. You actually filed instrument flight plans and flew various places both day and night. Our last six hops were to be a "road show". In order to knock out several hops in a row the instructors would take students on a road show and in our case we went cross country to Greenville Spartanburg, so Lt Bailes and Lt Mills could visit their families. We each flew three hops up and three back to Ellyson; the last hop for both of us would be our D-12 Check, which was our instrument check and final hop as a flight student.

We packed a bag for an overnight stay (RO1N = Remain Over1Night) and the three of us departed in our H-34 heading northeast. Lt Bailes and Lt Mills were in the cockpit and I was riding in the crew chief's seat down below.

Each leg of the flight Mills and I would alternate. The aircraft performed just fine; the weather was actually pretty good all weekend. On Nov 4th on the leg of the trip into Ellyson Field I flew my last hop as a Student Naval Aviator. It was at night with a slight mist and made the lights of Pensacola look even more majestic.

At Ellyson Field these days Winging Ceremonies occurred twice a week: Tuesday's and Friday's. Mills, Gibbs, Houck, me and four other Marines received those precious Wings of Gold on Tuesday, 7 November 1967 but really didn't get to celebrate until Friday the 10th of Nov, the Birthday of the Marine Corps.

The party was always held on Friday at the Ellyson Field Officers Club. For the newly designated Naval Aviators, tradition required that you went to the bar and placed twenty bucks in a pool to buy drinks for everyone. The bartender would mix you a special drink called an "OVERBOOST"; you dropped your wings into the mug, drank the drink in one gulp and caught your wings in your teeth.

Since it was the Birthday of the Marine Corps it made things even better and it was also the day Wiley got his wings. We also received our orders to the next duty station and were on our way the very next day.

Once again fate smiled on Marguerite and I; we had orders to the West Coast for training before going to Vietnam. Mills, Wiley and Houck were also heading west. Mel and several others got assigned to the east coast. "Word" was the west was best. Like most of the things I had accomplished thus far in the Corps, the finish was somewhat anticlimactic; it was the journey that was the exciting part. Marguerite looked fabulous at the ceremony and looked as proud as I felt when she pinned those wings on my chest. Without her, I doubt I would have made it.

Two brand new fearless Naval Aviators, Mel and me on "OUR" day, 7 November 1967

EPILOGUE

Lt John Mills was killed on his first training flight in California when the CH-46 he was flying crashed in the mountain training area. Lt Larry Houck was killed and Lt Don Wiley lost his left arm while serving in Vietnam. There were far too many others that also fell along the way, but of our little group, Mel and I were the only two who managed to make it to retirement relatively unscathed.

Mel, Wiley and me, 27 years after getting our Wings.

CHAPTER EIGHT

EVERETT

Marine Corps Helicopter Training Facility, Santa Anna,
California (LTA)
Marine Medium Helicopter Training Squadron 301 (HMT-
301)
Duty: Helicopter Pilot Operational Training
December 1967

I'd gotten my Naval Aviator Wings just about a month ago.
Because of the war in Vietnam no one was getting a full 30
days leave. The day after I had my wings pinned on my
chest I was on my way to California and HMT-301.
(Marine Medium Helicopter Training Squadron 301)
Since arriving, there had been no slack; it was fly, fly, fly.
We all knew things were going to be radically different
when during our squadron check in process, "They" told us
the day, date, departure point and flight number of the
aircraft that would be taking us to Vietnam. Nobody had
to tell us to pay attention or learn our lessons well. We
were to receive a minimum of 100 hours of operational
training in the UH-34D under as close to combat conditions
as "They" could create and so far, "They" had lived up to
everything "They" said.
    My first flight or hop in HMT-301 had been a real
revelation and my instructor had been Captain Everett
Haymore. Prior to actually meeting him, I was sitting in
the squadron ready room going over what the hop would
consist of and studying the emergency procedures that
would be covered.
    Captain Haymore entered the ready room and called out
my name. I was a little nervous since this was my first hop

here and I really didn't know what to expect. I jumped up and said, "Here Sir" before I thought.

Captain Haymore looked at me and said, "What the fuck are you doing?"

"I'm studying the training guide and the emergency procedures in the NATOPS manual (Naval Aircraft Training and Operational Procedures, the how-to book for a particular aircraft) for this hop Sir."

"Gimme that crap and call me EV."

I handed him my manual and training syllabus. He took it, promptly turned and threw the whole handful into the nearest GI can. (GI can= Garbage Can)

He said, "Come on kid, I'm gonna show you how to stay alive in Vietnam."

Then we went out to the aircraft and for the next hour and a half he proceeded to show me things I didn't know were aerodynamically possible in a helicopter. He frightened me more than once and a couple of times I was pretty certain I would die before getting back to base. Since it was my first flight here, it was called a FAM flight and the only time I touched the controls was flying out to the mountain training area and then back to base.

When it was over and we were walking back from the flight line to the ready room, Captain Haymore turned to me and said, "When I get finished with you, you will be able to do exactly what you just saw and you'll be able to do it at night." I didn't see how that would be possible.

I don't believe there was an instructor pilot in the squadron that had been back more than a year from Vietnam. Every one of them had seen quite a bit of combat flying and some of them had already completed two tours over there. "They" knew what they were talking about and Captain Haymore was the most respected one of the bunch.

EV had been good to his word and I was a completely different pilot now than I was just a couple weeks ago. I had flown several times with him and was very comfortable in the air. EV was one of those natural pilots that I would come to recognize and try to emulate. He was a task master and a "Nice Job" from him was truly a compliment.

Because of the war, we trained 6 days a week and today, Saturday, I was scheduled for an early morning hop with EV. This hop would be a check ride in the mountain training sites.

The San Jacinto Mountains were a few miles east of the Santa Anna facility and provided a great place to train a helicopter pilot heading to Vietnam. The mountains rose steadily and at the peaks were 10,834 feet above sea level, separating the Los Angeles area from the desert city of Palm Springs. From the highest landing site you had a spectacular view of Los Angeles to the west, the desert and Palm Springs to the east.

The Marine Corps had twelve mountain landing sites plus a large site, about two football fields long, called Blackstar. It was the lowest and where you started. From there, the sites were scattered through the mountains and as the numbers of the sites increased so did the altitude and difficulty. Site 12 was the highest and most difficult. It was located on the highest ridge and had been formed by using a bull dozer to push a flat spot big enough for a helicopter to land fairly comfortably. Down the top of the ridge, the forest service had made a trail running the length of the ridge; it was actually a fire break. It could have been loosely construed as a road but was pretty primitive. Depending on the winds, the approach was usually perpendicular to the ridgeline and when you landed, the helicopter was more or less sitting in the middle of the fire break/road, either looking into the L.A. basin or into the desert at Palm Springs.

This check ride was a test I had to complete before moving on to a more difficult stage of training. I had previously landed in all twelve sights but only at half the

maximum gross weight of the aircraft. Today, my task
was to land in all twelve at the maximum gross weight of
the aircraft. EV and the other instructors knew we would
seldom be flying around empty and would always be
expected to carry as much as the aircraft could hold on each
and every mission. If we got used to flying at the
maximum gross weight all the time, then a very heavy
aircraft in a dangerous situation would come as no surprise.

Since I was not yet and wouldn't be designated as a
HAC (Helicopter Aircraft Commander) for some time, I
was the co-pilot. As such, my place was in the left seat
and the HAC's was in the right seat. It was just opposite
of the fixed wing world where the plane commander sat in
the left seat and the co-pilot in the right. EV had
performed the HAC's duties for startup, pre-take off checks
and taxi but as soon as we reached the take- off position
turned the aircraft over to me.

He said, "Ok Red, you got it, let's go, Blackstar and
then one through twelve. If I have to take it at any point
it's your ass and if you're a good boy, I'll show you my
world famous ZERO SPEED full Autorotation from one
thousand feet to touchdown at the center mat when we get
back. "

I said, "Roger, I have control." I received takeoff
clearance from the tower and after takeoff headed almost
due east for the Blackstar landing site.

It was one of those gorgeous California mornings, clear
as crystal and just a little cool. EV tuned one of our
navigational radios to his favorite commercial radio station
and seemed to be enjoying the ride with a bird's eye view,
one of the perks of flying helicopters.

The hop was going well and I was steadily working my
way up the mountains. As I came out of Site 11, I made a
pretty wide swing out toward the east. The scenery was
such a stark transition from the green of the mountains to
the endless tan of the desert with only patches of green out

91

near Palm Springs. I was also trying to get a feel for the winds up here. A morning like this was unusual; it was cool and calm. In the afternoons, the winds and turbulence would build up to provide some real nasty gusts, but not this morning. The air was smooth as I made my turn to line up on site 12.

Approaching site 12 from the east made the landing zone more visible and was also more comfortable upon touch down because the site wasn't exactly level. Landing from the east the aircraft touched down slightly up hill which was much more comfortable than downhill.

I had a good steady approach going, 45 knots of airspeed, touchdown point framed in the windscreen, power coming up slowly so as to arrive at zero airspeed and zero altitude simultaneously. It was very dry and dusty so as I got in close to the touchdown point, the rotor downwash started kicking up a huge cloud of brown dust. At the edge of the landing zone I saw something flash and then I thought I saw something that looked like a blue blanket fly up. I immediately added power, dropped the nose slightly and made a quick turn to the left. If there was any flying debris out there I didn't want to fly through it and take a chance of getting something in the rotor system.

My wave off from the landing was a complete surprise to EV and he said, "What the hell are you doing?"

"I think I saw some type of crap being blown up by the rotor wash.

"Where?"

"At the 12 o'clock position on the zone, it was just a flash but I didn't want to take any chances."

"Ok, good headwork. Take it around again and we'll have a good look before we touch down but we need to land cause I gotta take a piss."

I set up for another approach and this time as we got in close to touchdown all I could see was the dust. EV said it

92

looked good and for me to go ahead and make my touchdown.

Just after touchdown EV set the parking brake and told me to roll the rotor turns back a bit while he got out and took a leak. He climbed down the side of the aircraft and took up a stance on the top of the right landing gear tire.

The dust settled and from the bushes about 30 yards in front of the aircraft emerged two long haired males clad only in blue jeans. The shoulder length hair blown around by the rotor wash was only restrained by the "Hippie Head Band" which I guess was part of their uniform of the day. They were waving their arms around wildly and although I couldn't hear them I could tell they were screaming at us.

From my position I could only see EVs' head and shoulders. He must have looked like quite a sight to these guys. EV was a big fellow, six foot two or better, a good two hundred thirty pounds. He still had on his flight helmet with the visor pulled down and his survival vest, so he looked even bigger. Standing there urinating from his perch atop the right main landing gear tire.

I saw him turn his head in the direction of the two wild men but it did not give him cause to stop his urination. He just looked at them and continued.

The two men were suddenly joined by two half naked females and the ladies began picking up clods of dirt and throwing them in our direction. This was neither effective nor bothersome. I could see the edge of the landing zone clearly now and the flash I'd seen on the first approach was from the chrome on a motorcycle that was parked at the edge of the landing zone right up against the bushes. Now I could see another motorcycle lying on its side. It must have been blown over on my first approach.

EV was still standing on top of the right landing gear tire having finished his business but was just observing the scene. He turned and climbed back up into the cockpit. As soon as he reconnected to the aircrafts' ICS (intercom

93

system) he said, "Can you believe those hippie assholes. They've ridden those bikes up here and are camping out. Probably know this is a safe place to smoke their damn dope. I have control of the aircraft."

Outside, the four happy campers were continuing their assault with dirt clods and were now starting to come closer to the aircraft and possibly becoming a hazard.

EV said, "Watch this."

He increased the rotor turns in preparation to lift off. This of course increased the rotor down wash to something akin to Hurricane force winds. The blowing dust and sand became an immediate deterrent to the happy campers and they started to retreat in the direction of the motorcycles at the edge of the landing zone.

EV lifted the helicopter into the hover and started to translate forward maintaining about a 15 foot hover. The rotor wash was now at hurricane strength and started moving all sorts of things around rapidly. The first to go were all the beer cans, then clothing, then heavier objects including the motorcycles. By his skillful handling of the helicopter, EV was using the rotor wash to literally roll the motorcycles and everything else down the very steep side of the ridge.

I would get an occasional glimpse of the havoc he was creating but I couldn't see the happy campers anywhere. EV continued to maneuver until he'd managed to roll those motorcycles a good 25 or 30 yards down the hill and here the bushes got too thick, and stopped the progress of the motorcycles.

EV said, "Well, that ought to keep those hippie assholes busy for a while and maybe they will think before they decide to trespass on government property."

He gave control of the aircraft back to me and told me to over fly the site again so he could wave. I did as instructed and then headed back to base. Due to other aircraft in the pattern the tower would not approve EVs' request for his world famous ZERO SPEED AUTO but he promised he'd show me some other time. I managed to do a credible job of faking great disappointment.

CHAPTER NINE

NAM 68/69

Travis Air Force Base
California
February
1968

Lt's Boroday and Houck and now Captain Spicer were
manifested on the same flight departing Travis Air Force
Base and heading for Okinawa. The guys in HMT-301
weren't kidding when they'd told us the day, date and
number of the flight we would be on to Vietnam. The only
real change was I'd been promoted from 1/Lt to Captain
just before we detached on leave.

   The LtCol from headquarters that told my class we'd all
be Captains within 36 months back in Basic School at
Quantico wasn't kidding either but even he got it wrong. It
had only been 28 months since he'd made that statement.
My class had been the last of the 18 month Second
Lieutenants. We were promoted to 1/Lt for only ten
months and now we were all Captains. It was mind
boggling for me. I'd left Vietnam in late August 1965 as a
grunt Corporal and I'm headed back in February 1968 as a
Captain, aviator, husband and father.

   The three of us had flown our last flights in HMT-301
on the 29th of January and were given just 25 days for
travel and leave before catching this plane. I'd taken
Marguerite and baby daughter Katie back to Omaha to stay
with Marguerite's parents while I was in Vietnam.

   The war in Vietnam had escalated dramatically and the
nightly news didn't cover much else. The TET Offensive
was in full swing; there was a very bloody fight going on
for Hue City and the combat base at Khe Sanh had been

under siege for about a month and I would be going right into the middle of the whole thing. With the current intensity of the war, the reports coming back indicated that helicopter pilots were rapidly becoming a consumable item so I wanted her to be close to family in case I didn't come back.

It had been colder than hell in Omaha and the days I had with my family there had been pure hell. The strain of the forthcoming separation was palpable; we could hardly talk to one another. It might have been easier if I had kissed them goodbye in California and left immediately. Some of the other guys had done just that. Marguerite and I were both aware of the path we'd chosen and knew the good came with the bad, but no matter, when you realize that everything you worked for is now on the line it makes things very difficult.

When I caught my flight out to California it was almost a relief for me in some ways but I could not get the look in Marguerite's eyes out of my mind. I had plenty of time to think about it because I left on the 23rd, a day early just to make sure I didn't miss my flight. It was a good thing because due to an Air Force transportation glitch I didn't arrive at Travis until the wee hours of the morning on the 24th only to learn that my flight would now depart in the wee hours of the morning on the 25th so I now had another 24 hours to wait.

I ran into Pete Boroday at the San Francisco airport waiting for transportation to Travis. By the time we finally arrived at Travis, checked in and learned of the delay it was noon. Pete was very excited about trying to see San Francisco and he knew I'd been in and out of there many times when I was a Sea Going Marine. I told him I'd be his tour guide for the evening, and hoped like hell it would keep me from thinking about that look in Marguerite's eyes.

We caught an Air Force bus into town and I took Pete on a whirlwind tour of the high spots. We visited the Golden Gate Bridge, the Presidio, had a drink at the Top of the Mark and the Marine Memorial Hotel and I saved the best for last. I took him down to Fisherman's Wharf, Number Nine Grotto. We were wearing our Winter Service Alpha uniforms and I told Pete I'd been told years ago that if you were a Marine and went to Fisherman's Wharf, be sure to go in uniform. I'd done it a couple times when I was enlisted and someone always picked up my tab out of respect for the Marine Corps.

There was a waiting list for tables of course and the Maître D' told us to wait in the bar. I told Pete to order a "Perfect Manhattan," a specialty of the house. It wasn't long before we got a table with a great view of the harbor. Oyster's Kirkpatrick and Lobster Thermidor were things Pete had never experienced. When we called for the bill the waiter said, "It's been taken care of gentleman." Pete was dazzled. We left the waiter a very generous tip. Pete told me it would be a night he would never forget.

Our flight was a chartered 707 and completely packed. After way too much milling around and manifesting we finally departed in the wee hours of the 25th. I thought it would be a straight flight to Okinawa but I guess due to the weight the fuel had been light loaded and we made a fueling stop in Hawaii at the civilian airfield.

Pete asked me what I was going to do for the two hours we had on the ground. I told him I was going straight to the bar and drink as many Hawaiian Rum drinks as I could hold. Larry Houck found a quiet spot and kept reading his book, but Pete stuck close enough to me to be my shadow. We managed to get down one side of the drink menu before our flight was called away.

OKINAWA

We'd left on the 25th but since we were crossing the International Date Line we would gain a day and 12 hours. When we landed in Naha, Okinawa it was already Tuesday the 27th. There were only six officers on this plane, and the three of us were the only Marine officers and the only helicopter pilots on the aircraft. Before allowing anyone to deplane, the Marine ATCO (Air Transportation Coordination Office) representative came on board, called our names and told us to follow him. Once off the plane and in the terminal he told us that we had been "Pre-assigned" by the First Marine Aircraft Wing to a helicopter unit "In Country". We were to claim our baggage as soon as it was unloaded and he would show us to our quarters for the evening. The ATCO had us manifested on a KC-130 flight for Da Nang departing early tomorrow morning. We later learned that the rest of the passengers would all be here for several days of processing before going "In Country". We were transported from the airfield at Naha, Okinawa up to Marine Corps Air Station Futenma, Okinawa for the evening.

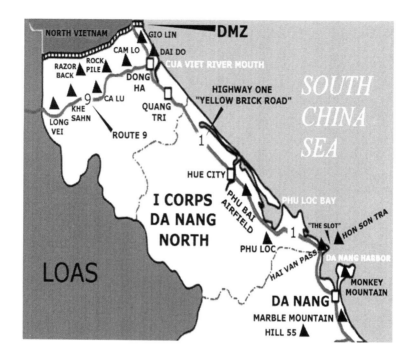

DA NANG, VIETNAM

Three tired and sleepy guys boarded a very crowded KC-130 for a flight to Da Nang. As the aircraft lifted off I thought about the last time I entered this country on the same type of aircraft. I could sense the apprehension most everyone was feeling. The last time I did this it was going to be a great adventure; I had nothing to lose but myself, the only thing I owned was a sea bag full of uniforms. Now it was not only my life, but the lives of two other people that needed me very much. I knew I couldn't dwell on this, I had to wall it off; I had to think only in terms of what was ahead not what I left behind. Eventually I would get back to what I'd left behind but for now it had to be just me and what I had to do.

As we got off the plane I knew that look on the faces of Boroday and Houck and I remembered what the Sergeant said to me the first time I landed here, so I said the same thing. "Relax guys, we won't be getting off in a hail of gun fire, it will be all right." I got an acknowledgement glance but the glance said, "We hope you aren't kidding."

I hadn't gone a hundred yards and I knew that this war, the one going on today, bore little resemblance to the war in 1965. I wasn't sure how you defined a war but from the sights, sounds and activity this was no longer a low intensity Guerilla war.

Since we were pre-assigned I thought things might be a little better organized. No waiting in those Southeast Asian screened "hooches" for your assignment and transportation. The three of us had been assigned to Marine Medium Helicopter Squadron 362, which was part of Marine Air Group 36. The squadron was supposed to be located at Hue Phu Bai Airfield, somewhere north of Da Nang, but nobody bothered to mention how we would get there. We all had assumed if we were being rushed to get in the squadron that some provision for getting us there quickly would be made, but that wasn't so.

I started asking around about transportation to Hue Phu Bai. I finally found a 1st Marine Air Wing ATCO representative and he actually had our names on a list and I found out there were three ways we could get to Hue. We could ride up in a truck that was part of a supply convoy, we could go over to the navy boat docks and try and catch a boat up there but since there was one hell of a fight going on in the city of Hue he didn't recommend either of those methods. He could however get us a ride over to the 1st Marine Aircraft Wing compound on the west side of the airfield and there was a helicopter pad there that helos from all over the place staged through very frequently. We could get a ride up to Hue Phu Bai on one of those.

Since we had no weapons of any type or field equipment I opted for the ride to the helo pad and figured it would be safer to wait there. Pete and Larry had no clue so at this point whatever decision I made was made for three. It was like I had two shadows instead of one.

The ride to the Wing compound and helo pad was uneventful. There were however, quite a few Marines and some navy corpsman piled up around the pad looking to hitch a ride just like we were. There were no shelters or bunkers anywhere near the pad and as far as the nearest water or heads I had no idea. I was surprised that the weather was gray, overcast, drizzling rain occasionally and even a little cool. We had on utilities and we had our baggage but that was it.

I started asking around trying to get some scoop on what was going on around here. I found a Gunny Sgt who was a member of HMM-362 who'd been on R&R (Rest and Recuperation) in Hong Kong for five days. He told me that this helo pad was used as the admin point for the squadrons to drop off and pick up mail and passengers. The squadrons would usually dedicate two aircraft per day to fly down from Phu Bai or Quang Tri for that purpose but because of the really lousy weather he wasn't sure if we would see much traffic today.

We waited all day and only one Huey came by the pad and it was from Marble Mountain airfield which was just a little south of Da Nang. The rain became a little heavier and the ceiling got a little lower all day and by late afternoon I was pretty sure we wouldn't see any helos from up north today. We'd rigged up a small shelter to help stay dry but no food, no water and no weapons wasn't going to get it. I had no idea what the hell would happen when the sun went down but I wasn't about to sit around this damn pad all night. I was going to find a place to spend the night, hopefully with a bunker, get dry and get fed.

I told Larry and Pete to pick up their gear and follow me. We headed back away from the pad into the more built up part of the compound. There were hooches and signs of life there. I finally found someone in a motor pool and asked if there was a transient barracks here or a mess hall. The Sergeant I spoke with didn't know about a transient barracks but pointed out an officers dining facility that was still quite a ways from here. It wasn't terribly encouraging but it was a start. We found the dining facility which was pretty primitive but more than welcomed. While we were eating I saw a guy in a flight suit with a VMCJ-2 squadron patch. My old buddy Rusthoven was in VMCJ-2, he was flying in the back seat of RF-4's. He was the reconnaissance systems operator that rode in the back seat and took the reconnaissance photos as the pilot put the aircraft in position. Very dangerous work these days but that was the mission of VMCJ-2. While we were in California we'd had a short letter from Russ saying he was on his way over, so he had to be here someplace. I got up and went over to the guy, he was also a Captain.

"Excuse me Captain but I noticed your VMCJ patch and wondered if you might know a guy by the name of Rusthoven?"

"Yeah, I know him; I even live in the same hooch. Why, you looking for him?"

"We go way back, it's a long story, but those two Lt's and I just got in country and are trying to get up to Hue Phu Bai airfield. We're H-34 pilots and have been assigned to HMM-362 up there. However, for the moment we are in bad need of someplace to bunk tonight. If Russ was around I know he'd give us some help if he can."

"My name's Jake Patterson, if you give me a few minutes to finish my chow I got wheels and I can get you over to our area. There are always a few guys on R&R or some such crap so I'm sure we got a few empty racks for the night. Just give me a couple more minutes."

"My names Bill Spicer and I damn sure appreciate the favor."

Patterson had a jeep and it was a little crowded with all our gear but we managed. He told us he'd come to Wing headquarters to drop off some photos of the Khe Sanh area and when they did that everyone always tried to time it so they could eat in the Wing headquarters officers mess, it was much better than most.

It was a pretty short ride but once again I felt naked being here unarmed even though it was a short ride. We were still out among the people and that familiar odor came back to me wafting on the cool moist air. I kept watching Pete and Larry closely and their eyes told the whole story.

Russ had just come back from a photo mission over North Vietnam and I was sitting on his cot in one of those hooches drinking one of his beers when he came through the screened door.

"Oh my God, who the hell let you in here and how did you find my cold beer? I hope like hell you've at least left me one."

We exchanged pleasantries and he got us all bedded down for the evening and then invited us to help put a serious dent in his beer supply. When I told him we were trying to get up to Hue Phu Bai airfield he and the rest of his hooch mates groaned and gave us their condolences. Evidently they considered anything north of Da Nang completely uncivilized. None of them had been up there on the ground but they'd seen it all from the air. We passed the night away listening to their stories. Larry and Pete had their first chance to hear "Outgoing" and some very distant "Incoming". (Artillery fire going away from the guns towards the enemy or mortar or artillery fire coming in from the enemy). There's always a question during your first experience of which is which. Only one experience for either is enough.

Enjoying Russ's hospitality for the night

HUE PHU BAI

Russ dropped us off at the wing helo pad at 0700 and told us we probably wouldn't see anything come by until mid-morning. It was still raining so I'd suggested we dig out our uniform raincoats. They weren't really designed for field operations but what the hell, they would keep us dry and we could always replace them some day. After a very mediocre breakfast and with a slight hangover, the three of us settled down under our temporary shelter to await the arrival of helicopters and hopefully a ride up to our squadron.

I don't know where everyone else spent the night but assumed they did much the same as we had, just found some place out of the weather to sleep. The Gunny from 362 showed up looking much the worse for wear and told me he'd found some old buddies that had way too much beer on hand and he did his best to help them deplete their supply. He also added that from here on out the beer availability would be mighty sparse.

At about 1000 I heard two H-34's long before I saw them. Everyone started looking in the direction of the sound and eventually they came into view. They were flying very low, just skimming the trees, and their approach to the pad was fast and simultaneous.

When the two aircraft were on the deck and had unloaded, the three of us walked out near the pad for a closer look. What we saw caused us to look at each other in amazement. These were two of the dirtiest, junky looking aircraft any of us had ever seen. The gunny had walked out with us.

"Captain, those aircraft aren't from 362. See those 'Bug Eyes' painted on the nose? Those guys are from HMM-163 at Quang Tri, north of us, so we probably can't catch a ride with them, but I'll ask. They may also be able to tell us if there are any birds from Phu Bai coming in later."

The Gunny went out to the aircraft and had a fairly animated conversation with the crew chief of the lead aircraft. He came back with some encouraging news, there were two birds from Phu Bai about thirty minutes behind these; there were currently two H-34 squadrons operating out of Phu Bai, HMM-362 and 363 but in any case we'd finally have our ride. The Gunny had also let them know there were three pilots here to be picked up and the pilots of the 163 aircraft were going to pass the word.

About an hour later a pair of CH-46 helicopters stopped by the pad and took the bulk of the passengers and one hell of a lot of mail. The Gunny told us they were from Marble Mountain and were probably on a mission for the 1st Division, not just the mail run for their squadron. A few minutes later another section of H-34's came in and landed.

"Hey Captain, these are our birds. See those camouflage painted turtlebacks right behind the transmission and Rotorhead? That's our markings. Back on the tail that funny little emblem is a Vietnamese God of War; it was given to the squadron years ago by the Vietnamese as well as the name, 'The Ugly Angels'. We are the only squadron with that marking."

Their approach to the pad was the same, together and fast until touchdown. If anything, the aircraft looked more beat up than the ones from 163.

"Damn Gunny do all these aircraft look this bad? I've never seen such dirty, beat up aircraft."

"Well sir, this ain't the training command. If these birds are up (meaning their mechanical status is ready to fly) then they are generally airborne and they take a hell of a beating."

We were finally on our way. The aircraft made a brief fuel and food stop at Marble Mountain Airfield, the home of MAG-16, and then headed for Hue Phu Bai.

Arriving on our squadron flight line was interesting to say the least. The whole place looked like a city dump with tents and above ground bunkers. The operations officer was the first person we met and we were told our welcome aboard would have to wait because the C.O. was flying. We turned in all our paper work, orders, log books, etc. and were issued a "Bullet Bouncer". It was a ceramic chest plate the pilots and crew wore that supposedly would stop a fifty caliber bullet. It must have weighed twenty pounds if it weighed an ounce but everyone said it worked. The flight equipment guys collected our helmets for painting, you didn't fly with a white helmet here; it was painted green and had the squadron emblem and your name on it. We were told to find a place to live and there'd be an AOM (All officers meeting) later this evening.

With that, one of the operations duty officers led us up to the squadron tent area. The hooches were hardback tents; a seven man tent stretched over a wooden frame, built about three feet off the ground, the typical Southeast Asian design. I was scrounging around for an empty space when a friend and classmate from OCS saw me.

"Hey Spice, welcome to Phu Bai. I got one primo vacant space in our hooch just for you. Besides, I think you'll like the company better, we got the best hooch here."

My friend was Tom Thurber from up in the northwest someplace. He was a very likeable guy and if he said he lived in the best hooch, I would have no reason to doubt it.

"Hey Tom, just lead the way, damn I'm more than ready to drop this gear someplace that I can call home at least for a while."

Tom showed me to a cot that was located behind a makeshift bar that the boys had built. It wasn't bad. The cot had an air mattress (normally referred to as a "Rubber Lady") and was vacant because the former occupant, another friend of mine, had recently been killed on a night medivac (Medical Evacuation) mission. That wasn't immediately explained and when it was no one dwelled on the matter.

At 1800, the AOM was called to order by the operations officer and then the C.O., or Skipper, talked about the current squadron operations and what the pilots should expect in the next few weeks. The squadron would be doing some supply missions up in the Khe Sanh, Dong Ha, Con Thien and Cam Lou areas and would be tasked for both day and night medivac around the Phu Bai area. Elements of the 5th Marine Regiment were heavily engaged in Hue City and the surrounding area. They were up against some well entrenched NVA (North Vietnamese Army). Last but not least the three "New Guys" were to be introduced. He called our names and had us come stand near him at the front of the operations tent. After telling everyone what wonderful pilots we were and what a great addition we would be to the squadron it was suggested by

the XO that we be given a "HIM". The skipper thought
that was a grand idea and in very loud unison all the
officers responded singing as best they could, "HIM, HIM,
FUCK HIM!!!!" With that heartwarming salute our
welcome aboard was concluded. Once again I was an FNG
(Fucking new guy).

FIRST MISSION

I was the first of the three FNG's to make the flight
schedule and on 5 March I was scheduled as the co-pilot
for a Major named Hunt. Everybody called him Major of
course, but when he wasn't around, he was referred to by
his friends and everyone else as "Light horse Harry." I
think he actually preferred that nick name. He was an
extreme short timer (meaning very few days left before
going home) and short timers didn't like to do real
dangerous stuff so close to going home. We were the lead
aircraft of a section for a "Milk Run" delivering stuff to
other helicopter units north of us up at Quang Tri. We
were to take off, fly directly up to Quang Tri, then Dong
Ha, then back to Quang Tri and finally come back to Phu
Bai. It was an easy run, and a good chance to break in an
FNG and show him part of the operating area.

The Major didn't have much to say in the briefing, the
wingman was a Captain named Jealous and they'd flown
together before. When we got in the aircraft the Major
looked at me prior to start and in very staccato fashion said,
"Ok, listen up, on your knee board keep track of every take
off and every landing, what goes on this aircraft and what
goes off. Write down the number of passengers and
estimate the weight of the cargo. Keep track of all the
radio frequency changes and make them on the radio, copy
down all 'save a planes' broad cast on guard, the map
coordinates of every place we land, don't touch anything
without my permission, I'm gonna start now, first nod
mags, second nod mixture, got it?"

I simply nodded and he started the engine. Just prior to
engaging the Rotorhead he told me to close my cockpit
door. I reached down and slid the door forward to close it.
When I got it in the fully closed position I turned my head a
full ninety degrees to the left and saw a bullet hole in the

Plexiglas. The hole lined up perfectly with a spot right between my eyes. I was still staring at it when I felt the Major release the rotor brake and the blades started whirling around. I wanted to open the cockpit window so I didn't have to see that damned hole but he wanted to keep them shut until we were up and away.

It had been much harder to get into the cockpit than I thought it would. With a bullet bouncer, survival vest, and pistol it was difficult enough just to climb up the side of the aircraft. Then you had to slide in between the cockpit window frame and the big piece of armor plating beside the seat. I liked the way the armor plate came all the way down alongside the seat but noticed with concern that when I reached out far enough to actually touch the throttle on the collective, my left hand was extending past the armor plate. I was fiddling with how I might operate the throttle without exposing my hand when the Major broke my thoughts by saying, "You have the aircraft."

When we departed the airfield the Major had turned the flight directly to the east heading for the ocean. The ceiling was only about 1000 feet. He told me that we needed to be above 1500 feet to be out of small arms range. If you didn't have 1500 feet then you went "Low Level" and flew at 10 feet weaving back and forth like a "Drunken Butterfly". He didn't want to low level all the way up to Quang Tri so he'd decided to go "Feet Wet" (fly out over the ocean) up the coast and avoid any chance of small arms all together.

I hadn't flown in almost a month so I felt really rusty. I stayed just below the clouds and tried not to scare or annoy the Major. A good half hour went by before he took control of the aircraft again and we turned inland heading for Quang Tri.

We followed our mission tasking, or Frag, to the letter and although we only got a couple hours total flight time for the day, it was routine. When we arrived back at Phu

Bai I had my first lesson in filling out the "After Action" forms. The sign hanging in the operations tent read, "After Action Forms are like taking a Crap, the jobs not over until the paperwork is done." Essentially you had to record on the AA form all the information you should have written down on your knee board during the entire mission. It was tedious and time consuming.

Paperwork completed, I'm officially a combat pilot now.

MEDIVAC WITH ROBBIE

Since my first hop I'd flown every day until today but all the missions were more or less new guy stuff. My friend Robbie Robertson came to me and told me I would be his co-pilot tomorrow on morning medivac. The medivac mission was divided into morning, afternoon and night. If you were on for the night, you were on all night.

"Spice, I heard you were up for your first medivac mission so I told operations to schedule you with me for the first time. There's some stuff I can teach you and show you that some of the other guys might not think about. So we will be on tomorrow from 0600 till 1200. It may or may not be busy, we just never know, but you've got to be ready for just about anything."

"Thanks Robbie, I'm glad it will be with you and I'll be ready."

Robbie was like me, he'd come to OCS on the meritorious NCO program, he'd had some sea duty and when we graduated from OCS he somehow managed to go straight to flight school so he was about six months ahead of me. He was already a HAC (Helicopter Aircraft Commander). It would really be nice to have a chance to fly with a contemporary, particularly a long-time friend.

At 0500 I was in the operations tent with a cup of really strong coffee for our brief. When Robbie came in the first thing he went to look at was the current intelligence map. He motioned for me to come over and have a look. Squadron S-2 (S-2 is the intelligence section) kept an updated map of the current tactical situation. On the map they identified both enemy and friendly positions and posted any unusual activity.

"Spice, you need to check this map every day before you launch; most guys don't, some of them don't want to know what's out there, but I think it's a good idea. Being an old grunt I'm sure you will too, and I especially look for any known or suspected locations of enemy automatic weapons that have been plotted. You've heard this aircraft can take a lot of hits and keep going, and that's true. It can take a lot of small stuff, but it can't sustain many .50 cals. I pay particular attention to the location of any of those or enemy units that probably have one. With the troop lifts or re-supply missions, it's not so much of a worry but with Medivac you really should know what's in the area.

I spent a few minutes going over the map. Robbie was right and up till this moment I'd had no reason to be concerned about the tactical situation because all I'd been flying were "Milk Runs".

One of the things I'd been working on was my maps. When we drew our bullet bouncers the operations officer had also given us a set of maps. Each pilot was responsible for his set and I'd spent a lot of time on mine marking in the locations of all the radio navigational aids and making reference points as to a bearing and distance from them. They were called Tacan Stations and were scattered all over our operating area. The references were to Tacan radial and bearing from each station. If I had to find a specific set of map coordinates, I could locate the coordinates on the map and look for the nearest Tacan radial and distance mark as a reference. It sure helped in navigation because the jungle is similar to the desert; from the air it all looks alike.

Next Robbie checked for activity this morning and we learned that some CH-46's had inserted a reinforced platoon sized unit in the hills west of Phu Loc Bay. From the Intel map my guess would have been a recon platoon looking to find NVA coming into or trying to get out of the Hue City area.

We were assigned an aircraft and Robbie took me out to help with the pre-flight. While we were looking over the aircraft, he introduced me to the crew we would be flying with this morning. Corporal Tygart was the crew chief, and the Corpsman was a Petty Officer First Class (equivalent to a S/Sgt) named Jones. It seemed everybody knew "Doc Jones," he'd been with the squadron about as long as anyone. The gunner was a Lance Corporal but he wasn't around at the moment.

Tygart and Jones looked me over with a somewhat jaundiced eye. Even though I was an officer and a pilot, I was still an FNG and if anything happened to Robbie this morning, I was the guy that had to get them out of harm's way.

I'd heard about Doc Jones already. Most of the guys said he just might be the craziest or bravest sonofabitch they'd ever seen and if they were hit, he was the one they all hoped would be there to help.

We got into the aircraft, turned it up and performed all the pre-launch checks, then Robbie showed me how to set up the cockpit and switches for a scramble start. Next we checked the machine guns, the ammo, and the medical equipment (stretchers and Doc's black bag). It was more of a check list for the crew than anything. After that we were ready; now we had to wait and hope we didn't have to launch. If we didn't launch all morning then that meant nobody got hurt, at least in this area.

The crew settled in right at the aircraft and Robbie and I went back into the operations tent to be near the ODO and the Double EE8 wired phone that would signal a mission. During the day, Medivac missions were classified Emergency, Priority, or Routine. Emergency, you launched immediately because some fellow Marine's life was in grave danger. Priority, you went as soon as you could; somebody was hurt, sick or wounded but it wasn't life threatening. Routine was just that, you got to it when you could. Unfortunately sometimes a routine medivac was someone in a body bag.

115

From 0600 to 0700 things were all quiet. The only activity were other crews coming down to brief and head out on their missions for the day, but shortly after 7 the Double EE8 rang. It had a penetrating, completely annoying sound and in the coming days, weeks and months I would come to hate that sound.

The ODO answered the phone and nodded at Robbie and me. He said, "Emergency Medivac" and started writing down the information. Robbie headed straight for the aircraft and as per my brief I waited on the information. The ODO checked the map and wrote down an approximate TACAN radial and distance to the set of coordinates, made a quick notation and handed me the paper. I could hear Robbie starting the engine.

I sprinted to the aircraft and wasn't quite strapped in when Robbie let the rotor brake go and the blades began to spin. I was still settling in and we were taxiing out of the revetment. I heard the tower clear us for immediate take off.

"Where the hell are we going?"

"Head for Phu Loc Bay, I'll dial in the FM radio frequency of the unit. Call sign is Picadilly One Four. There is supposed to be a gunship (UH-1 Huey rigged with four machine guns and two rocket pods) on station call sign Scarface 3-1. There is one emergency US, extent of the injuries unknown at this time."

"Ok, good job so far, Phu Loc Bay it is."

Robbie pushed the nose of the aircraft down and I noticed we were doing over 110 knots. Twenty knots over normal cruise speed. I got out the appropriate map and found the coordinates. I folded the map so that I could show Robbie what the terrain looked like.

"If there's a gunship on station we won't need the map. Make sure you clear everything away and your straps are tight. The zone will most likely be "Hot" so if we get in there and I get hit you take the aircraft and get us out of the zone, then do what you gotta do. If I'm hit going in, take the aircraft, wave off the approach and evaluate the situation. If I'm not critical, try and get back in the zone and get the medivac. Corporal Tygart, you guys are clear to test fire the guns."

There was an overcast at about 1500 feet, and it was drizzling rain, just enough to keep the outside air temperature cool and barely get you wet. Robbie was skimming along just below the clouds and navigating directly to the Tacan radial and distance given with the mission. I flinched when the FM radio crackled in my head set.

"Pestkiller Medivac, Scarface on Picadilly Fox Mike, you up?"

"Scarface, Pestkiller is listening ready for the brief."

"Pestkiller, Picadilly position is under heavy but intermittent enfiladed fire. I have engaged but have not silenced the gun yet. Best approach would be low level up the stream bed that leads west off the bay. I can observe and will call your pop up; LZ will be on your left. Wind is calm, main source of fire would be from high ground to the southeast, Scarface standing by."

"Roger Scarface, I copy all, standby."

I could see Robbie mentally picturing the situation. He asked Corporal Tygart if everyone in the belly copied the last transmission and they did.

"Ok then, here's our plan. We'll take Scarface's advice and go up the stream bed when we locate it. The wind is calm so when I pop out of the stream bed I'll try and slide the aircraft to the left and land with our tail in the direction of the heaviest fire. Gunner that will free you to engage if you can see the source, Tygart, that will put you and Jones away from the fire and free you up to help get the medivac in the cabin. When we lift off I'm going to pop up and dive right back in the stream bed until we are out of range of any ground fire, everybody got that? Let's go get that Marine."

117

We could see the mouth of the stream Scarface was describing. Robbie descended to just a few feet above the water and as we approached, the stream looked fairly wide, but where it started up hill it narrowed considerably and had a lot of overhanging vegetation. I wasn't sure we could go up the stream without hitting our blades.

"Pestkiller, Scarface has you in sight."

"Roger Scarface, Pestkiller is commencing approach, call the pop."

We were still doing over 110 knots when Robbie started up the stream bed. He was weaving his way up hill just above the stream managing to miss most of the foliage but I saw the rotor blades on my side whack a couple of things.

"Robbie we've hit a couple of bushes with the blades."

"Don't worry about it, that small stuff won't bother us a bit, just tell me if we are about to hit anything really big."

At this point for me it was a little like flying with EV, I was just along for the ride. I heard Scarface call for Robbie to pop out of the stream bed. He pulled the nose of the aircraft up and we literally popped out of the stream bed and were now sliding sideways toward a small grassy but flat plateau with one enormous tree right in the center. The plateau was about the size of a football field and the tree that dominated the center was at least 100 feet tall. The grass must have been about 2 feet deep. I could feel the aircraft coming out of translational lift, slowing down to almost a hover but still moving sideways. Snuggled down in the grass I could now make out Marines trying to conceal themselves from the enemy fire. Robbie was translating closer and closer towards the tree. I could see green and white tracers ripping chunks of bark and wood off the giant tree. I almost jumped out of my skin when our gunner opened up with a long burst from his M-60 machine gun. I looked to our front and thought I saw a Marine standing up and motioning for us to touch down. Robbie was looking out the right side and down at something. In order to put the medivac right by the cargo door he actually had to slide the aircraft over the top of the men waiting to load the wounded Marine.

"I'm setting it down are we clear on the left?"

It looked to me like our rotors might be just touching the outer branches of the tree but it wasn't anything very big. As we were coming down, I could see our left main mount was about to come down on a Marine in the grass. He was furiously rolling to get out of the way. Because of the drizzle and haze I had raised my dark helmet visor so I could see better. This wasn't a good idea but I didn't know what else to do. I was looking directly at a Marine in the grass and as he rolled clear of the left main mount tire our eyes met. In that instant I could read the terror in the young man's eyes. It penetrated to my core. As quickly as our eyes met he turned away aiming his rifle and started shooting at something towards our rear.

"Clear on the left."

Once on the ground Robbie told me to hit the stop watch function on the aircraft clock.

"Let me know when we've been on the ground for a minute. It's gonna take longer than we want to load this guy, he's hurt bad. More than a minute here and we could be in real trouble."

"Christ Captain, we got an amputee, got his left leg blown off about four inches above the knee. One of the guys puttin him in just went down, standby we're gettin him now; ok, you're clear to lift." I glanced at the stop watch and we'd been on the ground almost two minutes.

Robbie literally snatched the aircraft off the ground and immediately started a climbing right turn to clear the vegetation on the edge of the stream. He allowed the aircraft to descend rapidly to just above the stream bed and began increasing our speed and weaving his way back down the stream bed towards the bay.

"Captain, Doc Jones says he doesn't know if he can stop or slow the bleeding. Give it all you can or this guy may bleed out."

The instant they'd put the wounded Marine in the cabin down below I could tell it was bad because of that horrible sickening sweet smell of mutilated or bleeding bodies. It brought back some memories that weren't pleasant.

Robbie had the aircraft doing 125 knots and all I could think about was "Retreating Blade Tip Stall" and just knew that at any moment the aircraft would pitch up, roll over and we would all die. Robbie told me to change the FM radio frequency to "Delta Med" and then he called and told them we were inbound with an amputee. His approach to the metal pad at the medical unit was very fast but he stepped on the left rudder pedal which pushed the aircraft out of balanced flight. In doing this he was turning the aircraft so the fuselage was like a big barn door stuck in the wind and the drag he created quickly killed all the forward speed. At the last second he took out his "Side Flair" and managed to land quickly without too much rotorwash blowing up a lot of dust. As soon as we were on the ground the medical personnel came running with stretchers. From my spot on the left side of the aircraft I really didn't get a good look at the Marines being carried away until they were about twenty yards from the aircraft. It was a sobering sight.

As soon as we were airborne again Robbie had me switch the radio frequency to Phu Bai DASCC (Direct Air Support Coordination Center) they were the tasking agency for helo operations in this area.

"Phu Bai DASCC, Pestkiller medivac mission 3 dash 11 Alpha complete, standing by."

"Roger Pestkiller Medivac, standby to copy mission Bravo.

Robbie looked at me and we just knew it would be the same place so it came as no surprise that all the information was the same except there were more gunships from Scarface on station.

From my limited experience as a grunt I couldn't imagine what military genius picked that place for an LZ. (Helicopter Landing Zone) It was in hilly terrain and the only flat spot for miles around. From an enemy standpoint if you were going to pick the most likely spot that someone would try and land a helo, that little flat spot would be it. The fact that they were taking enfiladed fire told the story. Enfiladed fire is the worst type; it's when the long axis of the target aligns with the long axis for the beaten zone of a weapon. That little flat spot was a perfect killing zone. The NVA knew it and had probably been waiting.

"You have the aircraft, head us back for the mouth of the stream."

"I have the aircraft."

While I was heading back across Phu Loc Bay towards the mouth of the stream, Robbie pulled out a pack of Lucky Strikes and lit two. He reached across and stuck one in my mouth. I had the old H-34 doing 120 kts, so I was concentrating hard on flying and just let the cigarette hang in my mouth as I took a long drag. I could feel the tension in the aircraft, we all knew what we were facing again.

"Pestkiller Medivac, Scarface lead, say position."

Robbie keyed the mike and answered, "About half way across the bay from the stream."

"Roger Pestkiller, anchor present position. Be about a five minute delay, got some suppressive fire going in for the moment and some confusion on the ground."

"Pestkiller Roger anchor." Robbie made a circular motion with the fingers of his left hand and I started a turn to the left.

I made a couple of orbits and then Robbie pointed back to the west and I headed the aircraft for the mouth of the stream again. The cigarette had burned down until it was very short, I could feel some serious heat close to my lip.

Robbie reached over and took the butt out of my mouth. As he did so, the cigarette paper stuck to my lower lip. He tried to remove it as gently as he could, but it wouldn't budge so he gave it a pretty good jerk and it ripped the skin on my lip. He got the butt all right, only now I could feel and taste the blood that was starting to drip down from my lip onto my survival vest.

"Christ, you're bleeding, am I gonna have to Medivac you as well? Hey Doc, Captain Spicer is bleeding heavily from his lip, what should I do?"

"Well Captain, you could put a tourniquet around his neck."

"Naw, he looks gray in the face already. I have the aircraft. Scarface, you ready for me?"

"Pestkiller, start your approach when ready, try and set down in the same spot if you can. They have the three medivacs ready to load."

Robbie made the same approach as the first time and when he sat the aircraft down it was almost in the same tracks as our first landing. I didn't see the terrified Marine in the grass and I wasn't noticing the tracers hitting the tree like before but from the activity of the Marines, I knew we must still be taking fire, I just couldn't see it. I was trying not to be along for the ride. I was trying to follow every move Robbie was making with the controls. If I had to, I could take control of this aircraft and get us out of here, but I still didn't have a clue. I had one hell of a lot to learn and just hoped I'd be around long enough to learn it.

Over the next three hours we made five more approaches into that same zone and medivaced eight more Marines. During our last run, the afternoon Medivac had already launched in that direction. The fight raged on most of the afternoon and eventually some CH-46's under cover of a fixed wing attack extracted the rest of the unit.

After landing and parking the aircraft in a revetment, Robbie was already on the ground and looking the aircraft over for any battle damage before I managed to climb down. I felt spent, useless and horrified. I walked around the nose of the aircraft and Doc Jones was standing by the cargo door, Tygart was sitting on the right main mount tire and the gunner was still in the cabin. Tygart and Jones had the sleeves of their flight suit pushed up to their elbows. They were bloody from the tips of their fingers to well above their elbows. There was blood all over the front of both their flight suits, and the blood that had pooled up on the cabin floor was now dripping out the door onto the ground. The gunner was trying to straighten up the mess inside the cabin. I took a seat next to Tygart and lit a cigarette until Robbie said, "Ok, let's go, we got paperwork to fill out. Corporal Tygart as far as I'm concerned your aircraft is up once you get that mess cleaned up in the cabin.

As we were walking to the operations tent I said to Robbie, "I'm not too sure what the criteria for awarding a Distinguished Flying Cross is but I'd say I saw some Distinguished Flying today."

"Don't be talking about that kind of shit. That's our job, that's what we do. This squadron is too short handed to be sitting around writing up awards. We don't do that, other squadrons might but the Ugly Angels don't. If the grunts write us up that's one thing, but otherwise, this is our job, got it?"

Back in my tent I sat on my cot and stared at nothing. In the six hours we were scheduled for morning Medivac we'd flown for four and a half. Robbie came in with a large bottle of scotch and a couple of my tent mates, Ron and Tom.

"Robbie says you did real good for you first time Spice, he said you even kept your eyes open all the time."

Robbie produced a canteen cup and filled it almost to the brim with the scotch. He had one of his own. He handed me the cup and we touched them in some form of salute and said, "You did real good Spice, it's even more fun at night."

SLEEPING IN BIFF'S RACK

I'd had my first Medivac mission and even though I was still an FNG, I was starting to settle in as a member of the Ugly Angels. It's still March and there is a hell of a fight going on just down the road in Hue City and we had been occasionally receiving some rocket and mortar fire here at the base during the night.

My hooch mates, being the clever and good guys they were, had taken me right in and made me as welcomed as they could at least for the moment. Checking into a new unit was always a little unsettling but so far this was going pretty well and the living conditions, although lousy, were bearable. However, my friends offer to include me in their living space was somewhat misleading. Although it was a seven man tent, there were only six men staying there so I assumed there was an open space for one man. There had been, but when one of the guys was killed on a night medivac, these guys built a bar in that space. With great care and interesting craftsmanship the bar had been constructed using the wood from crates that 2.75" Rockets came in. The bar was lovely and took up a fair amount of space but they said, "Not to worry". Behind the bar was enough space for a folding cot and a small area to store a footlocker. There were a couple of large nails driven into one of the 2x4's which served as a place to hang a towel and flight suit. One of the guys said the inconvenience of the bar was a small price to pay in order to keep company with such a fine group. I guess I had to agree.

I adjusted to being the seventh man sleeping behind the bar; in fact, the bar actually afforded a little more seclusion. With the exception of the nights that my tent mates got rowdy or had rowdy friends in for poker, popcorn, and beer, then trying to sleep behind the bar was impossible and the impossible happened more frequently than I liked, but war is hell they say.

The entire group, that's Dave, Tom, Ron, John, Max and Me all slept on folding cots. I think some of these cots had been used in WWII. The seventh bed was an actual bunk. It was half of a barracks bunk bed. It had springs and a real mattress. The owner of this coveted object was the junior man in the tent. Everyone in the tent was a Captain except Biff. 1/LT Biff Steadman had somehow managed to scrounge up this real bed, complete with sheets, a blanket and pillow. He also had a metal wall locker that stood right beside his bed. He had the most combat experience, had been there the longest, was the type of old hand you wanted to stay close to and learn from. He was a 1/LT because he had acquired his wings the hard way. He came to flight school as a Marine Aviation Cadet, "MARCAD" and had to successfully finish flight school in order to receive his commission. We were all about the same age but that was the difference. He was also a bachelor, poker player, crap shooter, and drinker extraordinaire.

Our hooch was oriented east to west, with Dave, Ron and Tom living on the extreme west end. Max and John lived in the extreme east end and because of the room that the bar and Biffs' bunk took up; Biff and I lived more or less in the middle of the hooch. I didn't know Max or John very well at all. They seemed to stay pretty much down on their end no matter what was happening. The only thing I knew for sure about them was that even though they lived in the east end of the hooch, no one, and I mean no one could beat either of them to our bunker, which was just outside on the west end. At the first sound of incoming mortars or rockets the next thing I would hear was Max and John going out the screened door on the west end.

Besides the great company, the bar, and Biffs' popcorn machine, these guys had built the best bunker. It was a little taller, longer and wider than the other bunkers plus it

126

had several pieces of scrounged metal matting on top with a layer of sandbags on top of that. They had fitted it with battery powered lights and to keep from sitting on damp sand during long rocket/mortar attacks they had scrounged some plywood and made a floor. It wasn't just any wooden bunker floor because they'd found someone to paint an exact replica of a craps table layout on the plywood. This helped a lot, especially when Biff and the habitual poker players were asked to leave the bar area in the hooch because some people were trying to sleep. They would resume the game in the bunker or in those instances when there was no poker game but we were all in the bunker for a long time, getting a crap game going quickly was no problem.

I came into the hooch late one afternoon after a rough day of flying and found Biff packing his B-4 bag (a type of Military suit case, used mostly by Officers and Senior NCOs'.)

Biff said, "Man Spice, you look like you could use a drink".

"I sure could."

"Well, if I had one I'd damn sure give it to you but I'm fresh out."

"I know you don't have orders, where the hell are you going?"

"I'm going on R&R tomorrow, going up to Hong Kong for a whole 5 days. It's my second one."

"Well, you're a lucky SOB; I'll be on the waiting list for Hawaii forever."

"No, not forever but about seven months, all you married guys want to go to Hawaii and that's about how long everyone I know has waited."

"Then I'm gonna have another three or four months to wait."

Biff concentrated on his packing while I stripped out of my dripping wet flight suit and got down to my skivvie drawers and flip flops. I spread an old towel out on the bar and started the daily cleaning of my .45 cal pistol. I was just starting the reassembly when Biff said, "Hey Spice, would you do me a favor while I'm gone?"

"What kind of favor?"

"Just keep an eye on my stuff. You know, don't let them take my bunk, or hide it some place."

"Yeah, sure, none of us will let any of that crap happen."

"You don't know some of these sombitches; they'd do it just for fun. In fact, I got a deal for you, how about moving in and sleeping in my rack while I'm gone. I know it hasn't been fun sleeping over there behind that bar, so just go ahead and move in tomorrow and enjoy. I know those sombitches won't mess with you."

I thought about this for a second, sleeping on a real bed, with sheets, shit, are you kidding? I told Biff, "You got a deal; all your stuff will be safe with me, no problem."

I was flying co-pilot on a mission the next day that required a 04:30 brief for a sun up launch. We were going north to Khe Sanh; it would be bad.

We worked out of Khe Sanh, Dong Ha and Quang Tri, and didn't get back till almost dark. When I left, Biff was still in his rack and when I got back to the hooch, he'd made up the bunk with clean sheets and pillow case. He'd left a note, "Enjoy, but take care of my stuff".

The hooch was strangely empty but I could hear some merriment taking place in the next hooch which was occupied by the ground maintenance officers. They had obviously come across some extra goodies and attracted a crowd. They were always swapping and trading stuff with other units, particularly sea bee's if they were around. Their trades brought great treasures like a pallet of beer or a case of steaks. The nice thing about the ground officers and their trading was they were always most generous.

128

With the hooch empty, I saw this as my opportunity to enjoy my new sleeping arrangement. I stripped down and headed for the shower, then back to the hooch, clean skivvies and time for bed. I made sure to move my night time necessaries over from my cot behind the bar to the same position in reference to Biffs' bunk. I always kept my boots, flak jacket, helmet and pistol on the plywood floor right by the head of my cot. So at the first sound of incoming I could just roll out of the rack, scoop up my stuff and head for the bunker all in one motion. For whatever reason, I was usually the last guy out of the tent. I moved my stuff over and piled it down by the head of the bunk. The bunk was oriented differently than my cot. The head was toward the screen and the foot of the bunk was toward the middle of the tent.

I had forgotten what a bed felt like, just to lie on one but with sheets this was almost more than I could take. Previously my pillow had been my extra flight suit rolled up but now, a real pillow, wow. I'm not too sure how long I was awake after my head hit the pillow but it couldn't have been long.

I was sleeping so soundly I didn't hear the first few mortar rounds explode. What woke me was the screen door on the west end of the hooch slamming as the last of my hooch mates headed for the bunker. I hesitated just a second and then heard mortars exploding down near the flight line. I rolled out of the bunk onto the plywood floor and knew immediately that I was completely disoriented. It took a couple of seconds before I realized I was facing the wrong way. I needed to turn around toward the middle of the hooch and then turn right to get out the west end by the bunker. I could tell the mortars were coming in closer. In situations like this there was always a split second where you can't decide whether to drop and stay where you are or run for cover. It's probably a millisecond or picosecond, whatever it is, it's happening damn fast. Without thinking about it during this time I had turned myself around, put on the flak jacket, boots and grabbed my pistol. I was just gathering myself to make a rush for the screen door and the protection of the bunker when I saw, heard, and felt an incredible bright blue flash, an ear splitting SHARAAACK and felt shrapnel whizzing through the hooch. It was the unmistakable sound of a 122mm rocket exploding very close.

I burst through the screen door and rolled as I hit the sand. I was about twenty feet from the bunker but the entrance was on the other side, so I would have to crawl all the way around. I crawled straight to the bunker and got up as close to it as I could. Two more 122s exploded and I could hear the big pieces of shrapnel whizzing through the air well above the bunker. There was another blue flash followed by that ear splitting SHARAACK!!!! Again I could hear and feel the shrapnel whizzing through the air as well as smell the residual smoke from the explosive. This one had hit very close, I chanced a look and could tell it hit the corner of a hooch behind ours but the next row over. Four LtCol's lived in that hooch, including our former CO, LtCol Dick Kline.

There was a momentary lull in the explosions so I made a dash for the other side of the bunker and got to the entrance just a few seconds before the next round of explosions. I was the last guy in the bunker and it was pretty full tonight.

Jim Johannes was just inside the entrance wearing a flak jacket, helmet, flip flops and nothing else. He was the squadron flight surgeon, better known to the pilots as" Doc" or "The Quack". He was an interesting fellow. He'd been an enlisted Marine, got out, gone to college, then medical school, joined the Navy as a doctor and volunteered to be a flight surgeon with the Marines. He made some wisecrack that I didn't catch but I did notice his watch, it was about 1:30 in the morning. The Sonofabitches, I didn't even get a full night in Biffs' bunk.

The rockets stopped but down toward the flight line a few mortars were still coming in. We didn't know if it was over or if the bad guys were just reloading again. Johannes and I were staring out the bunker entrance and noticed a figure staggering through the darkness. The figure was staggering away from the hooch area and toward the flight line. Johannes said, "That's Col Kline, our old CO, he looks like he's been hit."

I told Johannes I was pretty sure that one of those rockets had hit on the corner of his hooch.

He said, "We got to go get him."

Johannes and I bolted out of the bunker followed by two more guys with a stretcher that we kept in the bunker just in case.

While we were dashing toward him we saw him collapse on the sand. When we reached him we could see he was bleeding from four or five "Through and Through" shrapnel wounds. Johannes looked him over quickly and said, "Let's get him on that stretcher and down to the aid station, I gotta go down there anyway and help with any other casualties."

Most of the casualties had been in the Officer hooch area. Two of the Lt Col's in the hooch with Col Kline were dead and the third, who was a squadron CO, was severely wounded. The four of us hung around the aid station and gave Johannes a hand until the regular medical crew got down there and then we headed back to the hooch area. The "All Clear" sounded while we were heading back.

The camp generators go off every night at 2200. (10:00 PM) This was to save the wear and tear on the generators and darken the camp. No sense making it easy for the bad guys. Tonight, the generators had come back on so that the damage could be assessed and any casualties discovered. As I approached my hooch I noticed that someone had already made a repair to the screen door. I also noticed a bunch of guys standing in the middle of the hooch. Along with John, Max, Dave, Ron and Tom there must have been another dozen guys.

As I came through the screen door everyone turned and looked at me like they had seen a ghost. I said, "What the hell's going on guys, is everybody all right?" They all parted and pointed towards Biffs' rack but no one said a word. There was a huge hole right down through the rack and the plywood floor underneath.

Somebody said, "Hey Spice lay down on the rack for a second." I didn't know what to say or do so I just lay down on the rack. If I had been in the rack when the hole was made, the huge piece of shrapnel that made it would have hit me right between the shoulder blades taking out everything in its path.

The boys had already figured out what happened. On the first 122 explosion that I saw, heard and felt, a huge piece of shrapnel had come through the tent about 3 feet above Dave's cot. It missed any of the wood structure but struck a glancing blow on Biffs' metal wall locker door. The glancing blow off the door caused it to go ricocheting downward right through the bunk and the floor, finally burying in the sand beneath the hooch. Max and John had already crawled under the hooch and dug it out while I was down at the aid station. The hunk was a twisted, jagged chunk about a foot across and weighed about two pounds. It matched up real well with the hole in the bunk. The guys presented it to me, all laughing. Somebody said, "We can't wait till Biff gets back. We know you promised to take care of his stuff, but Jesus Spice."

I left everything as it was but tucked in the sheets and blankets and made the bed look as neat as I could, I even fluffed up the pillow and put it on the head of the bed. Biff was gonna need a huge crow bar to pry the wall locker open cause the door was bent all to hell and jammed shut. I put the piece of shrapnel on the foot of the bed and got a sheet of paper from my letter writing gear. In letters as big as I could write, I printed, "To Biff, with love from the NVA".

We all learned the next morning that the severely wounded LtCol's squadron had attempted to Medivac him last night down to the big Navy Hospital in Da Nang. Evidently once "Feet Wet" they turned south out over the water and just disappeared. Nothing was ever found. Col Kline was taken to Da Nang later that day by C-130.

I was flying when Biff got back from R&R and was told that he just looked at his rack and didn't say much. By the time I got back to the hooch that day, Biff had mailed the piece of shrapnel home, found some way to make repairs to his rack and was lying there with his head on the pillow reading a book.

I said, "Welcome back Biff, how was the R&R?"

Without looking away from his book, he said, "It was great but that's the last damn time I'm letting you sleep in my rack."

MY NAME IS NOT MAX!

Although it is still March, still cloudy and crappy weather, it's going to be a good day because I am scheduled to fly with one of my hooch mates. We have an easy mission that requires us to fly down to Da Nang and back on a courier run to Third Marine Amphibious Force Headquarters.

As an FNG and Co-Pilot it was always more fun to fly with someone you knew well because they usually gave you most of the stick time so you could gain experience. The sooner you got designated as a HAC, (Helicopter Aircraft Commander) the sooner they had another HAC in the pilot rotation and that might just give them a day off the flight schedule once in a while.

Max had been my hooch mate since I got here. He was short, stocky, and powerfully built. He had rusty red hair, blue eyes, and forearms the size of Popeye's. He had a great sense of humor, a really quick wit, and a wry smile that fit right in with those blue eyes. I heard he'd gone to an Ivy League school and was on the rowing team and from the size of those arms he had to be good at it. Max was one of the quiet ones in the tent. He didn't gamble, was a moderate drinker and voracious reader. I believe if he had the time he could have easily read a book a day. There were many evenings when Biff and crew where playing poker and being generally noisy that I would see Max laying on his cot reading a book completely oblivious to the whole scene. I'd flown with him several times now and knew him to be an excellent pilot. He was always very generous giving me plenty of stick time and usually never said much.

Our flight today would consist of two aircraft because the old UH-34 was single engined. It was much safer for us to travel in pairs over here. We went single plane occasionally but avoided it if at all possible. Besides, if something did come up, two aircraft gave the situation greater flexibility and capability.

Max gave the other crew and me a quick brief and just shortly after our takeoff told me I had control of the aircraft and to take us to Da Nang. I turned our flight directly east in the direction of the coastline and once there made a right turn and headed almost due south out over the sea. I stayed above 1500 feet and far enough out to sea that we were out of small arms range from the beach.

Max tuned the old ARN-6 Birddog navigation radio to the Armed Forces Radio Network, and settled back to enjoy the ride. By selecting the right mixer switches on the communications control panel, Max could listen to music and news on that radio only and leave it up to me to listen on the UHF and FM tactical channels. The whole crew could have done this, but it wasn't a good idea, after all, somebody had to "Mind the Store".

Max never said a word until we got to Da Nang and then took control of the aircraft because I had no idea where Three MAF Headquarters was and it was just too hard to explain. We dropped off our package of "Special Stuff" and headed immediately for the Marine Airfield at Marble Mountain to refuel and hopefully get a nice meal.

For our return trip Max gave me control of the aircraft just after we got started which meant I was actually going to have a chance to taxi the old 34 onto the runway. Co-pilots almost never got this opportunity and the 34 was extremely difficult to taxi, requiring a delicate touch on the controls. To make things even more interesting there were no brakes on the co-pilots side of the cockpit. You had rudder pedals but no brakes. I mentioned this to Max and he gave me that Leprechaun type smile and said, "If you are doing things correctly you shouldn't need brakes." I managed not to need the brakes, got us airborne and headed back up the coast towards Hue Phu Bai.

135

When we were far enough north, I had our flight switch radio frequencies to a different control agency. Phu Bai DASCC (Direct Air Support Coordination Center) responded just as soon as I checked in with them. DASCC had an immediate emergency mission and we were the nearest aircraft available. I looked over at Max and he just nodded and took control of the aircraft.

Max keyed the radio mike and said, "DASCC this is Pestkiller 8 dash 1, go ahead with your mission we are ready to copy "

I got my pencil out and prepared to copy all the information on my pilot's knee board.

DASCC responded, "Pestkiller 8 dash 1, emergency extraction required, position approximately 20 miles off TACAN channel 72, 270 degree radial, contact Scarface 2-1 and 2 airborne and Night Stalker Team on Fox Mike (FM radio) channel 34.60." I got it all written down and Max nodded for me to read it back to them to make sure we had it right.

My read back was correct and the DASCC gave us clearance to switch frequencies to the tactical channels. I selected channel 72 on the TACAN and Max turned the flight towards the 270 degree radial. He took a moment to make sure our wingman had all the info and that his aircraft and guns were all functioning properly. Our crew took that as a cue to test fire the guns and make sure all was ready down below. My best guess was we were about 15 minutes out.

Max nodded toward the FM radio and I transmitted to the wingman to switch up FM 34.60, he rogered my instructions. I then switched our radio and the next thing I heard was, "Two's UP" (meaning that the wingman was now listening to that frequency).

Max immediately transmitted on the FM radio, "Scarface this is Pestkiller 8 dash 1, inbound your position with two, standing by."

"Pestkiller 8 dash 1, Scarface 2 dash 1, situation as follows, six souls, two WIA (Wounded in Action) in contact require immediate extraction. Scarface 2 dash 1 and two are still on scene, Scarface 3 and 4 are Winchester Minus (meaning out of ammunition) and have RTB'd (Returned to Base) for quick turn-around. I have Hellborne (call sign of an A-4 Skyhawk attack jet aircraft) 1, 2, 3 and 4 on station providing cover. Night Stalker has called for "Danger Close" drops but we have them in sight and we are working Hellborne close enough to hold the bad guys at bay for the moment. Night Stalker is moving very slowly towards a small clearing on a hill side, it's one of the few places suitable as a landing zone and everybody, and I mean everybody knows it. Contact Night Stalker Team this push (meaning radio frequency) when ready. You have the call."

I looked over at Max and he was staring straight back at me with the most serious look on his face I'd ever seen. He said, "This could be very bad."

"Yeah I know."

"No, I mean very bad and there may be a good chance that one or all of us may get hurt or worse".

"That bad?"

I didn't know exactly why but I heard myself saying, "In that case Max, I kinda like to know your full name. I've lived with you in a tent since I've been here, been rocketed and mortared with you, been shot at when I flew with you and all I really know about you is that your name is Max. I know more about our crew chief Cpl John P. Nose and Gunner L/Cpl Leedy than I do about you."

Max looked at me and said, "My Name is not Max!"

"It isn't?"

"NO!"

"Then what the hell is your name?"

"My name is Thomas J. McKnight."

137

Max continued, "Everyone calls you Spice, what the hell is your name?"

I said, "My name is William R. Spicer."

We sat there for a few seconds looking at one another all the while heading for the landing zone about as fast as the old 34 could fly.

I said, "Well, I can't stand the suspense, why does everyone call you Max?"

Max took a deep breath and seemed to relax a little under the circumstances. He said, "I'd just made HAC before the squadron moved up to Phu Bai from Ky Ha and one of the first missions I went on once we got up here was a Khe Sanh resupply. The siege hadn't started yet. I'm east coast trained so I wasn't used to flying in mountainous terrain and I was a brand new HAC (Helicopter Aircraft Commander). I was number four in the flight, the FNG spot and trying to keep up with the old hands. I took on this ridiculous amount of supplies with the intention of taking it up to one of the mountain landing zones. My crew chief even told me we were going to be too heavy but I told him to never mind I could "HAC" it. I lifted off at Khe Sanh lost my rotor turns and crashed. The good news was that the aircraft didn't burn which it usually does and no one got hurt. The bad news was that when they unloaded my aircraft and checked the weight of all the stuff I had on board, my aircraft was several hundred pounds over the MAXIMUM ALLOWABLE GROSS WEIGHT so there was no way in hell it was gonna fly. So everybody started calling me MAX GROSS, short for Maximum Gross Weight, and over time it got shortened to just Max. "

I said, "That's a hell of a story Thomas."

Max said, "Now that we got all that shit settled let's see if we can go save these Marines and not get hurt in the process."

Max called the wingman and told him to hold clear and act as the backup or rescue if needed. Then he called the team on the ground and told them we were now just a few minutes out and wanted to know their ETA (Estimated Time of Arrival) to the landing zone if they could provide one. The team answered back in a whisper that they were at the edge of the "Lima Zulu" and the "Company in trail" was about 2 to 3 hundred yards behind. Max told the team leader to prepare for pick up and that we would be approaching from the east coming up hill at low level. Max then called Scarface and asked him to overfly the pickup zone and drop a smoke grenade to mark it for us because we were coming in low and we'd never see it soon enough. If Scarface could do that then he wanted Scarface to direct Hellborne to drop uphill 2 to 3 hundred meters while we were getting into the zone.

Scarface was way ahead of us, called and said he had us in sight. Scarface over flew the zone and dropped a smoke grenade right in the middle and instructed Night Stalker to take good cover. Scarface then instructed Hellborne lead to drop it all 300 yards up hill from the smoke.

About the time we saw the smoke the ordnance from the A-4 drop went off. It was impressive and the good news was it was timed just right so we weren't going to be hit by the shrapnel from the bombs.

According to the direction of the smoke we were a little downwind for landing which isn't a good thing but Max was making it look easy. He'd told me that if he got hit going in to go ahead and make the pickup. Coming out of the landing zone I should head straight downhill.

Through all the smoke we could just barely make out a beleaguered looking group of Marines on the uphill side of the landing zone at the edge of the tree line. Max kept his approach coming and damn near air taxied across the landing zone to get as close to them as possible.

It took longer than expected to get them all on board but during that time the two Scarface gunships were working over the area above the landing zone with heavy rocket and machine gun fire. Max and I were pretty sure the A-4's had really done the job on any NVA up there.

With six Marines on board we were able to stagger into the air but didn't have a lot of power left for much evasive action and thankfully we didn't need it. We left Scarface and the Hellbornes to deal with whatever was left there and headed straight for the nearest Medivac facility.

When we dropped off the two wounded Marines the whole team decided to disembark, so as we lifted off the Medivac pad Max told me to take us home.

No one said a word all the way back to Phu Bai. In fact, no one said a word even after we parked the aircraft, and were walking towards the ready room tent. Max headed for the Aircraft Maintenance Tent to sign off the aircraft logs and enter the flight time for the day.

I kept expecting him to come into the ready room and operations tent but he never did so I filled out all the after action paperwork and turned it in to the operations clerks. I was just leaving the operations tent and I saw Cpl Nose standing by the Maintenance tent entrance, he was motioning to me. I went over to see what he wanted. He still never said anything but motioned for me to look at the aircraft log that Max signed.

At the bottom of the aircraft yellow sheet was a place for the pilot in commands signature. I looked at the name in the signature block and it read, Captain Thomas J. McKinight, USMCR instead of just Max.

EPILOGUE

Captain Thomas J. McKinight, USMCR went back to college and earned a law degree and eventually the rank of Colonel in the United States Marine Corps Reserve. He had a very successful career as a member of the Virginia Bar for many years.

Sadly in 2009 Max fell while hanging Christmas decorations at his house and died later from complications with his injuries.

Taken just a few seconds after he told me his name wasn't Max.

A DAY AND A NIGHT WITH VINNIE

THE DAY

It's still March and the cloudy, drizzly weather has persisted for almost a month. It's somewhat unlucky that the overcast is so high because the clouds wouldn't interfere with our mission today, which is to fly up to Khe Sanh and be working birds all day. If the overcast was lower we couldn't work the very high hills around Khe Sanh and the whole thing would most likely be cancelled. Although the action has diminished some, Khe Sanh is still pretty dangerous because of the NVA surrounding the place. So, with the siege and all, air operations in that area could definitely be hazardous to your health.

My job for the day was to be Vinnie's co-pilot on this mission. For some reason I had been Vinnie's co-pilot a lot recently and really didn't know why. Vinnie is 1/LT Vincente' Pilk, dark hair, dark eyes, olive skin and an accent not readily identifiable but definitely from back east some place. Vinnie was a real character.

Vinnie had only been designated a HAC (Helicopter Aircraft Commander) for a short while although he'd been "In Country" for six or seven months before I got there. Vinnie was a little different from most of the guys; some might have even called him hyper. I would have said it was more "Quirky" than hyper.

Under his flight suit he insisted on wearing a red and blue striped T shirt instead of regulation clothing. Despite some chastising and criticism he stuck with the T shirt. He said it was his "Lucky Shirt". He carried a long barreled .357 magnum pistol in a western style holster around his waist but always made sure the pistol was hanging right in front of his private parts rather than on the side. Even seated in the cockpit of the aircraft he would adjust the pistol so it was in front of his crotch.

Vinnie also had a terrible thirst. He could never seem to get enough water to drink so he carried two canteens of water at all times. When Vinnie was flying, water was a more important consideration than fuel. I'd been with Vinnie when we landed just to fill up his canteen with water.

Vinnie was a bachelor and would take an R&R quota to anyplace, anytime one was available. His latest was about a week ago and he'd gone to Singapore. I asked him what he did in Singapore. He looked at me with a straight face and said, "I took $1500 dollars with me and spent $1200 dollars on pussy and booze, then blew the rest foolishly on gifts for my family."

He also had a chess set that he'd acquired on a previous R&R to Hong Kong. It was beautiful. The set was in its own wooden box and when opened contained an inlaid wooden game board. The hand tooled chessman were very ornate, one set of pieces was gold, the other silver. He told me he'd paid $500 bucks for the set. No one had ever seen anything like it. When I asked him if he played, he said, "Oh no, I've never played."

"Then why on earth did you buy a $500 chess set?"

Vinnie said, "Cause it's pretty. And besides, for that much money, at midnight, the damn box comes open, those sonofabitches line up and have their own war, I just watch."

Vinnie loved to gamble. He was a constant member of the hooch poker or crap game. He loved the action and was always jumping around with excitement when the game got big. The bigger the action the better he liked it and the more he moved around. When it came to flying, Vinnie was also a little excitable but was a steady pilot and I never saw him flinch when things got tight. He would do his job.

This morning we were number four in a flight of four heading north. With the exception of going to Khe Sanh, I liked flying with Vinnie and think he felt the same about me. We had a great crew: Cpl Tygart and L/Cpl Villarreal.

They were two of my favorites, you never had to worry about the aircraft being right and they always knew what to do in a tight situation. Besides, Cpl Tygart was one of the best shots I'd ever seen with an M-60 machine gun, especially from a moving helicopter.

When we arrived at Khe Sanh, the flight was broken up into a pair of aircraft shuttling people and things back to Dong Ha and the other two aircraft resupplying positions with ammo, water, and food. Occasionally we'd have a passenger.

Khe Sanh combat base was just about as far north and west as you could get in South Viet Nam. To the north was North Viet Nam and to the west was Laos. It was in the mountains, and if there wasn't a war going on, the area would have made a wonderful resort. Before the war there was a banana plantation up there. Right beside the airfield that the Marines built was a beautiful waterfall.

The combat base and airfield sat on a small plateau, the only flat terrain in the whole area. It was surrounded by hills. Unlike the French back in the '50's, the Marines seized the high ground all around their base; whereas the French in a similar situation didn't and were annihilated. The NVA had recognized the similarity of the situation and were drawn to Khe Sanh in hopes of doing the same thing to the Marines. They overlooked one important thing, they were up against United States Marines and their plan wasn't working out quite so well. The Marines were taking a pounding but because they controlled all the high ground around the combat base and airfield the NVA had a constant uphill fight. The Marines were also masters at the use of supporting arms. Using their artillery, close air support and supplemented with daylight pinpoint bombardment by Air Force bombers, the Marines were making the NVA pay a terrible price.

For the Marines assigned there, Khe Sanh was pure hell. Marines don't like to fight from a static position, they like

144

to attack. But, this was the mission they were given and they were going to make the best of it. For those of us sent to help them, we couldn't do enough for our fellow Marines. They knew it, they respected our courage, and they also knew that without us their mission would be impossible.

The airfields metal runway was oriented basically north and south. On the east side of the field there was a series of revetments for parking helicopters. These were necessary if a helicopter had to spend very long on the ground. Khe Sanh was under constant observation as well as artillery and mortar fire. When you landed at Khe Sanh, or the nearby hill top positions, you were more than likely going to draw fire. That's why it was imperative not to stay on the ground too long.

From the air, the runway looked like a misshapen T. At the north end of the runway, the Marines had laid another large metal area across the axis of the runway that made up the T. It was called the passenger/cargo turn around. Before the siege got real serious, C-130 fixed wing cargo aircraft used to land here and it was in this area that they unloaded and turned around. Now the enemy fire was such that they couldn't safely land and be on the ground for any length of time at all. Now they would make low passes and drop the supplies at very low altitude. The supplies were on pallets and would slide up the runway to a halt near the passenger turnaround. Marines would break down the pallets and transfer the materials to the helicopters who would take the supplies up to the positions on the high ground.

The trick was for the helicopters to stay airborne or in a revetment until the Marines had staged a load for one of the positions on the high ground. When they were ready the helicopter would make a fast approach to the passenger turnaround, load as quickly as possible and hopefully get

145

airborne before any incoming enemy fire arrived. Sometimes it was a little frantic but the system worked.

Instructions were passed from the Marine HST (Helicopter Support Team) via radio to the helicopter as to where each load was to be delivered. The various high ground landing zones were identified by numbers that actually referred to their height above sea level. This information was taken from the lines of elevation on a map. Vinnie and I would be working 688 north and south and then 1013 the highest one up here, a very difficult place to land.

688 north and south were on a ridgeline to the west of the base and runway. The Marines held the ground between the base and the crest of the ridge. Over the ridge to the west was a lot of NVA, the Laotian border and the Ho Chi Minh trail. 1013 was to the northeast of the runway and base. It was a rugged and rocky peak that had a commanding view of the whole plateau around the base and surrounding area.

Vinnie made the first couple runs up to 688 north and then gave the aircraft to me and I made a couple runs up to 688 south. Things were going fairly smoothly, the aircraft was performing well, and seemed to have plenty of power. The weather was cooperating, it was still drizzling and cloudy but the hill tops were clear and visibility was pretty good. Even the NVA seemed to be sleeping in so far this morning because we really hadn't taken any fire at all.

Khe Sanh HST told us the next couple loads would be for 1013. Vinnie took over the controls and we headed northeast for the landing zone. It was more like a spot that you could rest two wheels on than a landing zone. It was impossible for a co-pilot in a UH-34 to shoot the approach because from the left seat you couldn't see where to touch the wheels down. So the co-pilots primary responsibilities going into 1013 was to make sure the HAC didn't let the rotor turns droop and lose power. If that happened and you lost your rotor turns it was going to be a very long fall to the bottom.

Vinnie did not like flying up here in the mountains. We had received our combat training in different places. His was in the flat woods of North Carolina and mine had been in the San Jacinto Mountains of California. So I was fairly comfortable up here, he was not. We'd done this together before and Vinnie would have me fly the initial approach until we got in fairly close and then he would take over until touchdown and I would just monitor what was going on. If something bad happened I was to take the aircraft and dive away from the zone, get the airspeed and rotor turns back. With the exception of the wind being a little gusty, we made the first trip without a hitch. We dropped off ammo, food, and water and picked up a couple Marines who were damn glad to get off that rock.

Vinnie had touched the aircraft down at 1013 on our second trip and things were going well. We had four Marines and a few supplies that had to come off. The Marines were off in a flash but there was some delay getting off the supplies. Vinnie had to hold the aircraft in a very awkward position and keep it steady.

I was sitting there watching the rotor turns and the manifold pressure on the engine when I noticed the oil pressure gauge just flicker a little and then start dropping. This was not good. If the gauge wasn't going bad, it meant we might be on the verge of an engine failure. I keyed the mike and said, "Vinnie, we need to go now." I had no more said that and Cpl Tygart called on the intercom and said, "Sir, we are clear to lift."

The second indication of engine failure besides dropping oil pressure was a rise in the engine cylinder head temperature and it was starting to rise at an alarming rate as Vinnie lifted the aircraft back into the air.

Vinnie pushed the nose over and we started the long descent to the runway at the base. A helicopter doesn't glide like an aircraft, it falls like a rock. If you have level ground below, you can autorotate (term used when landing a helicopter with no engine power) but with no engine power you are probably going to land on whatever terrain is just passing under nose of the helicopter.

Vinnie said, "Hey, look at that cylinder head temperature, it's really getting up there.

"No Shit, check the oil pressure, I think we are losing the engine."

About this time the last indication of real trouble appeared, an engine chip light. (A magnetic plug in the engine oil sump.) If there are metal chips in the engine oil they will adhere to the plug and make the light come on. Metal chips in the engine oil are a sign that the engine is starting to disintegrate.)

"Oh shit, this can't be good. You think we can make the runway or at least the passenger turnaround?"

"If it doesn't quit right now we gotta chance but keep your altitude, don't go any lower and don't change the power setting on the engine, just hold what we got."

"Ok, good idea"

We didn't need to say a thing to the crew, they were always listening on the intercom and I could hear them getting things ready for either a crash or hard landing.

We were at 1500 feet above the actual ground. This was plenty for a successful autorotation; it would all depend on the surface available for touchdown. If the engine quit right now, we were poorly placed because right below us was a big ravine with a rocky stream bed at the bottom. It would be a rough touchdown, a very long climb to get out of the ravine, and most likely we would have the NVA for company.

I was watching the clock and the last two minutes had seemed like an awfully long time but we were now close enough to the airfield that we would at least come down on

148

fairly level ground and under the protection of Marine guns.

You could smell the heat from the engine bay now. Vinnie said, "What do you think, time to come down, we are getting pretty close."

"Well Vinnie I hate to give up any altitude until that runway is passing under our nose but judging from the hot smell coming from the engine bay I think we better. If this Magnesium airframe catches fire at this altitude we will never make the ground."

Vinnie nodded and immediately started a descent. As soon as he reduced the engine power there was an awful grinding sound, the engine coughed a couple times and went silent. The good news was Vinnie had lowered the collective and entered an autorotation. The bad news was the runway wasn't quite under our nose. We weren't quite to the perimeter wire on the edge of the passenger turnaround.

I kept telling Vinnie, "Don't try and stretch a glide, pick your spot and go for it, we'll just have to take what's there, don't try to stretch it!"

At 250 feet above the ground Vinnie pulled the nose of the aircraft up slightly to kill off as much forward speed as possible. (This maneuver is called a "Flare" or "Flaring the Aircraft"). He was doing things right by the book. He held the flare as long as I thought he should and then pushed forward on the control stick to level the aircraft. He waited just a fraction of a second and started pulling up on the collective to cushion the landing as much as possible.

We still had a little forward ground speed maybe ten or twenty knots, we were heading down a slight incline and we were going to touchdown just short of the perimeter wire by the passenger turnaround.

I didn't think we were going to hit quite so hard but we did. The aircraft bounced and came down right in the perimeter wire. We plowed right through it and rolled onto the metal matting of the passenger turnaround. Once the aircraft got onto the metal matting, the smooth surface and the slight incline caused it to pick up speed. We rolled right across the passenger turnaround and were now starting to roll down the runway.

Heavy smoke started billowing out of the engine bay obscuring forward vision. Fire was a UH-34 crew's worst nightmare. The fuselage was made out of Magnesium to keep it light but Magnesium burns rapidly to a fine white ash. It would take about 40 seconds for a UH-34 to burn almost completely. The smoke might just be engine oil burning off but if it caught the Magnesium on fire, it would be time to get out of the aircraft.

The safest thing to do would be to turn the aircraft left into one of the revetments and get the hell out. If we got out now, the aircraft might block the runway and further hamper resupply efforts.

The smoke was really heavy now, black smoke, so I was pretty sure it was engine oil. I said, "Vinnie, turn left and put it in a revetment, Vinnie turn left and put it in a revetment." I looked to my right and Vinnie was gone, his seat was empty. I called on the intercom for the crew chief or gunner and got no response. I was alone in this aircraft.

I decided to stomp on the rudder and turn the aircraft to the left and put the damn thing in the revetment that was coming up on my left. However, for some strange reason when the UH-34 was designed, they put rudder pedals on both sides but only put brakes on the right side. The HAC was the only one that had brakes. There is a console between the pilot and co-pilots seat. Even though I was wearing my survival vest and bullet bouncer I managed to climb over the console into the pilot's seat. I tapped the brakes just to make sure they were going to work and as the aircraft approached one of the small taxi strips into a revetment I stomped on the left rudder and brake and turned the aircraft into the revetment. I let it roll in as far as I dare. The smoke was obscuring my forward vision. I didn't want to crash into the end of the revetment so I applied and locked the brakes and then reached up and applied the rotor brake. The blades were still going around but thankfully not very fast and the rotor brake brought them to a sudden stop.

I climbed down from the cockpit and took a look toward the nose of the aircraft. I couldn't see the source of the smoke but I could tell the whole thing was confined to the engine compartment. I couldn't believe the aircraft wasn't burning, but that was good news.

I turned to run out of the revetment and heard the first explosion. I wasn't surprised there was incoming, I'm sure all our smoke had given the bad guys something worthwhile to shoot at. The main control bunker was across the runway. To get there I would have to run about 200 yards or more across completely open runway and ground. I knew there were some trenches on the other side of the runway but that was still a long run over open ground.

When the Marines built the revetments they had to build metal taxi strips from the runway into the revetments. They'd dug a drainage ditch on both sides of the runway and where the taxi strip attached to the runway, it crossed over this ditch. The Marines had put a good sized culvert in the ditch and built the taxi strip over the culvert. It was the best cover I could get.

I made a dash for the culvert and crawled right in. It wasn't huge, but it was big enough I could crawl without too much problem. It was damp and muddy but it was comforting to know I had metal around me and about two or three feet of dirt above me.

At first I just crawled in far enough to get my whole body in and then I decided to crawl all the way to the middle. But, in the middle it was dark and I wasn't comfortable. The culvert was about 40 feet long, I couldn't tell how big around it was but it wasn't big enough for me to sit up. I could roll over but I couldn't back up. I'm not claustrophobic but I'm not really fond of wet, muddy, dark, tight spaces. I decided to keep crawling until I could at least see out.

I actually worked up a little bit of a sweat crawling to the end but once I got there it was worth the effort. I got myself into a fairly comfortable position, lit a cigarette and waited for the incoming enemy rounds to stop falling.

I don't know how long I waited, my watch was covered with a blob of mud, but after a period of silence I could hear footsteps pounding on the metal matting. A Marine jumped down in the ditch a few feet from the end of the culvert and peeked in. He seemed a little surprised to see me so close to the end of the culvert.

The L/Cpl said, "Sir, they sent me over to get you. The shelling has stopped for the moment. If you will follow me I'll take you to the command bunker with the rest of your crew."

The first thing I noticed as I entered the Command Bunker was an odor I'd never really smelled before. These Marines had been surrounded and under siege for over sixty days with nothing but sheer guts and supporting arms to keep them from being overrun and annihilated. These were some exhausted, grim faced men. I realized the odor I couldn't identify was fear. If anyone had ever told me that fear had an odor I would have laughed but I wasn't laughing here, it was palpable. These Marines knew that their existence was not just day to day but hour to hour.

I found Vinnie, Tygart and Villarreal in the corner of the bunker. Vinnie offered me his canteen cup which was full of hot coffee. With a big smile on his face he said, "Did you miss me?"

"It got lonely out there, where did you guys go?"

152

"Well you know the only thing I fear more than being shot in the privates is being burned, so I wasn't taking any chances."

Cpl Tygart said, "When we saw him going down the side of the aircraft we figured it was time for us to follow."

"How's our aircraft?"

"Your aircraft didn't burn it was just engine oil so I think if we fold the blades and get the lifting eye attached to the rotor head that someday it might get hauled back and fixed."

"I knew you'd have a plan."

An hour before our squadron mates were going to quit for the day they told us to get ready and they would give us a ride home. No one was anxious to spend the night here because we would most likely have to sleep in a culvert so the four of us made our way to the aircraft, got the blades folded and put the lifting eye up on the rotor head. Vinnie and I looked over the engine compartment and still could not see any visible signs of an engine failure other than a huge oil leak. We'd done all we could do.

By 1900 (7PM) we were back at Phu Bai in the horrible hooches. We'd cleaned up and Vinnie was already in the poker game. Someone asked Vinnie how Khe Sanh had gone today. Vinnie looked up from his cards, took a sip from his beer, squinted a little and said, "About like you'd expect. Man they got good coffee up there."

Passenger Turn Around at Khe Sanh, complete with mail bags waiting.

Bottom left hand corner is a revetment wall. Sandbags are at the entrance of culvert I spent some time in.

Runway at Khe Sanh. The revetments are to the right. The slight haze or smoke just to left of the runway was from incoming round. The lead aircraft is up and away.

THE NIGHT

The operations department kept track of who flew what mission when. Everybody took his turn no matter what. I'd had my initiation on day medivac several times, but now, I'm up for my first night medivac. Night Medivac was the single most dangerous mission we had. Just before I got here we'd lost a whole crew and since I'd been here I'd lost a hooch mate to a horrible burn. The Operations officers were also very careful about what two guys they put together for this mission. Unlike day Medivac, which was flown with only one aircraft plus a gunship escort, Night Medivac consisted of two UH-34s. On day Medivac you launched for Emergency, Priority, or Routine requests. On Night Medivac you only launched in cases of an Emergency. The lead aircraft was the actual Medivac bird and carried the Corpsman; the second aircraft was the chase or backup aircraft in case lead went down or if there were

155

more Medivacs than he could carry. The lead aircraft was always reluctant to call down the number two aircraft because that pilot was not quite as experienced and also there'd be no backup if both aircraft were loaded with injured Marines.

Just a few days after our Khe Sanh mission, Vinnie came up to me and said, "Guess what Spice?"

"OK, I'll play, what?"

"You and I got night Medivac. It's your first one and you're scheduled with me tonight."

"Yeah, I know and I couldn't think of a better guy to break me in."

"Well I just wanted to let you know in case you didn't, it's my first one as a HAC. I'm gonna get a couple of those little flash lights the medical people have, you know the one you press the clip and the light comes on, you can put them in the pen pocket of your flight suit. You want me to get you a couple."

"That would be nice."

"You got a regular flash light; you know that GI kind with the interchangeable lens from white to red, don't you?"

"Yeah, I got one."

"You need new batteries or anything?"

"No, I got new batteries in there and I have a spare set in my survival vest. Look Vinnie are you worried about flying with me tonight? Don't worry I'll be ready."

"I'm not worried about flying with you, I'm glad I'm flying with you, I like to fly with you, I'm just worried about NIGHT FLYING PERIOD!!!

"Me too."

"Greg Armstrong is the lead tonight and Lavigne is his co-pilot. Our brief is at 1700 so I'll see you there."

Armstrong was also a Captain but he'd been here for quite a while much like Robbie. When we showed up at 1700 for the brief he was all business and made it clear that

156

as the number 2 he would not call us down into a zone unless it was absolutely necessary. After the brief we pre-flighted our aircraft, set up the cockpit for a scramble start, and briefed our crew. Cpl Tygart and L/Cpl Villarreal had been assigned another aircraft while Tygart's original aircraft was undergoing an engine change. After that, we returned to the operations ready tent and settled in to wait.

I'd checked the Intel board before the brief and so had Armstrong. He gave me a funny look while I was studying the map. I noticed there was a battalion making a sweep along the coast southeast of Phu Bai. They weren't all that far away. The sweep was to the south along the coast which was smart because their left flank was the ocean and wouldn't pose much of a threat. I mentioned that to Armstrong and he simply nodded.

It was just a few minutes after midnight and that damn Double EE8 went off. I really hated that sound because I knew what it meant and always felt as if my heart just stopped. Vinnie and Lavigne had gone out to the aircraft long ago. Armstrong was waiting for the operations duty officer to get all the info written down and I was looking over his shoulder copying the info as he wrote it down. As soon as I saw the map coordinates and the Tacan reference I looked up at Armstrong and said, "It's that battalion down on the coast." He walked over to the map and had a look for himself.

"You're right, let's go, at least it will be flat and we don't have to worry about hills."

We ran out to the aircraft. Vinnie was asleep on a stretcher in the cabin, Villarreal was stretched out on the troop seats and Tygart was sitting on the right main mount tire. When he saw me coming he woke them up. By the time I got up the side of the aircraft and into my seat Vinnie was strapped in and ready to start the engine.

Both aircraft were airborne very quickly and as per the brief we turned on all our running lights and tried to be as visible as possible. It was our job to head directly to the position at altitude, 1500 feet or better. Armstrong was going to fly behind and slightly below us with no lights on at all. Hopefully once we got overhead the pickup zone the bad guys would see only one aircraft and the lead aircraft could then start his descent into the landing zone unnoticed at least until he got the aircraft on the ground.

We were overhead the zone in less than fifteen minutes and Vinnie started a right hand orbit. We could see the phosphorescent glow of the surf line. About 100 yards off the beach was a tree line that was about three hundred yards wide, and then there was a huge open patch of nothing but white sand, a kind of a "No Man's Land" maybe three hundred yards wide and then another tree line that extended back way into the darkness. The Marines were in the first tree line with the ocean to their back now and the NVA were in the other tree line. We could see some occasional tracer streaks going back and forth across the "No Man's Land" or open area, but had no feel at this point for the intensity of the fire or the possible size of the NVA unit in the other tree line. The FAC (Forward Air Controller), or "one four" as they were known, told Armstrong he had four emergency medivacs, one with uncontrolled bleeding and needed him to land immediately.

Vinnie continued his right hand orbit and Armstrong started his approach. Since I was on the left side of the aircraft I couldn't see what was going on.

"Holy shit, Armstrong just touched down. When he turned on his landing light that whole fucking tree line lit up, did you see that?"

"No Vinnie I really can't see much from over here."

Tygart said, "I saw it Lt, if they didn't get somebody else hit when that happened I'll be damned surprised."

As soon as Armstrong shut off his landing light the firing stopped. Armstrong came up on the radio, "Dash two they've got more than four medivacs down here. Shut

158

off all your lights now and I'll call when I'm lifting from the zone. Start your approach when you hear my call. Come in from the ocean side, touching down facing west towards that big open area. Wind is not a factor. Coming out make an immediate left climbing turn back out towards the water. Whatever you do don't go straight ahead very far into that open area; the bad guys are really thick in the other tree line. I'm calling for gunships now."

Vinnie and I exchanged glances while I was shutting off all the aircraft lighting. We knew this would not be good at all.

"Tygart, you guys ready down there? I know we don't have a corpsman on board but just do the best you can."

"We got it all covered Captain, we're ready."

We heard Armstrong call that he was lifting from the LZ and Vinnie started his descent. We were out over the water and although it was very dark we could see well enough to know where the LZ was without the FAC trying to illuminate the zone. Unfortunately before we could tell him to hold the illumination he popped an illumination grenade in the landing area. Now everybody knew an aircraft was coming in for a landing.

Vinnie kept his approach heading for the zone.

"We might as well take advantage of the illumination since it's there."

The flare in the landing zone was so bright I couldn't see much else and things were getting brighter as we were getting pretty close to touchdown. I could feel the familiar shudder of the 34 coming out of translational lift and into a hover. The FAC suddenly came up on the radio.

"Pestkiller Dash Two, wave off, wave off now."

Vinnie immediately turned the aircraft smartly to the left and added full power to make a climbing left hand turn. My job was to keep my scan going on the instruments in case Vinnie got disoriented I could take the aircraft and using the flight reference instruments get us up and away.

159

The sharp turn really got my attention and it took a second or two to realize he wasn't disoriented even though we had about 45 degrees angle of bank.

"Pestkiller Dash Two, keep going, keep going, the fire is too intense for you to try and land. I'm trying to organize some suppressive fire standby, standby."

We orbited for about five minutes and really didn't see any more fire from the far tree line. We both knew they were waiting for us to try again.

"Pestkiller Dash Two, OH SHIT, dash two start your approach, my radio operator is hit bad if you don't get in here this time he's gonna die, OH SHIT, he's gonna die, COME ON, COME ON!!!!"

"We are heading down now, don't, repeat don't illuminate the zone."

"Hurry man, GODDAMN HURRY!"

I stayed on the instruments until we were very close to touchdown and then looked up. Vinnie made a very fast and terrific approach, turned on his landing light at just the last second and shut it off the instant he touched down. There was a lot of scurrying around the aircraft and you could feel personnel being loaded onto the aircraft and then smell that horrible sickening smell of blood and damaged bodies.

"We've got five guys on here Lt you're clear to lift."

Vinnie lifted the aircraft into a hover, dropped the nose slightly and as we started forward pulled in full power on the collective. We were too heavy to turn or climb immediately so we had to go straight forward to gain air speed. This took our flight path out into the "No Man's Land" strip a little farther than either of us wanted but we had no choice. Vinnie had just started to make the left turn when three things happened almost simultaneously. The entire tree line lit up. It was like several hundred little white flashes occurred at the same moment. At the very first flash, Tygart fired right back at the sight of the flash. I

160

didn't think it was humanly possible to react that quickly, and our dash lights went out. We couldn't see any of the instruments.

Tygart was screaming, "I got that sonofabitch, I know I got him!" Vinnie was very busy trying to continue our turn and I quickly reached up to my shoulder pocket and pulled out one of the little medical lights Vinnie had acquired earlier, stuck it in my mouth and bit down on the little metal clip which turned it on. Now at least we could barely see the instruments.

Vinnie leveled the aircraft momentarily and as he did so there was a very bright flash off to our right coming out of the tree line, followed by two more in rapid succession.

"Keep turning Sir those are RPG's, keep turning!!" (RPG is a Rocket Propelled Grenade)

Vinnie reacted immediately and now had enough airspeed to make a very positive climbing left hand turn. One of the RPG's went under us and two went behind us, but during the turn I could see them exploding harmlessly in the sand of the open area.

Since I'd been here, I'd seen a couple instances where I knew there were people shooting at the aircraft but I never had any idea of the volume of fire. The guys were always saying that anyone who could shoot at us did and that we took a lot of fire we never saw, but tonight I saw it all and I couldn't believe we didn't get hit. The guys were right, every time we showed up any bad guy that could shoot, took a pot shot at us whether it was a good shot or not.

"You have the aircraft."

"I have the aircraft."

I headed the aircraft straight for Delta Med. I could see two gunships coming in the vicinity of the tree line and hear them talking to that poor FAC on the ground. Very quickly the first gunship started making a strafing run on the tree line and I could see the bad guys shooting back. It was going to be a hell of a fight and I hoped we didn't have

161

to come back again tonight. Armstrong called on the radio to say that he was heading back and wanted to know our status. Vinnie told him to wait at Delta Med; we were inbound with five more.

"Hey Lt, I think we got the bleeding stopped on this one guy and he'll probably make it. Not bad for a couple aircraft mechanics. Sorta like fixing a damn hydraulic leak."

As the medivacs were removed from the aircraft, the medical people gave us a thumbs up which we were glad to see. Armstrong had already gone back to the airfield at Phu Bai.

"You have the aircraft, take us home."

"I have the aircraft, Phu Bai it is."

It was a little after 0300 when we got back. While we were sitting there hoping we wouldn't get another mission tonight Vinnie broke out a deck of cards and began playing solitaire. He had a cup of coffee sitting nearby.

"You know, I think they ought to make those little medical flash lights standard issue for flight crews or at least keep a box of those things here in the ready room tent."

He picked up the cup of coffee and took a sip.

"You know Spice; it's too bad they can't make coffee as good here as they do up at Khe Sanh."

DAI DO

The end of March finally came and the first two weeks of April brought much better weather, the end of the siege at Khe Sanh and the battle for Hue City. Things actually quieted down for a while but we were still in the miserable hooches at Phu Bai. We hadn't received any incoming rockets or mortars since the beginning of April and the squadron ground officers were saying that we were due for a good deal, possibly a move out to one of the LPH's (Helicopter Aircraft Carrier) that we'd seen loitering off the coast from time to time. HMM-363 had been assigned to one for a while but they had been sent south to Marble Mountain. So there was an empty carrier deck out there and that meant real beds, much better food, hot showers and Air Conditioning!!

My hooch mate Ron Harkless came to me on the night of the 12th and told me that the skipper was sending the two of us out to LPH-2, the USS Iwo Jima, to meet with the ship's personnel and discuss the living arrangements prior to us moving aboard. So the ground officers were right as usual.

The next morning Ron and I flew single plane out to the Iwo Jima which was holding station about 10 miles off the coast and just about abeam the mouth of the Cua Viet River. Once we'd landed on the carrier we were escorted below decks and taken to a place called HDC (Helicopter Direction Center) it was the control center that provided the helos radar information or mission information when you were working off the ship. The control tower controlled the flight deck but HDC controlled everything else. On this class ship the HDC officer is always a Marine and usually a Major. Although he is a Marine, he's ship's company, and is responsible to the Captain for the helicopter operations around and from the ship. It's a big and very busy job.

The Major was a fellow helicopter pilot by the name of Roberts. He introduced himself and welcomed us aboard. Just about the time he finished his welcome the Captain called down from his bridge on the intercom and wanted to know who we were and what

squadron we represented. I recognized the voice immediately.
Before the Major could answer I said, "Major, who's the Captain
of this ship?"

"Captain Sheppard, why?"

"Not John Tyler Sheppard."

"The very one, do you know him?"

"Ask the Captain if he remembers a Corporal Spicer that was
the Admiral's orderly on the Carrier Division Staff."

"Captain, one of these pilots down here wants to know if you
remember a Corporal Spicer that was on the staff of Carrier
Division One."

"Yes I remember him very well."

"Well Sir, Captain Spicer just landed that H-34 on your flight
deck. He's one of the representatives from HMM-362, the Ugly
Angels."

"Well you send his ass straight up here to the bridge."

The Major was going to get a guide to take me to the bridge but
I told him it wasn't necessary. Ron was the senior man anyway so
I left him to deal with the details and headed straight up to the
Captain's Bridge. When I stepped through the hatch onto the
bridge I remembered to salute and request permission to come on
the bridge.

"You sure can Marine, get your ass over here and tell me all
about where you've been, it's obvious you've been very busy since
I last saw you on the Kitty Hawk."

He stuck out his hand and when I offered mine he grabbed me
and gave me a huge pat on the back. We went over to his chair on
the port side of the bridge and had a nice visit. I filled in the
blanks and he listened intently. When I left the bridge he told me
with a grin on his face that if our squadron gave them any trouble
while we were on board, I'd be the first guy he looked up. On my
way back down to HDC I kept thinking how strange it was to see
him again. He was a collector of nautical antiques. When the
Admiral wasn't using me in port, he allowed Captain Sheppard the
use of me and his car, so I'd driven him to lots of nautical junk
yards in several countries.

On our return to Phu Bai, Ron briefed the Skipper on the arrangements we made. The squadron got the "Word" the next day to start the move aboard the Iwo Jima.

The flight schedule for the 14th reflected an "All Hands" evolution to pack up and start loading aboard the Iwo. The Squadron had 24 aircraft on hand and most of these machines had been in Vietnam a long time. They were also flown to their structural limits damn near every day. Of the 18 we had up, half were being used for the move aboard and the rest were carrying out working bird and medivac missions assigned by the Group. Once we were completely aboard our tasking or frags would come exclusively from the SLF or Battalion via the ships HDC.

I was scheduled as my hooch mate Tom's co-pilot and since I was the contact point with the ship we were working on the load aboard. As soon as a section got packed up their gear was loaded aboard and flown to the ship.

Twenty four hours later HMM-362 was now aboard the Iwo. The six of us could have all lived in two man rooms on the Iwo, but we didn't want to break up our hooch group so we moved into a junior officer, six man bunk room, and still referred to it as "our" hooch. Some of the Lt's that wound up getting our two man rooms thought we were crazy.

We thought we might have a few days to settle in but we were sadly mistaken. Our mission for the 16th was carrier qualification. After flying aboard and making several landings on the 14th we were informed by the ship that we now needed to "Carrier Qualify". As it turned out it was a pretty good idea and not only provided training for us but the flight deck personnel as well.

In addition to the carrier qualification, we had a little trouble settling in on the ship. I wound up seeing Captain Sheppard a couple of times, and finally discovered there was a big disconnect between some of his department heads and his XO about having Marines on his ship. The XO, who was in charge of the officer's mess, wouldn't let the pilots or the infantry officers eat their meals because they weren't in the uniform of the day. For the Navy, that was a nice washed Khaki uniform and in the evening they even wore ties. We had two choices, flight suits or utilities. The infantry officers quite often had come aboard ship just for the day and only had the clothes on their backs. The XO and a couple of the Commanders on the ship were also very upset because we were all carrying guns. The SLF Commander and his XO damn near started a huge fight between the ship's officers and the infantry officers and our pilots. It wasn't the Captain's fault, it was some of his officers who had little to no experience with embarked Marines, especially those Marines that were actually fighting a war; it was a new experience for them. Captain Sheppard was more than understanding, took the manner in hand and things got sorted out in a hurry.

During our move aboard we'd also flown most of the SLF ALAPHA staff aboard and now that we'd all settled in we started loading elements of the Battalion as well. We weren't told exactly what units of 2/4 we were bringing aboard, we just kept flying back and forth from the beach to the ship until the Grunts and HDC said we were finished.

Since we were now exclusively in support of the SLF and Battalion, it seemed strange that if they weren't busy, neither were we; it was a welcomed change of pace. We got a few frags to take SLF and Battalion personnel to Dong Ha for meetings but so far the flying had been very light. We used the time to work on our aircraft, rest and take advantage of the good living, but still had the feeling something big was about to happen.

On the afternoon of the 27th after a very quiet morning all pilots were called to the ready room. The Skipper had been notified by the SLF Commander that he wanted a troop lift conducted ASAP. Operations had posted a hand written schedule and we were to launch two flights of four aircraft, go pick up some Marines and take them to a location designated by the SLF. That's all the information we had.

I was scheduled with the Skipper. As soon as we were all rendezvoused the Skipper headed the formation directly for the mouth of the Cua Viet River. We flew up the river towards Quang Tri and somewhere close to there was our pickup LZ. The

166

Call Sign was Dixie Diner 14. They were well organized and waiting for us. These Marines were traveling pretty heavy, packs, plus all their 782 equipment. They weren't going all that far, I wasn't real sure where we were unloading them but it was east of the pickup zone somewhere along the north bank of the river. The entire flight carried four loads each and then it was back to the ship.

Early on the morning of the 28th we were once again summoned to the ready room. Something big was brewing but not even our ground officers had any good rumors. I was scheduled as co-pilot with one of my hooch mates, Biff.

There was to be another lift but this time we were taking Marines from the ship. These Marines were also heavily loaded. I could see extra water and at least 5 Magazines on each man. I saw some of the officers carrying extra sixty millimeter mortar rounds with them and that only happened when things were very serious.

Once again after rendezvous the entire flight headed directly for the mouth of the Cua Viet River. It was the first major river south of the DMZ and the North Vietnamese border. It was a great terrain feature, easy to identify. I wasn't sure how far below the border the river was but from 2000 feet at the mouth of the river you could see the next river, the Ben Hai, and beyond that you were looking into North Vietnam. This was no place for a picnic.

Mouth of the Cua Viet River. UH-34 below to left is lead.

The Skipper started dropping the flight down to just above the water and we flew straight into the mouth of the river. Not much more than a click (term for 1000 meters) was a small creek, a tributary that led off to the north. Essentially it paralleled the coast line. I didn't know how far north it ran but according to my maps it ran about half way up to the DMZ. The Skipper referred to it as "Jones's Creek". There wasn't any name in Vietnamese on the map, so Jones's Creek was good enough for us.
Right near the mouth of the creek, where it fed into the Cua Viet River was a huge sand bar almost big enough to be called an island. We flew right over the sand bar and made a right hand turn following Jones's Creek to the north. We flew up the creek about a click, maybe a little more and the Skipper led us into a flight landing on the east side of the creek, where the Marines got out and deployed very quickly. The skipper simply reversed his course and we all headed back to the ship which was maintaining station about 8 miles off the mouth of the Cua Viet. Back on the ship we were instructed by SLF operations to standby for a possible re-launch.

HDC told the ODO that we now were responsible for a day and night medivac package. Since we were all standing by it wasn't going to be a problem. The afternoon passed very slowly and still we had no news from the SLF or Battalion on what was actually going on. At 1630 HDC called the ready room on the intercom and told us to scramble for an immediate launch, it was an emergency lift. We all scrambled for the flight deck and manned the aircraft we'd flown earlier.

The Skipper took the same flight route into the pickup LZ which was the exact location we'd put these Marines in earlier today. We landed as a flight once again but the Marines were spread out all over the place. They were scrambling to get aboard and definitely in a big hurry.

The Skipper broadcast on the radio that as soon as you had a load to lift and head south down Jones's Creek. We were moving the Marines back to a position near the mouth of the creek, just a few hundred meters north of the junction of the creek and the river.

Biff and I noticed the Marines weren't even bringing their packs, just rifles and water. This wasn't a good sign, something was radically wrong. Since we were the last two aircraft in this formation, Biff wanted to make damn sure we didn't leave anyone when we took off.

We'd landed facing to the north, parallel to the east side of the creek bank. We were pretty heavy so as we lifted off we naturally had to head north a little in order to gain enough airspeed to make a 180 degree turn and head south down the creek. As we attained flying speed Biff started a right hand turn keeping the aircraft low, about ten to twenty feet off the ground. He'd just rolled out of the turn and we were now heading south, flying parallel to the east side of the creek when the gunner, Gunnery Sgt Cooper said, "We're taking fire on the left!!"

As I was turning my head to the left to look out my cockpit window the crew chief Sgt Johns said, "We are taking fire on the right!!"

I kept looking to the left and turned my head just far enough to see four fully uniformed NVA soldiers about as startled to see us

169

flying by at ten feet as we were to see them. One was blazing away with his AK-47 and the other three appeared to be either trying to change Magazines in their weapons or bring them to bear on us. Gunny Cooper was firing a very long burst on his M-60. I couldn't see his results but I don't know how he could have missed because those guys were only about forty yards from us as we went by. I really don't know how they missed us. I snapped my head to the right but didn't see what Sgt Johns was firing at, but I could see dirt and dust kicking up in front of the aircraft. Biff was staring straight ahead concentrating on the task at hand.

Well off in the distance we could see the dust kicked up by the other aircraft landing. Biff was keeping the aircraft about ten feet off the ground, weaving like a "Drunken Butterfly" and doing at least 100 knots. After that one quick encounter we didn't see any more NVA but that didn't mean they weren't out there.

The Skipper called for the flight to rendezvous "feet wet" just east of the mouth of the Cua Viet River. We were the last section (2 aircraft) in this flight and the Skipper called for us to detach, hold "High and Dry" until the flight reached the ship. We would be the temporary day medivac until the flight was back aboard, and the regular day medivac aircraft were prepared.

Biff gave me control of the aircraft and lit up a smoke. He pointed in a southerly direction and made a motion for me to start climbing up. I flew to a point south of the river and leveled the flight at 2000 feet setting up a right hand orbit. Biff continued to smoke but looked over and gave me a thumbs up, indicating he was satisfied with the position I'd placed the flight. We couldn't see anything going on down on the ground north of the river and the radio was completely silent. We continued to orbit watching and listening until the HDC called for us to return to the ship. Biff let me make the landing back on the ship.

The next day, Biff and I were surprised that we were assigned to be the backup for Night Medivac lead. If anything happened to the lead aircraft on night medivac tonight we would take their place. If nothing happened we'd get a good night's sleep.

We were very aware that seeing NVA soldiers very near our pickup zone was not a good thing. We were also very surprised that some type of action hadn't taken place. All of us were hoping that someone would tell us what the hell was going on ashore, but nobody was talking.

The afternoon medivac package didn't launch, so at 1800 those assigned for the night went up, and got their aircraft ready.

Capt Ben Cascio and Lt Larry Houck were in the lead aircraft and my pal Robbie and Lt Bowers were the chase aircraft. Ben was a very experienced and skillful pilot and so was Robbie. This was a very strong team that had tonight's assignment.

After dinner I went up on the flight deck just to walk around and watch the sunset. I used to do that when I was enlisted on sea duty. With no air operations the flight deck was peaceful and quiet not to mention the sunsets were spectacular. I stayed up there until it was completely dark and then went down to our "bunk room".

I was awakened from a nice, sound, air-conditioned sleep when I heard the two aircraft turning up on the flight deck and very soon after I knew they'd taken off, I fell sound asleep again. I couldn't have been asleep long and suddenly there was a flashlight shining in my face. It was the Squadron ODO (operations duty officer).

"Spice, get up!! You and Biff are on. Cascio's been hit real bad."

Biff slept on a bunk about 6 feet from me and the ODO woke him next. Neither of us said a word. We were up, dressed quickly, and headed straight for the flight deck. Corporal Flagg was our crew chief and the gunner was L/Cpl Leedy. I wasn't sure about the Corpsman. I thought I saw "Doc" Jones come running out but for some reason I assumed he was with Cascio. I'd also seen Petty Officer Huhn, one of the other Corpsman, up on the flight deck earlier in the evening. The important thing was that we had a Corpsman aboard.

When we were given clearance to take off the ship was on an easterly heading taking it away from the beach. Biff dumped the nose slightly to gain airspeed and then started a climbing left hand turn back towards the beach. The sky had been cloudless last evening, and this morning we had good visibility in that pre-dawn darkish gray sky.

Biff continued his climb and turn to 1500 feet above the water. As soon as he stopped the turn and leveled the aircraft we could see the tracer rounds ricocheting up into the air. There were at least three streams of tracer rounds going in all directions. (The Tracer round is a bullet that has material on the end of it that glows when fired, so the person can visually "Trace" the round and see where it hits. Usually red in color for lower caliber weapons 7.62 and below, .50 caliber, particularly the NVA rounds were green and white. In a machine gun belt, usually there's one "Tracer" every four rounds. If the fire looks like a steady stream of tracers, there are one hell of a lot of bullets flying through the air.) The only good news here was that all these tracers were red.

As soon as I saw the tracer rounds ricocheting off the ground and bouncing as high into the air as we were I reached up and turned off all our external lights. Biff started increasing our altitude and we continued to head for the beach. HDC had given us a heading for the mouth of the Cua Viet River as well as the map coordinates, YD 252710, but they weren't necessary now; all we had to do was head directly for the tracers.

Our UHF radio was on the HDC frequency and our FM radio was on our "Squadron Common" frequency. Since we'd launched the radios had been silent. Biff leveled the aircraft at 2500 feet and told me to take control. He then told Flagg to test fire the guns and we heard the crew both fire a quick short burst. He looked over at me then back toward the beach.

"Looks pretty bad, got any ideas?"

"It would be nice to know what happened and what's going on but nobody's talking."

"Yeah I know, let's see what we can find out from night medivac chase before we switch to Dixie Diners frequency."

He pressed the radio key on the control stick and said, "Any Pestkiller aircraft this frequency this is Pestkiller one two, over."

"One two this is medivac chase, over."

"Chase, this is one two, Whiskey Tango Foxtrot, over?"
(Whiskey Tango Foxtrot meant What the Fuck?)

"One two, chase, we are just lifting off the old pad located on the south side of the mouth of the Cua Viet. Lead took grenades in the LZ while picking up the medivacs. Shrapnel took out Cascio's' left eye, Bush is wounded but not bad. Houck managed to somehow get the aircraft out of the zone but had no lights or electronics. I joined on him and used my landing light to illuminate the pad for him and he managed to get it on the ground and shut down. I've got the crew and medivac's aboard and we are heading for the ship. I think Dixie Diner needs you bad cause I'm sure they have more medivacs now than they did when Cascio went into the zone. All hell is breaking loose down there. From what I could make out by looking down it appears that the Marine and NVA lead units accidentally bumped into each other in the dark, somehow became intermingled and didn't know it. Nobody seems to know who's who or where their lines are. I'll call on UHF when I'm lifting off the ship. Good Luck."

"Roger, you call on UHF when inbound to help me but stay at or above 2500 feet with all your lights on, I'm running totally dark, no lights and will be at 2000 until called down. One Two out."

"Medivac chase roger, out."

Biff took control of the aircraft and had me switch the FM radio to Dixie Diner 14's frequency.

"Dixie Diner one four, Pestkiller Medivac."

"Pestkiller, one four, say your position."

"I'm running lights off and have the tracers in sight."

"Roger Pestkiller, can you see where the two main streams of tracers are crossing?"

"Roger I can see them clearly."

"I'm right below where they are crossing. Hang loose we are trying to get things under control a little. There's no way you can attempt a landing at the moment, you'd have no chance, repeat no chance."

"Roger one four, we will be standing by, it's your call."

Biff gave me control of the aircraft and using hand signals directed me to orbit at 2000 feet and clear of the area that the tracers were ricocheting. The minutes seemed to drag by. Robbie called on the UHF that he was just off the ship and inbound but of course he couldn't see us. Biff told him we wanted to keep it that way. If we got a chance to go in for a pickup he hoped we'd be on the ground and back in the air before the NVA knew we were there.

A good ten minutes went by before Dixie Diner called us. We could tell by the amount of tracer fire that things had settled down a little at least for the moment, but the tracers hadn't stopped completely.

"Pestkiller Dixie Diner, I had a couple medivacs down here but there may be more now, it's hard to tell. One guy is going downhill fast. I can't guarantee the zone is completely cool. It's your call. They get after you too much wave it off."

"Pestkiller roger, are we clear to fire in any direction during the approach or while on the deck?"

"Negative Pestkiller, we don't have any idea where our troops are deployed at the moment."

"Exactly where are you? Are you lying out in the open or are you in a hole of some kind?"

"I'm in a good sized shell hole and the wounded are in the next hole over, maybe fifteen yards."

"Is there any way you can mark your position for me without illuminating yourself or giving away your position? Can you flick a Zippo lighter, light a heat tab, flash light, anything."

"Stand by Pestkiller."

Biff had maintained a right hand orbit so he could continuously observe the area down there and also keep the exhaust stacks pointing up. The exhaust stacks were on the left side about two feet below my cockpit window. At night the engine exhaust gave off a blue flame or glow that was pretty visible.

"Ok Spice if he gives me a light of any kind I'm not going to look away. I'm gonna get us down there in a hell of a hurry. There isn't much wind at all so I want to sit us down facing south.

174

We know the bad guys are coming from the north and I don't want to go an inch in that direction when we come out of that zone. You stay glued to the gauges, and if you think I've got vertigo take it, level the wings and get us the hell out of there, get back up to 2000 feet and we'll try again. If anybody gets hit going in I'm still gonna try and get those guys out. Everybody got that?"

"Pestkiller Dixie Diner we found a flash light, got the red lens in. Are you in a position to observe?"

"Good enough Dixie Diner, when you're ready."

A few seconds later Biff lowered the collective actually entering an autorotation to increase our rate of descent. I couldn't see shit from my position even if I was looking but I was glued to the flight instruments. We were in a 45 degree angle of bank turn to the right and descending at 1500 feet per minute. We were coming down like a falling rock. He increased the angle of bank and pushed the ball out of center so we were no longer in balanced flight. This also increased our rate of turn and descent. I had a quick glance to my right and he was looking directly out his open cockpit window. We were still turning and now less than 500 feet of altitude. Our descent rate was almost 1800 feet a minute. He needed to start rolling out and adding power pretty soon or we were gonna hit the ground pretty damn hard.

"Less than 500 feet Biff."

"Ok, I got it."

The right hand turn continued for another 45 degrees of heading the altitude kept coming down, we were less than 200 feet now and suddenly the aircraft rolled out of the turn and the power came up very quickly. He pulled up the collective and added throttle banging the rotor and engine needles together at the same time. The old 34 was shuddering pretty heavily. The radar altimeter red warning light came on at 50 feet above the ground and the shudder continued, now very pronounced as we came out of translational lift. There was a slight side flare of the aircraft to kill off the last few knots of airspeed and then touchdown.

I heard Cpl Flagg saying, "I see them, I see them, unplugging to help out!"

175

We never liked it when the crew chiefs unplugged from the intercom."

I'd turned the red dash lights down as low as I could but when I looked up I couldn't see shit. I looked over a Biff and his head was still turned to the right looking out his open cockpit window. I could hear and smell the wounded Marines being loaded into the aircraft. It was that horrible sickening smell of blood and torn bodies.

I looked to the right again and was shocked to see two streams of tracers some distance from the aircraft on the right hand side. I saw Biffs' head come up and knew he saw them too. They didn't appear to be coming at us. I think we both thought it was our Marines trying to cover our departure but we weren't sure.

"We got 4 on board you're clear to lift sir!!"

Biff added full power and literally snatched the aircraft off the ground pushing the nose down to gain airspeed quickly. At sixty knots he pulled the nose up sharply adding power to maintain the sixty knot rate of climb which was the best rate of climb we could get, over a thousand feet per minute. We could see a stream of red tracers well below the aircraft and watched the rounds ricocheting majestically off into the darkness. Biff maintained the climb and started weaving back and forth to try and keep them from tracking us. Once over the river he turned east and headed straight for the ship. I suddenly remembered to turn on our external running lights.

We called HDC and told them we were inbound with 4.

"Pestkiller Medivac Lead, this is chase."

"Go ahead chase."

"I've got your lights now; I'm about a mile in trail. If you have to go back I'd do the same again.

"Lead Roger."

After we landed and they took the medivacs below we could hear some whistling from one or two of the blades. HDC told us to shut down, for now there were no more requests for medivacs. We looked the fuselage over using flash lights but couldn't find any bullet holes. Two of our blades had damage to the rear portion of the blade, but nothing to the leading edges. If we took hits in the blades we never heard them. We could have blown up some debris in the landing zone, there was no way to tell where the damage came from.

Since our aircraft was going to need some work on the blades, the guys assigned to day medivac took over. Looking back towards the shore we could see more tracers ricocheting well up into the air. We still had no idea of just what was happening but we knew for those Marines in there that hell was in session. We'd only been airborne about an hour but it had been an interesting hour.

The 28th had become the 29th so Biff and I weren't back on the schedule until the 30th, but we also didn't get any sleep because of all the flying during the day. All hell was breaking loose in there along Jones's Creek.

On the 30th I flew twice and the fight was intensifying. I was scheduled with the Skipper again on the 1st of May. We flew all day long flying in ammo, water and replacements. Off the ship we kept low heading straight for the mouth of the Cua Viet River. Then turning north up Jones's Creek we damn near air taxied up the creek looking for Marines or NVA. The fighting was taking place on both sides of the creek. The Marines appeared to be using the creek as a central rallying point. Wounded were being brought to the creek and by landing in the creek we could keep the cabin in defilade while trying to load and unload cargo or personnel.

The scene on both sides of the creek was surreal. We could see Marines and NVA engaged in hand to hand combat. This was the most vicious thing I had seen so far. It was difficult if not impossible for the crew chiefs or gunners to fire because of the intermingling of the Marines and the NVA. Although we had aircraft dedicated to the medivac mission, we were all taking medivacs back to the ship now.

Aircraft from Quang Tri had now been pressed into service and we could see gunships and CH-46's working with units to the west of the creek. There were air strikes being run to the north of us

177

and destroyers had been brought in close to the coastline to provide naval gunfire support. We still had no idea of what the hell was going on here.

Back on the ship, the aft hangar bay had been converted to a huge Triage. They were putting the stretchers up on saw horses and even our squadron flight surgeon, Lt Jim Johannes and corpsman "Doc" Jones were doing minor surgery on some of the wounded. One of the hospital ships had been brought up to the north to save run time.

None of us had seen anything like this. Khe Sanh and Hue had been terrible and bloody fights, but the viciousness of this one was staggering. Near the village of Dai Do and the area on both sides of the creek the fighting was particularly heavy.

Landing craft were coming alongside the carrier with Marines from somewhere. These Marines were coming up the combination ladder into the hangar bay, picking up a rifle, helmet and other equipment taken off wounded Marines and then put on the port aircraft elevator and taken straight to the flight deck. We were taking these guys in as replacements.

The main battle lasted for another 48 hours, and then things seemed to quiet down almost immediately. The level of violence of the fighting just couldn't have continued much longer. The battle was like an out of control fire that simply burnt itself out. For the first time in several days there were no air strikes or naval gunfire taking place. No artillery coming in from Gio Lin or the Dong Ha area, it was actually quiet over the battle field.

We had reports that Hotel and Golf companies were down to 30 or 40 men. Normally a Marine company had 240 men. There were so many wounded that we'd filled up the Iwo and the hospital ship and we flew for three more days transporting wounded down to the big Navy hospital in DaNang. The worst part was flying the dead down to the mortuary in DaNang. One of my hooch mates, Tom Thurber drew the short straw and led the flights down for a couple days. They had to throw away the flight suits they were wearing when they finished and the smell of death stayed with those aircraft for weeks, even though they were washed inside with diesel fuel.

Finally, once all the dust had settled, the Skipper called us all into the ready room and tried to tell us what the hell had taken place. It seems that a full Division of NVA, the 320th had crossed the Ben Hai River heading south. They had been met head on by 2/4. The Marines had no way of knowing that their Battalion size force was up against a complete NVA Division. The Battalion had done an amazing job, but were so outnumbered that by the time the fight was fully developed there was another Marine Battalion,(1/3) some U.S. Army and ARVN (Army of the Republic of South Vietnam) units involved. It had been one of the most violent and deadly fights of the war. Its remote location and short duration didn't allow time for much to be reported about the battle. The Skipper had no idea how many enemy had been killed, but had been told that this particular NVA Division essentially no longer existed; they had been completely wiped out. That was it, that's all we knew and the details would take a while to be reported. For us it was on with the next missions.

Two weeks after the big fight the Iwo left station heading for the Philippines, and we were back living in the horrible hooches of Phu Bai.

Holding near Jones Creek, waiting to go back in for another Medivac. Crew Chief waits in cargo door way with his M-60 machine gun.

Coming back to the ship.

SWIMMING WITH ROBBIE

May is a pretty warm month in Vietnam, but this day, May 22 seemed particularly hot. What made it seem particularly hot was because the squadron was back ashore, at Phu Bai, living in those horrible hooches. We'd been back ashore almost a week now and hadn't had a decent night's rest.

A week ago we were living and working off a ship. We'd been heavily involved with the battle of Dai Do just after getting aboard. Although the flying had been intense and dangerous, the living was really easy. Air conditioned rooms, a real bed with linen, three hot meals a day and a nightly movie, if you didn't have night Medivac. The ground guys spent more time ashore than we did but at least when they came out of the field it was back to the ship, not to some camp with hooches. So we were all spoiled or contaminated by the good life.

However, the Navy told us to get off the ship, the Iwo Jima deployment was over and the ship was going home. We were to assume our duties back at Phu Bai until a replacement ship arrived, "On Station". So we were back with MAG-36 and back living in the horrible hooches. Compared to the ship's air conditioned rooms the night time temperatures were nearly unbearable and being back on cots didn't help matters at all. We could adjust to a lot of things, but the heat was kicking our asses.

This morning it's hot already and I spent the night trying to sleep on a cot with perspiration dripping off every part of my body. I'm really looking forward to getting airborne and a chance to cool off. I am scheduled as the co-pilot for one of my best friends, Capt Henry Angus Robertson III, Robbie. Robbie has been one of my main mentors since I joined the squadron, plus we'd known each other a long time.   I'd flown with him a lot and always enjoyed being in the cockpit with him.

We were part of a four aircraft flight being sent north to Dong Ha for duties as "Working Birds" today.   Once there, we would be given specific tasking.   We might work all day for the same unit or have several different assignments. Our flight of four was airborne by 0600 and we made the transit up to Dong Ha at 1500' which after last night felt cool and refreshing.

After checking in with Dong Ha DASCC (Direct Air Support Coordination Center) Robbie and I were given a separate mission from the other aircraft.   We were assigned a VR (Visual Reconnaissance) mission.   The DASCC gave us a radio frequency, a set of map coordinates for the pick up and said it was a "Take and Wait, Until Detached" mission.   This meant we were to go, pick up whomever at the coordinates and take them wherever they wanted to go until they sent us home. Didn't sound too bad but it did sound like a long day.   The really worrisome part was we were single plane.   Normally the UH-34 aircraft did not operate single plane because we were single engine, it was much safer if we went in pairs.

I didn't recognize the pickup coordinates as any Marine positions so I broke out my maps, found the spot and gave Robbie a heading to go find the place.   I switched the FM radio to the frequency we'd been given and Robbie immediately gave them a call.   It took them a while to answer up and we told them we were inbound for the VR pick up.

The landing zone wasn't well marked and we knew this was not a Marine Unit.   Parked all around the landing zone were the biggest amphibious landing craft we'd ever seen. I'd seen pictures from WWII of these things but they were much smaller then and were called "Ducks".   After touching down in the LZ, Robbie pointed to a large sign near one of the tents.   I couldn't quite see the whole sign but it said something about an Amphibious Tractor Battalion, "Sunders Wunders".

"Sunders Wunders". Notice the man standing by the very large front tire.

I could see three men walking briskly towards our helicopter but being on the left side I couldn't see them get in. Robbie said, "Holy Shit, we got three full Army Colonels as passengers". This was pretty unusual; these guys were obviously on a mission to see where they would set up to operate or planning a big amphibious operation. One of the three Col's passed a map to the crew chief, and he passed it up from under our seats to us. The map had three red circles on it marked, 1, 2, and 3. We assumed this is where they wanted to go and in that order.

We found the first two spots with no trouble; one was the Cam Lo Bridge and the other a road junction between Dong Ha and Quang Tri. Our passengers didn't want to land, they had us orbit the locations and the crew chief said they were talking and making notes. Before heading to the third spot we made a quick refueling stop in the Dong Ha fuel pits and then started for location number three. We were familiar with the entire area we'd been flying over and maybe that's why the Army had tasked the Marines to take these Colonels around.

The last spot was at the mouth of the Cua Viet River. If you followed the river east from the Quang Tri area you came right to it. We had to fly right past the area of the battle of Dai Do. We'd been all over this area. Where the river ran into the South China Sea was an easily identifiable land mark. North of the inlet there had been lots of bad guys prior to the battle for Dai Do, but for the moment it was a pretty safe area. South of the inlet there was nothing but several miles of wide open sandy country and beautiful white sand beaches. There were no villages or people.

We stayed above 1500 feet and were making a few orbits of the inlet when our crew chief keyed the mike for the intercom and said, "Hey Captain, these Colonels want you to land on the south side of the inlet." Robbie told the crew chief to have a real good look for anybody on the ground and then we would land.

Robbie made a smooth landing near the high water mark on the beach because the wet sand wouldn't blow up near as much. The Colonels hopped out and began walking around like some tourists who'd just gotten off a plane to start their vacation. They were dressed in army fatigues, cartridge belts with one canteen and a .45cal pistol. They also had flak jackets and helmets. However, they had no radio, no rations, nothing to help if anything went wrong. One of the Colonels waved goodbye to us and Robbie said, "What the Hell, are these guys kidding?" Robbie sent the crew chief out to ask what their intentions were. We were both laughing about how we would explain what we did with three army Colonels and how the bad guys got them. This might be a quiet area for the moment but you never knew when that would change, we didn't know the current enemy situation; we didn't see a soul but that didn't mean there weren't some around.

The Colonel that had waved goodbye pointed to his wristwatch and then held up 2 fingers. Then he pointed toward the ground with his index finger in a pumping motion. I said to Robbie, "I think he wants us back here on the ground in 2 hours."

"I think you're right."

With the crew chief back aboard the aircraft, he confirmed our interpretation of the hand signals. We lifted off and started a wide spiraling climb to 1500 feet. Robbie said, "This is bullshit, we can't fly around for two hours keeping an eye on these crazy bastards because we will be out of gas. I don't want to go back to Dong Ha and shut down because if something happens, there is no way we can get word to them and they could be stuck out there way longer than the Marine Corps would want them to be, so I'm out of ideas.

I said, "Why don't we do a good VR ourselves of the area south of the inlet, there shouldn't be anything there except maybe a few palm trees and damn few of those, if it looks all clear we could go just far enough south that they can't hear our engine noise, land and shut down. We won't be able to see them but if there's gun fire we could damn sure hear that."

Robbie thought about this for a moment or two, all the while heading south along the beach. He told the crew chief and gunner to have a good look at the area for any signs of human traffic. After a good 15 minute look we were all convinced that area was completely void of anything. Robbie continued to circle and then started an approach to the beach heading north. The ocean was on the right side, his side of the aircraft. He was going to land at the high water mark again because the wet sand would be nice and firm. He made a smooth touchdown and we shut the helicopter down.

We'd been on the ground about 5 minutes and it was hot. Robbie said, "God damnit, here we are at the water line of the beautiful South China Sea sweating our tits off and we should be in that water having a nice swim and cooling off, who's up for "Swim Call?"

I said, "Shit, I'm all for that."

Robbie said, "How about Cpl Nose and L/Cpl Henderson, you guys wanna go swimming?"

The response from the crew was a polite but positive, "Negative Sirs".

Just entering the water for a refreshing "Dip". Little did we know.

The crew offered to man the machine guns and keep a watchful eye for bad guys but they weren't stripping down out here and going swimming for "Nobody". Robbie told them to suit themselves.

We had climbed down out of the cockpit. I was sitting on the right tire wondering where I could find some shade and Robbie was standing by the main cargo door, the crew chief and gunner were sitting inside the cabin. We looked at each other and started pulling off boots and flight suits. We decided to wear our skivvies to save ourselves and the crew any embarrassment. Robbie was first heading to the water. He didn't get in very far and made a plunge. I was right behind him. The water wasn't ice cold but cold enough to be refreshing; it was wonderful. We both floated around in the surf letting the waves wash over our bodies. Looking back at the helicopter I could see Cpl Nose and L/Cpl Henderson standing near the machine gun that was mounted in the cargo door. I waved and they just shook their heads.

The surf wouldn't be spectacular in the South China Sea unless there was a big storm but there were three or four foot waves coming in and breaking. The drop off was much sharper than either of us expected so the waves came in and broke fairly hard. I swam out far enough to try and catch them building up, hoping to "Body Surf" a little. Robbie seemed content splashing around closer to shore. We'd been in the water for about ten minutes and I finally caught a wave just right and it took me all the way into shore. When it broke and I was trying to get up in the shallow water I got momentarily tangled up in something that felt slimy and thought it might just be seaweed. The mess was there just for a second and then gone so I didn't think too much about it.

The next time in I ran into another mess of stuff, Robbie was just getting up and started cussing about this damn stuff that kept sliding across his body.

"I think its seaweed."

"There ain't no sea weed in the South China Sea, this ain't the California coast with kelp beds and it ain't the Sea of Japan."

I realized he was absolutely right. I said, "It can't be jelly fish or we would have been stung by now."

Robbie was standing in knee deep water. He kicked hard as if he was trying to kick whatever it was that kept sliding over our bodies and legs. He was successful, his kick knocked a really ugly looking sea snake clear out of the water and up onto the beach. The snake immediately went right back into the water. Cpl Nose and L/Cpl Henderson both started screaming about sea snakes everywhere.

A wave came in and hit Robbie in the back, knocking him face down in the water. He didn't say a word but got up and started walking towards the shore. I was out a little further in water just over my waist and I had started walking toward the shore. I could feel all this stuff or these things just sliding over my legs and still thought it was sea weed or something. It wasn't until I got to ankle deep water that I realized the things sliding over my body were sea snakes. Looking back I could see a huge writhing ball of these things.

Robbie and I made a serious dash to the high water mark and then worked our way back to the helicopter. Our crew kept pointing toward the water yelling "See em, See em, there's a whole knot of them just working their way down the surf line."

We watched them for a minute or so, then looked at each other, shrugged our shoulders and started getting dressed. We both agreed that with the exception of the sea snakes it was the most refreshing thing we'd done since we left the ship and given another chance, we'd do it again, snakes or not.

We picked the Colonel's up right on time and took them back to their LZ. Robbie said that he thought they looked as if they realized that being alone out there for two hours was not such a good idea. They waved goodbye and we headed back to Phu Bai. On the flight back the sea salt from our swim dried very quickly on our skin, making us feel very itchy but we still felt it was worth it.

Our crew blabbed the whole story of what we had done, so by morning everybody knew about the sea snakes. The

CO made mention that if there were to be any "Swim Calls" they'd better be listed as an official function on the flight schedule.

On June the 2nd the USS Princeton was "On Station" and we were ordered to load the battalion and ourselves back aboard and resume Special Landing Force operations. There were no complaints from anyone we knew. Each ship and crew has their own personality. The Princeton was an old WWII carrier converted into an LPH. It was old, but compared to living in a hooch it was a luxury hotel.

In the process of loading back aboard the USS Princeton, a big event happened for me. I was assigned to fly with the Skipper and it was during that hop after I'd made about three landings from the left seat he said, "Why don't we just make this your HAC check?"

"You are giving me a HAC check from the left seat, the co-pilots seat?"

"Why not, if you're a HAC you should be able to 'Hac' it from any seat."

He didn't touch the controls for the rest of the day and the next day I was on the flight schedule as the HAC, the Aircraft Commander, it was my airplane. At first I thought I would be nervous but I suddenly realized I could now do anything with this aircraft I'd seen anyone else do and I knew there was no reason to be nervous. I really was ready to be a HAC.

We conducted several successful combat operations from the Princeton until the 10th of July. Unfortunately the ship was ordered to the Philippines for repairs, the battalion was ordered ashore for R&R and we were ordered back to Phu Bai and the horrible hooches for duty once again with MAG-36.

Our arrival at Phu Bai was full of surprises. There were major improvements being made at Phu Bai, especially to the living areas, positive proof that since the end of the TET Offensive, the bulk of the fighting had moved further

189

north, up where we had been working. The Sea Bees had moved in and were in the midst of building metal Quonset Huts just like they had down at Marble Mountain in DaNang. There were plans for real flush toilets. However, after flying all day we learned that there were no hooches available because they were all full. With the Sea Bees and the army units that came to protect them, the base was overcrowded. The best that could be offered was a cot in an unfinished Quonset hut.

We were so tired that at first it didn't seem like such a bad deal until we saw what they meant by an unfinished Quonset hut. What we had was a concrete slab over which had been erected the galvanized metal shell that formed the half- moon shape of the Quonset hut. The ends were completely open. These structures sat in the middle of an open sand field about 100 yards from the perimeter wire of the camp. There were no bunkers or toilets and the nearest shower was a good quarter mile away back in the old hooch area.

Located just inside the wire were huge circular rubber bladders filled with water. We were told they were used as settling ponds for the water purification plant. There were metal stakes that held up the sides of the bladders and they reminded me of an above ground swimming pool about four feet deep. The type you might have in your backyard.

With great care the cots had been placed about 2 feet apart the length of the Quonset hut in three very straight rows. You had to be very careful not to put your ass in someone's face when you bent over to undress. Getting in and out of the rack was also going to be tricky, trying not to kick your neighbor. There was no place to store anything, so it all had to be rolled up and placed under your cot. We stood sweating through our air conditioning withdrawal in shock and contemplating a night in our new surroundings.

After picking out a cot and stripping down to our skivvies, we had a good look around. I thought May had been hot but July was a whole different deal. With white sand all around us so hot you couldn't walk barefoot on it, an eighth inch metal roof above you radiating heat that you could watch shimmer, what you had here was an oven for people. It wasn't a Sauna, it was a goddamned oven. With the ends wide open you were also gonna be fresh meat for the mosquitoes. The topper was that the only source of drinking water was your canteen if you had one and could find a place to fill it. There were big signs posted that the water in the settling ponds was not potable.

I was so tired and pissed off I really didn't even want to think about walking across that hot sand to find the mess hall but Robbie had taken the cot next to mine and he bugged me to at least go and look. Hopefully we could find a water source to fill our canteens.

I finally stretched out on my cot and read a book until the light faded. There was no electricity yet in the huts and the army that was guarding the perimeter for us advised against the use of flash lights this close to the perimeter wire. The brightest full moon I'd seen in a long time came up and I slipped outside of the hut to see if I could read by the light of the moon but the sand was too hot to sit on and the metal of the Quonset hut was too hot to lean on so I went back to my cot.

I gave up trying to sleep about midnight. I sat up on my cot and lit a cigarette. I was staring out the end of the hut looking right at those bladders of water. Those big bladders of cool water, glistening in the moon light. I stubbed out my smoke, stood up, slid into my flip flops, grabbed my pistol and towel and was going to head for the bladder in the middle of the group. I was trying to ease out between the cots without making too much noise when I heard Robbie say, "Where the hell do you think you're going?"

"I'm going swimmin."

"Where the hell are you going swimming this time of night?"

"I'm going right out there and get in one of those bladders and float around until I cool off and can sleep."

He didn't say another word, just got up and followed me out. When we got to the bladder I'd selected we hung our towels, pistol belts and skivvies on one of the metal support rods and slipped over into the water as quietly as we could. It was blessed relief, actually after being so hot the water felt quite cool. I wasn't getting out of here for a while. In fact, if I could find a way to sleep without drowning I wasn't getting out until morning.

We'd been in the water about thirty minutes before the first mortar round exploded and we heard the first distinct rattle of an AK-47. We both froze. Robbie said, "Just great, the Army guys told us they hadn't been attacked for almost two weeks and these sombitches gotta pick now to try and start a fight."

A couple more mortars came in followed by a lot more automatic weapons fire. The Army had some Quad forty millimeter weapons mounted in a track vehicle. I didn't know the official name but they called it the "Duster." The Duster to our far left started firing almost down the line of the perimeter wire followed very closely by the Duster to our far right doing the same thing. It was obvious there was a probe of the perimeter on this side of the camp. The volume of fire kept increasing. There were spot lights sweeping the wire, tracers flashing overhead, all hell was breaking loose.

Robbie came close to me because of the noise to say that he thought we needed to stay put; we were probably in the safest place. I nodded my agreement and then started to laugh. He got this strange look on his face and said, "What's so goddamned funny?"

"I was just thinking how this is gonna look if we are killed. I can see the headlines in the Stars and Stripes newspaper. Two naked Marine Captains found dead after love tryst in camp swimming pool."

Robbie blustered and said, "Now that's not f---ing funny and this is the last damn time I'm ever going swimming with you."

We gave it a good thirty minutes after the attack was over and we'd heard the all clear sounded in the main part of the camp and then eased out of our swimming pool and went back to the Quonset hut. I was actually cool enough to fall asleep quickly. No one had missed us during the attack and after the sea snake thing we thought it best not to share our experience.

THE MAIL RUN

The Ugly Angels had a system for keeping track of the types of missions the pilots and crewmen flew and it was the general intent to spread things around so no one pilot or crewman got all the shitty missions all the time. In 362 it was the "Missions Log" and as far as most of us were concerned, it was the "Holy Book". The daily flight schedule and mission assignment was made up by checking the log to see whose turn it was to fly a particular mission. Once the flight schedule was written, the die was cast and there would be no changes. This was a hard and fast rule because previously, every time someone changed the schedule or assignments, invariably, someone got hurt or worse. With a double digit loss rate of aircrew this was serious business and no one broke the rule. Even suggesting a change was to chance invoking the Skipper's wrath.

The Mail Run was the one mission that no one wanted to miss because your entire responsibility for the day was to fly outgoing mail and passengers down to the Wing Headquarters in DaNang and bring back the incoming. This was like a day off, except you got to fly, see some nice scenery, have a good meal, hopefully get to use a real flush toilet and just generally feel you'd had an all too brief glimpse of civilized life. DaNang was a rear area; down there people lived in buildings, they had flush toilets, hot food, hot water showers and electricity 24 hours a day. Compared to that, our living conditions were pretty primitive. We lived in tents and it all went downhill after that.

It wasn't necessary to leave early in the morning, an eight o'clock take off was just fine. You took off, flew east a couple of miles to the beautiful South China Sea and turned south along the coast line. You had a Wingman and

194

you flew just far enough off the coast that the bad guys couldn't shoot you and just high enough to take advantage of cooler temperatures at altitude. You could tune in one of your radios to the Armed Forces Network and listen to music for your flight down to DaNang, where you would land at the First Marine Air Wing helo pad.

At ninety knots cruise speed it took a little less than an hour before you arrived at the Wing pad. This put you low on fuel but you needed to be, in order to be light enough to lift more weight taking off from the Wing Pad. From the Wing pad we always headed straight for Marble Mountain airfield. It was the home of MAG-16. The airfield was just south and east of the DaNang airfield and it sat right on the beach. Most guys felt they had the best living conditions, especially mess hall, of anybody in the Marine Air Wing. At Marble they lived in Quonset Huts; some of them even had air conditioners. When you arrived there you took on the maximum fuel load, then taxied to transient parking, shut down and went straight to the mess hall for lunch. Sometimes you could even find a fairly recent Stars and Stripes newspaper and if you were lucky, you just might have a chance to read this newspaper while sitting on a real toilet.

Once you got all those things out of the way it was time for the return trip. Takeoff weight wasn't a problem; we taxied the old 34 onto the runway and made a rolling takeoff. After takeoff at Marble Mountain we always made a quick turn to get back out over the ocean and then turned north. Until you got across the entrance to the DaNang harbor you had to stay low because of the aircraft coming in to land at DaNang, but after that we always climbed for cooler air.

Today it was my turn for the "Mail Run" and I was really looking forward to the mission. It was also Glenn Russo's turn for the mail run but we were both HAC's. I had recently been designated as a Helicopter Aircraft

195

Commander (HAC). Operations told me that messed up their rotation for the moment because there was an imbalance of HAC's and co-pilots, so if I wanted to go, one of us would be the HAC and the other the co-pilot. Glenn was about six months senior to me and I certainly didn't give a damn about what seat I would fly in, I just didn't want to miss my turn at the "Mail Run". I looked at Russo and said, "I'll be your 'Mixture Man' let's go to DaNang. He laughed and said," you're on."

The weather was just beautiful, it was hot, but there wasn't a cloud in the sky. Once "Feet Wet" (term for being out over the water) we both settled back and enjoyed the ride. We shared the stick time and it was nice having an experienced guy to "Mind the Store" while you enjoyed the ride. Everything went exactly as it should until the return trip.

We'd done the standard turn out to "Feet Wet" just after takeoff at Marble and were heading north along the coast staying low until we got across the mouth of DaNang harbor. The mouth of the harbor was marked by two mountains. To the south was what we called Monkey Mountain and to the north was Hai Van Mountain. Highway one, the "Yellow Brick Road," ran around the harbor and then turned north right over Hai Van, running through the Hai Van Pass. Both of these mountains were pretty good sized. I didn't know much about Monkey Mountain's composition but Hai Van seemed to be one very large hunk of rock that had become heavily forested over the years. Just east of the pass, the mountain made a fairly sheer drop down to the ocean and from the air the stone face of that drop off was dark gray. Just to the east, not more than a mile offshore was another much smaller mountain, more like a large rock formation that jutted up out of the sea. On our maps it was titled Hon Son Tra. It also had become forested over time and its exposed rock edges were the same color as Hai Van. The open space between these two was referred to by most pilots as the "Slot". It was generally here that we were climbing to or just leveling off at the altitude for the return flight up the coastline. We did not normally take any ground fire when in these areas.

As we leveled off at 1500 feet we were just about in the middle of the "Slot"; Glenn was flying at the time and I was enjoying the opportunity to relax and give my closest attention to Hai Van Mountain passing to my left. Glenn seemed to be doing the same with Hon Son Tra on our right. Suddenly the crew chief came up on the intercom and said, "We are taking Fire from 3 o'clock." (The nose of the aircraft was always 12 o'clock, so we were taking fire on the right side of the aircraft.) About the same moment I noticed the unmistakable green and white tracers drifting past the nose of our aircraft. Just as Glenn started to take evasive action and the crew chief was returning fire we all could hear the hits. The enemy bullets sounded like they were above us and banging into the transmission and rotor head. The old 34 could take a lot of hits from small stuff but the green and white tracers told us this fire was .50 cal and this aircraft just couldn't take a lot of that, especially in the rotor head.

Our wingman normally referred to as "Dash Two" was flying on our left side in a cruise position which allowed him to be shielded from the fire we were taking. I gave a quick look out to my left to see if he was ok. He was taking evasive action as well and unless the bad guys started shooting at us from both sides dash two was in good shape for the moment.

Glenn and I looked at each other at the same time. His evasive actions had taken us down to about two hundred feet above the water.

I said, "I think we took a couple hits up in the rotor head, transmission area."

Glenn just shook his head in agreement then said, "All the temperatures and pressures are normal for the moment and I don't feel anything strange in the controls".

I said, "How about it Cpl Funderburg, L/Cpl Vincent everybody ok? No leaks, fires or anything bad down there?"

Funderburg came back, "We're ok down here sir, I got about thirty rounds off right into where I saw the muzzle flashes, if I didn't get them I scared hell out of them but we do have some transmission fluid starting to leak down now and it's more than a one or two rag leak.

Russo and I looked at each other and then at the transmission pressure and temperature gauges and then at the hydraulic gauges for the flight controls. Everything was still normal.
Russo told Funderburg to keep an eye on things and give a shout if anything got worse.

We were in no position to hang around and take on the fifty cal, nor was it something you did in an UH-34. Russo had me dial in DaNang DASCC and we reported taking the fire. If they could shoot at us they could also shoot at incoming aircraft to DaNang Airfield. DASCC said they would launch gunships to check it out. We were just on the edge of their area and switched to Phu Bai DASCC and reported the same thing plus our problem of possible damage.

By now we were well out of range of the fifty cal and coming up on a small inlet area that had a beach on both sides of the inlet. I could see Russo eyeballing in that direction. I told him I agreed with getting closer to shore but that was a really small inlet and I didn't know what the enemy or friendly situation was. Just ahead was another inlet only much larger. On the map it said Cua Bein or Vinh Bein but I just knew it as the entrance to what we called Phu Loc Bay. I told Glenn that was the best one if we had to land, the beach was at least 200 yards wide, it was very straight there, and from what I could see of the water line, it looked as if we were dealing with low tide for the moment. Glenn just nodded his head and turned the aircraft slightly left towards the shoreline and started looking out into the distance to see what I was talking about.

I thought I could smell hot hydraulic fluid or transmission oil and quickly looked at the gauges again. Just as I was finishing my glance at the gauges Cpl Funderburg came up on the intercom and said, "Sir, we got a big leak on the transmission deck and it's raining hot red stuff all over the cabin. " Glenn and I looked at each other and nodded.

I said "I'll get the landing check list while you line us up to land on the beach. I would take the beach on the north side of the inlet".

"That's exactly where I'm headed, call dash two and tell him what we are doing. Can you believe this shit? Some hard core sonofabitch had to work his ass off to row a fifty cal out to that damn rock and then piss ant the damn thing up the hill. If Funderburg didn't get him I hope the gunships grease his ass."

I called the wingman and told him we were landing to check out a big leak and to assess the damage from the hits we took and suggested he hold "Feet Wet" at or above 1500 feet just in case. We also wanted him to notify the DASCC that we were landing and to try and get in touch with any other squadron aircraft in the area.

Glenn made a nice roll on landing. The beach here was quite flat and very smooth. It was low tide and at the high water mark there was about a three foot berm of sand. I made a mental note that the berm would afford good protection if we took fire from the tree line on our left. From where we landed there was at least 200 yards of open beautiful sand beach and beyond that was a dense looking tree line with lots of underbrush. Not good because the bad

199

guys had a great place to hide and a completely clear field of fire across the beach. Since we were the only big, green helicopter on this beach we would be pretty easy to find.

We shut everything down to have a good look. While Glenn and Funderburg were climbing up on the transmission platform Vincent and I were keeping a sharp eye on the tree line. I heard Funderburg say, "Holy Shit, look at this Captain." I knew that couldn't be good. Glenn motioned for me to come up and Funderburg came down to make room.

We'd lost a lot of transmission fluid from a line that had a big nick from a .50 cal round. The leaking line was workable but the big problem was one of the fifty cal rounds had hit a mounting bracket and pretty much cut it in half. It was a miracle it hadn't caught fire or worse, come loose. There are four mounting brackets; these four brackets are what hold the fuselage, the rotor head and transmission together. We'd managed to land with only three points of attachment holding us together. The NATOPS manual (the book that tells you all about the aircraft systems) doesn't cover this type of situation. We knew we could probably have continued on losing transmission fluid, the book said in emergency situations you would fly for up to 45 minutes with no fluid but never mentioned how far you could get with only three of the four bolts that held the machine together. Glenn and I looked at each other and we knew we'd better get the wingman in here to take the mail and get someone to get us a ride home, there was no way dash two could carry it all. Besides the mail, we also had other documents that didn't need to be piled up on a beach near Phu Loc bay.

While Glenn was on his survival radio with the wingman, I had Funderburg and Vincent get the machine guns out of the aircraft and set them up on the high water berm about twenty five yards in front and back of the aircraft. As soon as we could get dash two down here and get him loaded with all the mail, we would move further away from the aircraft because if there were enemy in the area, it would soon become a target.

Dash two came in and landed about fifty yards in front of our aircraft. This was a good move because the beach sand was firm enough here to allow him to roll the aircraft for takeoff and he could carry more weight with less power required. With the addition of our load to his, he would be pretty heavy.

Dash two had three passengers on his aircraft and while Glenn and I kept a close eye on the tree line, the four crewmen and three passengers quickly transferred our load. With the noise of dash two's aircraft it was hard to hear but I thought Glenn was trying to tell me something. He was shouting and pointing towards the tree line. Just as dash two was lifting off and I was trying my best to duck the blowing wet sand I saw what he was shouting about. At the south end of the tree line, closest to the inlet, was a person in the typical conical white hat and black pajamas. It also looked as if this person had a long white beard. I finally heard a shouted word from Russo, "Papasan"; he looks like an old Papasan. (Term generally used to describe an elderly Vietnamese male, in traditional garb)

With the loud departure of Dash two, the beach was suddenly very quiet and the only sound was the sloshing of the surf on the beach.

Glenn said, "I think we ought to go over and talk to him, see if there are any bad guys in the area. I'm not too sure how long it will be before help arrives."

"I agree. You want me to go over and talk to him?"

"No, I'll go; you stay here and make sure I'm covered."

"I think I'd better go with you just in case there is trouble, Funderburg and Vincent will cover us without my help."

"Ok, let's go."

I yelled, "Funderburg, Vincent, Capt Russo and I are going over to the end of the tree line and check out that old Papasan, see if there's any bad guys in the area. Keep us covered. If any shit starts, rake hell out of that tree line. Push comes to shove, start swimming away from the shoreline."

Funderburg and Vincent just nodded and gave us the "Thumbs Up".

We climbed up over the sand berm and started walking toward the tree line. We kept about 10 yards between us so one round wouldn't get us both. We both kept a steady gaze on the old Papasan and he did not move as we approached.

The sand was very loose and made walking difficult, plus we had another 100 yards of beach to cross. By the time we reached the old Papasan we were both sweating profusely. The Papasan never moved and didn't change his facial expression. He seemed to be staring right past us in the direction of our helicopter or the sea.

I spoke to him using a traditional Vietnamese greeting which sounded something like, "Chow ung ma joy". Loosely translated it meant, "Did you eat any rice today". My Vietnamese was extremely limited and Russo's' was non-existent. The Papasan did not respond but shifted his gaze to me, then to Russo, then back toward the helicopter or the sea.

Russo was next to break the silence.

"Papasan, any VC, any VC?"

The Papasan's expression never changed, he continued to stare out toward the sea. After a fairly long pause he said in very good English, "No VC, No VC, Beau Coup NVA!"

We didn't speak French but we both knew what beau coup meant, LOTS of BAD GUYS!!!

Russo and I immediately turned and headed back toward the beach and the security of our machine guns. We gave some consideration to running but we thought it best to appear unrushed because we were pretty sure we had to be under observation. If the NVA were in the area they wouldn't start anything big right now, they would wait until another aircraft came in to rescue us and make it worth their while to start a fight.

When we arrived back at the beach and jumped down off the berm onto the wet sand, I made my way down the beach to Vincent and Russo went up the beach toward Funderburg. We both looked back at the tree line for the Papasan and he had disappeared. We exchanged looks and knew this wasn't a good sign. If this was a peaceful area, we would have drawn a crowd of people, women, kids, elder villagers all coming to see the helicopter and the Americans. The Papasan had taken a chance doing what he did and it was a very helpful warning that big trouble was nearby.

We heard and saw the approach of a helicopter before we got the call on our survival radios. It was one of our guys from 362. In fact it was good old Robbie. He said he and another aircraft were inbound and for us to be ready to get aboard quickly. Russo gave him a brief on the beach conditions, wind, and warned him about the possibility of NVA along the tree line. Robbie was gonna have his wingman use their two M-60 machine guns to rake the tree line while he was coming in to pick us up if he was taking any fire.

Keeping as low as we could, Vincent and I with the machine gun started moving up the beach toward Russo and Funderburg's position. We joined up but stayed a good 20 yards apart and set up so we could shoot at the tree line.

Robbie was starting his approach and his wingman was now laying down covering fire. I thought I saw a couple muzzle flashes. Funderburg cut loose with a long burst but I couldn't tell where he was shooting. If Robbie's aircraft was taking fire during his approach I couldn't tell.

We were now a good 100 yards up the beach from our helicopter and Robbie touched down right behind us. We stopped firing just before he touched down and began running around the nose of the helicopter for the main door which was on the ocean side. We were barely aboard when Robbie lifted off and started turning out over the ocean. We were in a big sweaty pile of bodies and machine guns on the cabin floor.

I took a seat and was just fastening the seat belt when I saw Cpl Wilson, the crew chief, unfasten his safety belt and get up. He turned to look at the battery compartment which was located to his right on the forward bulk head of the cargo compartment. He went straight to the compartment and started undoing the cover. I now could smell that acidy, sulfur smell of a battery that was probably getting very hot. He got the cover off and undid the quick disconnect from the battery and pulled it from the compartment. This is no little car sized battery, it's more like 2'x 1'x 1' and very heavy. Not to mention this one was boiling over and that the pilot, Robbie, was violently maneuvering the helicopter to keep from taking any hits.

Cpl Wilson was trying to reach the open cargo door to throw out the boiling battery. Just as he got close enough to the opening to throw the battery, Robbie rolled the aircraft to the right and Cpl Wilson and the battery were now headed out the open cargo door. In a reflex action, I undid my seat belt and jumped up grabbing the collar of Cpl Wilson's flight suit and the back of his bullet bouncer. It stopped him and allowed the heavy battery to keep going out the cargo door opening. That was the good news; the bad news was I was down wind of the air rushing into the open cargo door area. As the battery went out, the rushing air sucked off the boiling battery fluid and slapped me right in the face with it. I screamed; it was hot and it hurt. Cpl Wilson and I were falling backwards away from the cargo opening and we landed in heap with Cpl Wilson on top of me.

My first thought was I would be blind; my second thought was WATER, GET WATER ON MY FACE AND EYES!!!!!!! On my cartridge belt besides my pistol I carried a canteen of water. I was yelling WATER, WATER at the top of my lungs and was fumbling to get my canteen out all at the same time. I managed to get the canteen out and started pouring water on my face when Cpl Wilson grabbed my canteen and took charge of the water pouring.

Robbie and his crew had been on a Medivac mission earlier and were heading back to base when the call for help came in, so besides the crew chief and gunner, there was also a Navy Corpsman on board, my lucky day. The corpsman had immediately figured out what happened and what needed to be done. He pulled Wilson off me and jumped a straddle of my chest jamming his fingers in a position to hold my eyes wide open so there was no way I could blink or close them when the water was poured into my eyes. I couldn't believe how much water those guys had on that helicopter. The relief was instantaneous and they kept irrigating my eyes until they used up all the water.

The corpsman finally got off my chest and I lay there on the cabin floor enjoying the coolness of the big puddle of water around me. After blinking a few times I was greatly relieved that I could see Cpl Wilson's slightly chubby face with its ridiculous moustache. I glanced over at Russo; he was on the aircraft's intercom providing a play by play of what was going on to Robbie. Russo motioned for me to stay on the floor and leaned over and yelled that we were getting ready to land at a Battalion Aid Station.

Although I could see, my vision was very blurry which I assumed was from all the irrigation. I felt I was out of danger but when you land at an aid station with a Medivac, they take nothing for granted. I was trying to get up off the floor and get off the helicopter but found myself on a stretcher moving very rapidly towards a triage tent.

As soon as I felt the stretcher being placed down on something hard, I had a flash light in my eyes and then the irrigation started again. A little more controlled this time but the flow was heavy. While this was going on someone was scrubbing hell out of my face and then began applying something that felt like a salve on my face.

I never heard Robbie lift off and wondered why and when I heard someone use the term "Medic," I realized this was an army aid station. Before I knew it I was being carried back out to Robbie's helicopter and off we went again. The medics at the aid station had placed dry gauze bandages over my eyes and I'm sure things looked way worse than they were. At least this time I got off the damn stretcher and had a seat. I was seated next to Russo who squeezed my arm and yelled in my ear that we were heading off shore for a hospital ship. This really was my lucky day and I knew Robbie would get me taken care of with the best.

At that time in Vietnam, we were fortunate to have two hospital ships, the USS Sanctuary and Repose. They seemed to alternate every month or so and I suppose it depended on how full of casualties they were. I didn't know which one was out there but I really didn't care because it would be the best medical care available.

Just minutes after landing on the hospital ship I was in a dark room with an ophthalmologist. He put some drops in my eyes that stung like hell and then locked my head into some type of device so that the only thing I could move was my eyes. He then began a very thorough examination of my eyes, eye lids and face. He said nothing while he worked and I just did what he asked and enjoyed my first air conditioned air in a long time. In fact, I was getting a little chilly because my flight suit was still soaking wet, but it actually felt good.

After what seemed a long time, he switched off the bright lights that had me seeing spots and finally spoke. He said, "Captain, you are a very lucky Marine. There is no damage to your corneas so your vision should not be affected in any way. There are some pits, or holes that the acid burnt into the white portions of your eyes but this will not affect your vision. The fact the battery fluid was boiling even for a short time most likely reduced the potency. Your greatest risk over the next couple of days will be from infection. The quick actions of irrigation most likely saved your sight and because the irrigation was persistent for some time, hopefully it washed away all foreign material or residue. However, under the circumstances and in this environment there is still a chance that you could get an infection in one of those pitted areas. I'm going to apply some antibiotic salve to your eyes and bandage them up for twenty four hours. After that we will take off the bandages, and have a look. If everything is ok, I'll give you some drops that you will need to apply for a while but you will be on your way back to your squadron. Ok?"

"No problem here Doc."

Twenty four hours on a clean, air conditioned hospital ship was a hell of a good deal, even if I had my eyes bandaged. To keep me from taking up a bunk for someone who was really hurt, they asked me if I would mind sleeping in the bunk of someone that was away from the ship on an R&R trip. I said, "A real bed, are you kidding?"

What they didn't tell me was that it was a nurse's bunk and that she had three roommates. They all figured that since my eyes were bandaged and I was a fellow officer, that this would be ok. Well it was, but what was I gonna tell the guys when I got back to the squadron, they'd never believe me.

As good as it sounded I was more than ready to leave. I just wanted to get these bandages off and see again, I was tired of being led everywhere. It was a terrifying experience being blind for 24 hours. I was amazed how quickly my other senses were heightened, especially smell and hearing.

The Doc was good to his word and it was great to see and move without assistance. Everything was still a little blurry but it was mostly due to the salve.

It was afternoon before one of my squadron mates arrived to pick me up and take me back to base. There were a few guys in the ready room tent when I got back. I had new sunglasses, a bottle of antibiotic eye drops and a note to the squadron flight surgeon. There was some joking around, and they didn't believe me about the nurses. Of course they wouldn't have believed me if I said I'd slept with them all either. After things settled down, I asked the operations officer when I would be back on the flight schedule.

He looked at me and said, "Tomorrow asshole, you've already had the Mail Run and a day off on the Hospital Ship, so you're on for Medivac tomorrow afternoon, and you won't be up for the Mail Run again for ten days, any questions?"

Hospital Ship, either USS Sanctuary or Repose. Helo Pad on the stern.

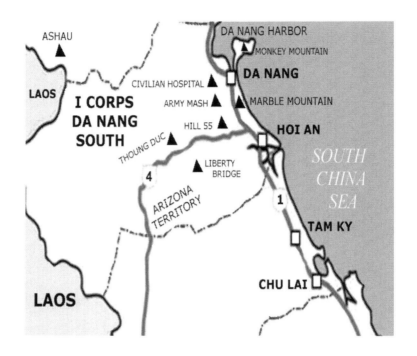

BAD AFTERNOON AT THOUNG DUC

HMM-362 was now "Down South" from where we'd been operating for most of the last year. UH-34 Squadrons were slowly being disbanded, the pilots dispersed, and the old aircraft sent home. The Ugly Angels had been the first Marine UH-34 squadron in Vietnam and would be the last out.

The squadron was in a real state of flux. All my mentors and hooch mates were gone. Dave had been horribly burned and was Medivaced, Biff, Ron, Tom, John and Robbie had all rotated home. We had a new CO, XO and a bunch of FNG's to replace those pilots who had been killed, wounded, or rotated out. To make things even more interesting we were now assigned to a new Air Group, MAG-16 at Marble Mountain airfield.

We were being tasked with missions in the southern part of I Corps, dealing with new control agencies, and a different enemy. In northern I Corps, so close to the North Vietnamese border, our battles had been almost exclusively with the NVA (North Vietnamese Army). Down here it seemed to be a mixed bag of NVA, the local Viet Cong, and any little old lady with an AK-47 in her shopping bag who felt like emptying a 20 round Magazine into a passing helicopter.

Up north the operations were exclusively Marine, but down here in the DaNang area, operations were conducted by all services. It seemed as if they all had their own war going on and no one seemed to be in charge. Besides the Marines, there was Army, Air Force, and Navy. The Air Force inhabited the airfield at DaNang; the Navy had a huge supply depot and very large Navy hospital. The Army had two different medical units and combat units in the field. The Army also had Special Forces teams operating out near the Laotian border and no one seemed to know what the hell they were doing. In the middle of all this were Vietnamese units trying to blend in with both the Army and the Marines. The final touch on this military potpourri, at the very southern border of the I Corps operating area, was the exclusive domain of the Republic of Korea Marines Blue Dragon Brigade (ROK Marines)

In the eastern part of the new area, the terrain was different; flat with lots of rice paddies. There were long tree lines that stretched along the paddy dikes which offered good concealment for bad guys. As you got further west, out toward the border with Laos, the terrain became mountainous again. It was out there, where the mountains met the rice paddies, that the encounters with the NVA were much more frequent.

The first few days of operations were a zoo for us, trying to get snapped in on all the new stuff. The bulk of responsibility was falling on three of us who were experienced flight leaders. Buzz Knight, Al Nichman and myself. The squadron was immediately saddled with the Medivac mission, both day and night. So for us, the first several days were either morning, afternoon or night Medivac.

We had different gunship coverage for the Medivac missions, which seemed like a good thing. Up north we didn't receive gunship coverage unless it was an emergency Medivac during the daytime, and we did not receive gunship coverage at night unless requested. Down here in MAG-16, gunship coverage was automatic for any emergency Medivac mission and the gunships would lead out and establish communications for you. As the Medivac pilot, you were ultimately in charge of how things would be accomplished because you were the guy who had to land in the zone. Since the gunship established communications with the ground unit we just listened, our silence gave consent. If we wanted to do something different all we had to do was speak up. It was certainly different but nice to have a few less things to worry about going into a hot zone.

On the first rotation I drew the short straw and started on the night shift, Buzz got the morning and Al the afternoon. We'd been at this a few days now and having very good luck until Buzz returned one afternoon with an aircraft literally ready for the scrap heap. Luckily no one had been hurt but the aircraft had holes from stem to stern, the engine had been over boosted, the transmission and rotor head had been over sped beyond limitations and the rotor blades all had holes.

When Buzz parked his aircraft Al and I went out to have a look, so did everyone else. Buzz looked at the maintenance officer and said, "You might as well haul it down to the scrap heap, everything has been over torqued, over sped and over boosted, but I got the bastards out.

Al and I asked, "Which bastards did you get out?"

"Some Army Special Forces team out near a place called Thoung Duc started screaming for an emergency extraction, they did have wounded so I went after them. They got something going on out there but they got no air support or supporting arms, they are sitting ducks out there for the NVA."

We didn't hear anything more about Thoung Duc for several days but we were notified that the Army team Buzz rescued put him in for a Distinguished Flying Cross. Buzz was in the ready room just finishing up the paperwork from having morning Medivac and I was just getting briefed to assume the afternoon Medivac mission. I'd already turned up the aircraft and briefed the Corpsman, Crew Chief and Gunner so we were all set to go if we got a mission.

Buzz was hanging around the ready room basking in the glow of the good news about the DFC when that damn Double EE8 field phone went off signaling us to launch. My copilot went to the field telephone to take down the information, radio frequency, call sign, nature of emergency and coordinates.

As he was turning to follow me Buzz asked, "What are the map coordinates?"

My co-pilot was a FNG named Jim Potts but I'd heard everyone call him "Weird Harold." I'd never flown with him before and was surprised he was on the flight schedule with me. This was his first Medivac mission and I knew he'd be twitched to the max. Lt Potts replied with the numbers that made up the coordinates.

Buzz looked at me and said, "That's Thoung Duc, watch your ass."

We were airborne and heading west before the gunship but the gunship cruised about thirty knots faster than the UH-34 so I wasn't worried about him catching up. I'd

213

done a good map reconnaissance of the area and knew if I picked up the correct river it would run me straight back to the mountains and where the river came out of the high ground was Thoung Duc. It was a very small village.

The gunship, call sign Hostage, waved as he went by. I could hear him attempting contact with the landing zone and I listened to the brief. There were three emergency US, they were Army. They were taking intermittent fire from the high ground to the west. The fire was mixed .50cal and mortars.

Well this was just great news, fifty cal machine gun and mortar fire in or on the damn landing zone from the high ground to the west. Enfiladed fire onto the LZ, how could they miss? What military genius put men in this position with no support? The gunship called me on the radio and wanted to know if I copied the brief and I said I did.

I formulated my plan and keyed the radio mike, "Listen up, I will be making a high speed, low level approach up the river. In the zone, you call me when you see my aircraft and again when I'm abeam your landing zone. I'll be making a sharp right hand low level turn into your LZ. Hostage, I'll be below 100 feet the whole time so you are clear to fire anytime." They both acknowledged my instructions. I made sure my crew was ready and they were all set.

I heard the "in sight call" from the soldier in the LZ and very shortly the abeam call. I was looking hard trying to see the LZ. I had hoped it was on the river bank but it was on the other side of the village huts uphill from the river bed maybe 100 feet above the river. I was at 50 feet over the river and flew just a little past the abeam position and then made a very hard right hand turn, more or less standing the old 34 on her nose. (The Pilots called this type of approach technique a "Button Hook") The LZ wasn't very big and there were lots of civilians very close but I managed to slip the aircraft onto the ground about forty feet from the Medivacs.

The civilians were trying to push forward and get on the aircraft, they were completely panicked. The army guys did a good job of holding them back while my crew got the wounded on board. I felt, rather than saw, a couple of mortar rounds go off and the civilians all scurried away from the aircraft. The soldier with the radio started screaming for me to lift off. The gunship pilot was also telling me to get the hell out of the zone. He was firing his rockets into a target on the hill behind me. The outside air temperature was really hot which greatly effects helicopter performance. I didn't have a lot of power available and was just barely able to lift out of the zone without over boosting the engine. As soon as I was clear of the wire and huts by the LZ, I made a sharp right turn diving for the river so I could pick up airspeed and get out of range of the guns.

We were hauling ass down the river and I asked the Corpsman for the seriousness of the wounds. All three were hit with shrapnel and although serious, no one had lost a limb or had a bad chest wound. I was thankful for that and started a climb to get above 1500 feet. Hostage called me and told me he was detaching to refuel and rearm.

I headed straight for the nearest Army medical unit. The main unit was near Monkey Mountain but now there was one closer to Marble Mountain so I went there. After dropping off the wounded we headed straight for Marble to refuel and hopefully shut down.

While we were refueling the call for another mission came in from DaNang DASCC (Direct Air Support Coordination Center). Lt Potts was taking down the information and got ashen faced when the coordinates were the same as before; we were going back to Thoung Duc.

We had the same gunship and he was way ahead of us. When he called me on the radio to tell me he'd been trying to get some artillery or air to use on this trip he said that he was having trouble getting it all coordinated because it was an army operation and we couldn't determine where or how many army troops were in the area. I told him we would just do the same again and hope for the best.

The bad guys were ready and waiting this time. Hostage and LZ control told me I was taking fire as I came up the river and made my turn. Hostage rolled in and started shooting as I was landing. Two more soldiers were wounded, one very badly. This time there were no other soldiers to control the civilians and some got aboard before we could even get the Medivacs on the aircraft. They were climbing up the side of the aircraft; they were holding onto the struts, it was a chaotic scene. I saw a couple of mortar rounds hit among the huts; one was white phosphorus which is terrible stuff. It sticks to skin and the air makes it burn like a Fourth of July sparkler. I saw a little girl go down after being hit with the damn stuff. I could see the green and white tracers going over my aircraft and I could see some of the mob falling as they were shot. I couldn't believe that we weren't being shredded by the enemy fire.

I had always prided myself that I could remain cool under fire. I made sure I never raised my voice or yelled at my crew no matter how tight things were getting, I always thought I could keep cool and work my way out of danger. But this time, I could see us all dying right here, right now. I was scared and my legs were shaking so badly that I had to put my hands on top of my knees and push down as hard as I could to keep my feet on the rudder pedals and the brakes. I looked over at Weird Harold and he was looking straight ahead with his arms folded. For his first Medivac mission he'd drawn a beaut; he was petrified.

For the first time ever I found myself screaming at my crew chief, "Get these damn people off this aircraft right now, I don't care if you have to shoot them get them off now!" I could see what was going on outside the cabin door and could sense the chaos that was happening in the main cabin. It had to be hell for those three young men down there. Hostage was on the radio telling me to get the hell out of the zone, that he was out of ammo and making dummy runs trying to fool them into stopping shooting. Over the top of the whole scene I could still see the little girl that had been hit and probably her mother trying desperately to comfort her.

There was another burst of fire and a few more people fell and I knew it was now or never. I didn't announce to anybody that I was going to try and take off I just applied all the power I dared and tried to lift the aircraft. I was so heavy it just barely bounced. I couldn't lift straight up. I needed to roll it forward and bounce just a little to get airborne and there were people in the way but I didn't care I did it anyway. The aircraft staggered and skipped along the ground, it ran through the wire at the edge of the LZ and started rolling down the incline towards the river before it finally shuddered and started to fly. I had as much power as I could get on the engine without blowing it up and now was not the time to blow an engine. I let the aircraft settle towards the river and got level about twenty feet off the surface of the water. The best I could do was sixty knots. I couldn't climb, I couldn't do anything but just hold what I had and hope for something better.

About a mile downstream from the village, the river was very shallow and there was a huge sandbar in the middle. I was having fore and aft control problems with the aircraft and when I asked the crew chief what was going on he said we had civilians all the way in the tail cone of the aircraft and he was trying to get them out but there wasn't room in the main cabin.

That was it; much more of this and the aircraft was going to come out of the sky despite my best efforts. I decided to try a modified roll on landing, on the sand bar. I told the guys down below what I was doing. I looked over at Weird Harold and he was still staring straight ahead.

The aircraft touched down softly on the sand bar. The sand was smooth and firm and I didn't have to wait long for it to roll to a stop. I told the crew chief to throw off all the damn civilians. He said, "Sir, some of these people are badly wounded."

I said, "Ok, throw everybody off that isn't wounded and we'll take the civilians to that Vietnamese hospital after we get the soldiers to the army medical unit."

I couldn't believe the number of people that got off that aircraft. True, they were small and didn't weigh all that much but no wonder the aircraft was barely flying. The civilians didn't seem to object and started moving off the island even before I took off. I guess for the moment they knew they were out of harm's way. The crew chief said it must have been a record but he didn't get to count.

This time when I lifted off things were much better, the aircraft was performing as it should. I did suspect that there was damage to the rotor blades from all the junk that was blown up by the rotorwash as we were trying to get out of the Landing Zone. I made sure I got back up to 1500 feet just to stay out of small arms fire. The gunship pilots thought we'd had it when we landed in the river. As I lifted off they called on the radio wanting to know if I could make it this time. I told them I could, so they detached to re-arm and try and get some supporting arms standing by.

DaNang DASCC was calling for another mission before we got off the army Medivac pad. I told Weird Harold not to even write it down; I knew the coordinates by heart now. He just nodded. I still had to get the civilians off and headed for the only civilian hospital in the area. The hospital didn't have a helo pad just a big, empty, dusty open space by the hospital. I really hated it because we kicked up a good sized dust cloud. We had a lot of lookers but no one came out to help. My crew carried the wounded up and placed them on the porch of the hospital. If we left them out by the aircraft we'd blast them with sand when we took off.

As we headed back for Thoung Duc, I noted that we had two gunships waiting on us. The lead said there were three members of the team left there, two were wounded and we needed to get them all out. I told him we'd do our best and that my plan for the approach would be the same. I would have liked to try something different but the terrain just wouldn't allow it. I couldn't go in high because of the enemy situation up on the hill and I couldn't come in from the other side because of the hill so I was stuck coming up the river. The bad news was the NVA knew it too.

The last time out of this zone, the last thing I saw out of the corner of my eye was that little girl. I'd completely lost my fear, after that one shameful moment when I allowed myself to be so scared, I had regained my cool. Why, I don't know, but getting ready to go back into that zone didn't bother me in the least.

I told my crew, "Ok, you know what to expect. The Vietnamese will mob the aircraft no doubt. Get the soldiers on board and there's one little girl that's badly burned from white phosphorous. I don't care if you have to shoot people to get to her, get her on board this aircraft. Any questions?"

From down below I got a resounding "No Sir." The crew chief told me he'd also seen the little girl and knew who I was talking about.

This time getting into the landing zone I wasn't so lucky. The enemy fire wasn't as intense because the gunship had started firing at the hillside before I got there but the LZ was full of people. At the last second I had to swerve to my left and land outside the wire. The bodies of the fallen were right where they were hit. The soldiers were several yards away, caught up in the crowd of civilians. The crew chief said, "Sir, you're gonna have to pick up and slide sideways over the wire or land on it or the soldiers will never make it. I didn't hesitate; I lifted the helicopter into a hover and started sliding to my right over the wire and into the edge of the civilian crowd. I just hoped I wasn't landing on bodies, either alive or dead. The crew chief and corpsman jumped out of the helicopter and moved forward to assist the soldiers. There was a huge shoving match but my crew got the soldiers aboard. The crew chief moved back out into the crowd and when he re-emerged he had the little girl in his arms. All the while there was mass confusion going on in the main cabin. I could hear shouting and cries above the engine noise. I had no idea how many people were down there. I saw the crew chief get aboard and then a few bodies go flying out the door.

He said," Sir, you are clear to try and lift, but I don't know if we are gonna make it."

I said, "Cpl Wilson, we are gonna make it, I'm gonna get you out of this zone and I'm gonna do it right now."

I put on all the power again and started to roll forward and bounce a little. The first bounce knocked several people off that were hanging on the aircraft strut. A burst of green and white tracers sent most of the rest scattering for cover.

I half bounced, half rolled through the wire and was heading down the incline toward the river again. I felt the old 34 shudder and knew I was flying at last. I didn't waste any time; I headed down river for that big sand bar and landed. Most of the other group I dropped there had moved away but there were a few still sitting along the river bank as if they were waiting on a ride. This time the only civilian we kept on board was the little girl.

220

Hostage called to see if we were ok and I told him we were doing fine. He said he was staying there, he had a couple flights of fixed wing in bound and he was gonna kick some serious ass.

I had deliberately gone back out there without fueling because I wanted to be as light as possible coming out of there. If I hadn't I don't think we would have gotten out of the zone. Now fuel might be a little tight but if I had to set it down somewhere at least I would be a lot closer to help. I headed straight for the army aid station helo pad and dropped the soldiers off. The last guy off the aircraft was on a stretcher, I was looking straight at him as they carried him away. He gave me the "Thumbs Up" signal and then blew me a kiss. I just waved back at him.

We lifted off and headed straight for the civilian hospital. Once again we blew up a big cloud of dust and collected a large crowd of the curious. It was not a routine thing for a Marine helicopter to be delivering civilian casualties to this hospital.

Cpl Wilson had the little girl in his arms. He started walking toward the front entrance of the hospital. The huge crowd of the curious came rushing forward to see what it was all about and then at the sight of the little girl and her horrible burns they all turned and ran. No one would take her or help Cpl Wilson. He tried desperately to get someone to come over and take her or help him find a spot for her, even the nurses and older people ran.

I had locked the brakes so the aircraft wouldn't roll. Before I knew what I was doing I realized that I was waving my arms and screaming at the top of my lungs, "You rotten, chickenshit sonofabitches I'd like to kill you all, every Goddamn one of you!" I'm sure Weird Harold thought I was losing my mind and I think I was. Cpl Wilson was walking back toward the aircraft with the little girl still in his arms. I could see the anguish on his face and the tears streaming down his cheeks. I screamed at Weird Harold, "Hold the controls, I'm getting out."

I climbed out of the cockpit and down the side of the aircraft. I went straight to Cpl Wilson and without saying a word took the little girl from his arms and headed right back toward the front door of the hospital. The curious had come forward again and as I got close they ran again.

The hospital was an old French colonial building painted yellow, had white columns and a porch. Four stone steps lead up to the porch and a set of large white double doors for the front entrance. I went straight up the steps and in a pure rage applied a kick to the double doors that sent them flying open. The doors banged against the walls. There were several people inside this large hall. I'm sure a few were nurses and then I saw a man in what looked like surgical scrubs. I saw an empty gurney against one wall and went straight to it placing the little girl down as gently as I could.

I heard myself screaming, "White Phosphorus, White Phosphorous." I turned around and they were all staring at me. I'm wearing a dusty flight suit, bullet bouncer, flight helmet, and have a pistol belt. I looked at the male I assumed might be a doctor and saw him bite his lip and shake his head slightly. Everyone ran except for two of the nurses and the doctor. They just stood there. I dropped my hand to my pistol holster and the two nurses grabbed the gurney and rolled the little girl down the hall. The male in the scrubs didn't move but gave me a look that said "what do you expect me to do?"

I didn't look back as I walked to my aircraft. In my heart I knew the little girl would probably die. The Vietnamese couldn't help her and they would just put her on the floor somewhere so they could use the gurney and let her die. I was at the aircraft and trying to get back up to the cockpit when I finally realized I couldn't find the hand holds to climb up the side of the aircraft because of the tears in my eyes.

I told Weird Harold to lift us out of there and take us straight to the Marble Mountain fuel pits. I called the DASCC to check in and they told us we were relieved for the day. We'd been so busy that the squadron had reconstituted the mission with another aircraft. That was fine with me because I was pretty sure this one was gonna need some work.

It took Weird Harold forever to fill out the paperwork. It's the co-pilot's job to fill it out and the HAC's to look it over. I just wanted to get out of the squadron area. I didn't want to answer any questions about Thoung Duc, I didn't want to think about that little girl; I just wanted to be by myself.

We lived on the ocean side of the runway and when the aircraft weren't making noise and the wind was right you could actually hear the surf. I went straight down to the beach; I wanted to be alone. I felt completely drained, almost numb and a little ashamed. I'd done my job. I hadn't chickened out when the chips were down but I'd yelled at my crew chief, I'd been more than a little scared and I'd never done that before. I guess the reason I felt ashamed was that I realized I wasn't a "man of steel," that I was human like everyone else, and maybe that's what really scared me.

THREE DAYS SEARCH AND RESCUE AT CHU LAI

A few days after my Thoung Duc mission, the CO calls me in and tells me to take a section (Two Aircraft) down to Chu Lai and assume the duties as Search and Rescue for three days. This assignment comes out of left field; we've never had a mission like this before. I guess the look on my face told him I thought this was some kind of a joke. He raises his eyebrows and says, "No Shit, I want you to do this. It's a good deal for a change and it should be like three days 'In Country R&R.'"

I replied, "Yes Sir".

"Oh, by the way, take the new XO with you as your co-pilot and let operations pick your wingman."

"Yes Sir".

When I left the CO's office I still thought this might be a joke and went into operations just to make sure. It wasn't a joke. The new XO, a Major Setzer was way ahead of me. He was talking to the operations officer and things were all set up for tomorrow. I told the Major I would see him tomorrow and he jokingly said, "Don't forget to bring your toothbrush."

Chu Lai was a Marine airfield about sixty miles south of DaNang. Most of the Marine fixed wing assets were there. A-4 Skyhawk (attack close air support jets) and F-4 Phantom (Fighter/Attack) aircraft operated from there. I'd never been there, never had any occasion to even think about the place but knew that when we called for close air support that's the place the jets usually came from.

Curiosity got the best of me so I started asking around about Chu Lai and the SAR mission. Turns out for those UH-34 and CH-46 squadrons in MAG-16 here at Marble Mountain it was a rotating mission and considered by all a "good deal". Since we had been up north in a different air group we knew nothing about it but now that we were the last "34" squadron "In Country" and were members of MAG-16, our turn had come for this mission. A Ch-46 pilot that I knew from flight school said, "Yeah, it's great, you can catch up on your sleep and read a book or two, not much happens down there for the SAR. It's pretty quiet and you get to see a lot of fast movers takeoff and land."

DAY ONE

The new XO had been cooped up behind a desk for the last several years and had finally gotten orders to Nam. I knew he wanted this mission and would hope to get maximum stick time helping him get "Back in the Saddle".

Our brief time wasn't until 0900, which was more than gentlemanly, so I actually took my time and had breakfast in the mess hall instead of the usual "smoke, a coke, and a puke". It felt strange and I guess I was really more used to getting up in the darkness and launching at first light. I think I actually preferred it that way.

I met the Major and my wingman for the mission, 1/Lt Joe Lavigne, and his co-pilot 1/Lt Ed Crews. Both were very quiet guys and very steady pilots.

I said, "Good morning Major, the weather looks great and since you've been cooped up the last several years, why don't you take us to Chu Lai this morning and I'll just 'mind the store' in case you need any help."

He broke into a broad grin and said, "Thanks, that's just what I was hoping you'd say."

He briefed our mission/flight and did a nice job getting us down to Chu Lai. I was glad to see he took us out over the ocean and made the whole trip "Feet Wet"; things were a lot safer if you could do that.

As we were making our approach to the airfield we could see a single CH-46 aircraft lifting from a pad near the tower. The tower controller told us to land on that pad, that it was strictly for the SAR aircraft. We thought the 46

225

crew would at least give us a brief or say something but they didn't.

Once we landed a Captain from air traffic control came over and told us that one aircraft had to be on duty 24 hours a day starting right now. I told Lt Lavigne to take his crew and go to lunch wherever that was and the Major and I would stand by until they got back. I also told Joe that he would have the duty all afternoon and I would take the night shift, from dark till dawn. I think he was greatly relieved.

The Major headed straight for the little wooden cabin that was the designated billeting spot for our stay. I don't know where this thing came from but it sure wasn't anything Government Issue. It was actually mounted on skids. He wasn't in there long and came out in a rage. The Captain from air traffic got the full brunt of his outrage. Seems the CH-46 crew had trashed the place as a present for our arrival. After I had a look, it wasn't my idea of humor either. My crew chief and gunner were pretty disgusted as well and said they would clean it up but the Major would have none of it. He took his camera in first and took some pictures and then told the Captain he didn't give a shit where they came from, but there had better be a work detail over there to clean the mess up, and he would inspect their work. He also wanted the names and squadron of the previous occupants. I left to go set up our aircraft for a scramble start, and find out something about the local area.

Although we were ready to launch in case of an emergency, there just wasn't very much going on for the moment. So if sitting in the shade of the control tower in near 100 degree heat was somebody's idea of "In Country R&R," it certainly wasn't mine. I took the time to get some gear from my aircraft and clean my .45 caliber pistol and listen to the Major continue with his tirade. He'd managed to generate quite a bit of action and interest. Several Field

Grade Officers, (a field grade officer in the Marine Corps or Army is a Major or above) had come over from the Air Group side to check out the commotion. They would look, shake their heads and leave. It seemed strange to see so many "Heavies" (That's a Captain and below term for Field Grade Officers). For the last seven months our squadron had two Field Grade officers and for a while we only had one, the CO. Down here amongst the fixed wing outfits "Heavies" seemed to be a dime a dozen.

Joe and his crew came back and were raving about the officer's mess. They said the officer's mess looked like a beach hotel and the crewmen said the same about their facility. I really didn't care so much about the setting but was definitely interested in the food. They said the quality of the food matched the setting. I was encouraged.

Joe had also managed to scrounge up a couple of maps/charts of the local area which would be very helpful if we launched. He and his crew assumed the duties and I spent the afternoon going over the maps and charts, making some notes. I had intended to go over to the other side and check out this place but the Major had taken off in the jeep so I was stuck here until he got back.

About 1700 (5PM) I caught a ride to the other side of the airfield and the Marine dropped me off at the officers' mess. Lavigne and Crews weren't kidding; this place was really very nice considering the circumstances. I nosed around for a couple of minutes, saw a couple of familiar faces from OCS days and got directions to the eating area. I was just taking a tray and getting in the line when I heard a voice with that great Texas accent say, "Welcome to Chu Lai Spice".

I turned around and standing right behind me was a good friend from OCS, Basic School and Flight School. Captain Dee Habermacher, call sign "Habu".

"Habu, how the hell you doing, how long you been here?"

227

"I'm doing just fine but I haven't been here all that long. Let's get our food and get caught up on what's been going on."

Dee and I had a little bit of history as contemporaries and competitors. I'd known him since his first day in the Corps and when I volunteered for Helos in flight school it opened up the slot for him to achieve his dream of flying jets. He was exceptionally grateful and I was happy for him. I hadn't seen Dee or his family since we parted company at Saufley Field in Pensacola. He headed for NAS Meridian for jet training and I went to Whiting and then on to Ellyson Field for helicopter training, so this was a real treat for both of us.

Dee told me that he'd only been here a week and had flown a few close air support missions and tonight was his first night mission, some type of pre-planned radar controlled drop (TPQ) which according to him should be pretty easy. I asked what time he was taking off and he told me 2000 (8PM).

I filled in the blanks for him and told him I'd been here about seven months, that I'd volunteered for helos because I wanted to be sure and "get where the action was" and boy did I get my wish. I added that this mission was unusual for me and that I would be his SAR for the evening.

Dee told me he was glad that I had his back this evening. He was a little scared since it was his first night mission and I told him who wouldn't be; I was always scared on a night mission. He added that the aircraft were getting pretty tired and he was a little concerned about the condition of some of them. I laughed and said, "What Marine Corps aircraft isn't tired after several years over here. At least you're flying one with an ejection seat; the crew and I are strapped in that magnesium, gasoline burning sonofabitch till it gets back on the ground, one way or the other." We both laughed and then Dee had to say it,

"Well you're the dumb sonofabitch that volunteered." I had no reply.

We didn't discuss the fact that he just got here and I'd been here for seven months. We both knew the answer. The Marine Corps needed a lot more helicopter pilots than they did jet pilots. Helicopter pilots were trained at a lot faster rate because the need was so great at this time and the losses were very high.

We finished our meal quietly and Dee told me he would try and look me up tomorrow. I told him I would like a tour and maybe a chance to look up some of the other guys. We shook hands and departed.

I hitched a ride back over to the other side and found the Major and my crew sitting in the shade of a very clean little cabin. I took a peek inside and noted that not only was the small window air conditioner working but some thoughtful people had actually put clean linen on all the bunk beds; this was definitely an improvement. I wasn't sure what sleeping in there would be like, the last time I had a chance to sleep in an air-conditioned space had been aboard ship.

I told Joe and his crew they were relieved and asked the Major to relinquish our jeep so they could go to the other side for meals or whatever. I also told Joe he could do whatever he wanted but he needed to be close enough to back me up if things went bad.

It had been a fairly quiet afternoon. The fixed wing world operated on two types of missions, Pre-Planned and On Call. Pre-planned was exactly that. An order for an airstrike would come down from the wing telling the group and squadrons to conduct an airstrike on a target at a certain time and place. Hence, Pre-planned. The request was usually generated by the infantry in support of an operation they were about to conduct or were conducting. The On-call close air support was completely different. The air groups here at Chu Lai were tasked to have aircraft armed, manned and ready for an immediate launch if the infantry called for or was in need of close air support. This was very serious business if the Marines were involved in some type of fight at that moment and needed immediate help. The "On Call" could also be airborne if the need seemed imminent. So all these missions were driven by how busy or engaged the infantry was at that moment in time. They stayed pretty busy but the fixed wing operations were a little more orderly or organized than on the helo side of the house. When these guys launched they knew where they were going and what they were going to do. For the helo guys it was completely different. When you launched you might have some idea of where you were going and what you were going to do but it didn't necessarily hold true. You might start out on a resupply mission and wind up on an emergency recon extraction. You might start out in the early morning and not get back until well after dark; it was a completely different ball game.

We'd been on duty about an hour and four aircraft, (A-4's) were taxiing into position for takeoff at the far end of the runway. I checked my watch and it was exactly 1900 (7PM). I just assumed it was a night mission similar to Dee's but an hour earlier.

The runway was made of aluminum matting like all of the expeditionary airfields over here. This one was eight thousand feet long and had arresting wires at both ends which was a fairly typical arrangement for a Marine tactical airfield. The control tower was usually located at the midway point of the runway but that wasn't the case here. The runway was oriented north and south, basically parallel with the coastline, but for some reason the tower was located closer to the northern end of the runway. I think the field had been enlarged after the control tower was set up.

I heard the roar of a jet engine at the far end and knew the lead aircraft had applied takeoff power. I was sitting on

230

the left main wheel of my aircraft staring back down the runway watching the aircraft accelerate towards me. They made individual takeoffs but were only seconds apart. I could see they were loaded down with lots of bombs hanging under each wing. I also noticed they used up a fair amount of runway and they all broke ground or lifted off at about the same spot on the runway. Then it was all quiet for quite a while.

The only aircraft to do anything in the next 45 minutes was a KC-130 Hercules, an aerial re-fueling tanker but used for lots of other things. This one landed and dropped off several pallets of cargo, about a dozen passengers, and then took off.

About 1945 I heard A-4's start up, and begin taxing. I looked around for my crew. The crew chief, Cpl Wilson and gunner L/Cpl Sills were inside the helos main compartment sprawled out on the seats. The Major was inside our clean cabin enjoying the fruits of his efforts. I called to him and told him that one of these aircraft was flown by one of my buddies. He came to the door of the cabin to watch.

"I've got the evening flight schedules right here. These are individual TPQ missions that will be launching just a few minutes apart. What's your buddies name?"

"Habermacher, Sir."

"Well, he'll be the last one of these four to go."

It was good and dark now and I watched with great interest as the first three took off. I noted that they all lifted off at about the same point on the runway. It was really cool watching them take off and I wondered what it would be like. Finally it was Dee's turn.

The engine roar of the aircraft was unmistakable and I watched intently as the aircraft hurtled down the runway. It must have been a great sensation for Dee. However, the A-4 didn't look right, the aircraft looked much slower and didn't seem to be accelerating at the same rate as the others

231

I'd seen earlier. It also looked as if it was slowly drifting to the left towards our position. I knew that something was wrong and about to get much worse. I heard myself screaming at my crew to "Scramble" as I was climbing up and getting into the pilots seat.

I was about ready to engage the blades when I heard the first explosion, followed very quickly by a couple smaller explosions. It couldn't have been more than a couple hundred yards from us but my aircraft was facing down the runway. The explosions and the aircraft were behind me now.

I engaged the blades and was getting ready to lift into a hover so I could turn around and see what was happening when I noticed the Major wasn't strapped in. He was doing great but just a little out of practice. He'd performed the duties of a co-pilot during the scramble start and decided to worry about strapping in later. While I waited a second or two for him I called the tower and told them that SAR was ready to lift, standing by for instructions.

Tower came right back, "Pestkiller SAR see if you can determine whether or not the pilot is still in the aircraft, crash and fire trucks are on the way."

While I was talking to the tower the Major signaled me with a thumbs up indicating he was ready to go and I lifted into a hover and immediately turned to the left finally getting a good look at what had happened.

I heard the Major say, "Jesus Christ!"

The A-4 was engulfed in a fire ball that was a good eighty feet high. There were 500 pound bombs scattered all over the place. Fuel had spilled out of the aircraft and besides the main fire ball there were puddles of burning fuel and some of the puddles had bombs laying in them. I couldn't see the cockpit of the A-4.

My first thought was to try and get close enough to use the down force of the helicopter rotor wash to blow the flames away from the cockpit. By doing this we should be able to see if the pilot was still in there. If he was, I would try and hover over the cockpit blowing the flames away until the crash crew could get in there and get him out.

If I went straight at the burning A-4 I really couldn't see very well over the nose of my aircraft so I continued to turn the helicopter until I had the wreckage on my right side. That gave me and the crew chief the best view. All the while I was translating or sliding the helicopter sideways towards the fire ball.

As I got close I could really feel the heat and realized that I was moving way too slowly into the fireball. Even when I added more power the rotor wash wasn't sufficient to blow the flames down enough for us to see the cockpit. I also noticed all the bombs once again and realized how hot they must be getting. I knew they wouldn't be fully fused but also knew that with enough heat they might explode "Low Order". I didn't know what a 500 pound bomb would do if it exploded low order but I knew my Magnesium aircraft full of 115/145 aviation fuel was poorly placed sitting over the fire and these bombs.

I told the Major we weren't going in fast enough and I was going to back off and try again. I knew in my mind that all this was happening extremely fast but it felt like everything was in slow motion and all very clear.

This time I got us going sideways about as fast as we could and still maintain control. As I got closer to the burning A-4 I rocked my aircraft to the left and applied full power to arrest my sideways flight. This maneuver was like hitting the fire with a huge fan blowing over 100 miles an hour. It worked this time. The rotor wash blew the flames away from the A-4 and suppressed them down far enough that I could hover directly over the cockpit.

I didn't see it at first but Wilson started screaming, "The cockpits empty, the cockpits empty, the pilot has ejected!" I could finally see the empty cockpit. The canopy was gone and the ejection seat was missing. I wanted to make sure the ejection seat was missing, because that indicated the pilot had actually ejected from the aircraft and not just popped the canopy and tried to walk out of the fire ball. There was no point looking around close to the fuselage; he would be someplace else.

Cpl Wilson came up on the intercom and reported that the fire ball was building rapidly towards the back of our aircraft and now might be a good time to back away. I couldn't see what he was talking about but knew he was right.

I applied a little power and started translating sideways backing away from the burning A-4 and fire ball while still looking for any sign of a pilot or chute. The Major told me when we were finally clear of all the bombs on the runway. As soon as I knew the cockpit was empty I told the control tower. They acknowledged my report but said nothing else. Now that we were hovering clear of the fire ball I called them for further instructions. They asked us to remain airborne until crash crew had the fire under control and the pilot was located. I acknowledged the instructions and told the Major to take control of our aircraft and fly out towards the beach and shoreline. We could orbit there until the tower called with further instructions. If we hovered around using our landing light to look for the pilot we would only be making it more difficult for the crash crew by blowing sand and dust all over the place. The crash crew had arrived on the scene and they appeared to have lots of extra help looking for the pilot.

The Major flew us out over the shoreline and set up a nice comfortable orbit over the water and the beach. There was no moon this evening and he commented how dark things seemed. He also wanted to know if we would Medivac the pilot and I told him it would all depend on how badly he was injured. If the medical unit couldn't handle his injuries here we could take him to DaNang or to a hospital ship if one was nearby.

The control tower called and said that the pilot had been located and was on his way to the medical facility; he was alive and the extent of injuries was unknown at this time. They also requested that we remain airborne until the entire mess was cleaned up, they didn't want us coming back and landing while the Explosive Ordnance Disposal guys were cleaning up the bomb mess. Crash crew was busy spraying water on the bombs to cool them down so EOD could then get them off the runway. The runway was closed for quite a while and when we got back we needed to refuel.

By the time we landed back by the tower the Major was showing signs of fatigue. He jokingly told me he'd just doubled his night flying time for the last several months. I laughed and told him to hang on, it wasn't daylight yet and we weren't done till then.

After refueling we all assumed the same positions as before. I was seated on the left main tire again looking down the runway, the Major was back in the cabin and Wilson and Sills were asleep in the main compartment.

I was watching the second flight of four heavily loaded F-4 phantoms take off when the Major came up with the good news and the bad news. Bad news was the injured pilot was my friend Dee and the good news was he wasn't burned, but was hurt. He'd injured a foot during the ejection and got beat up quite a bit, but he would be ok. He was also finished for this tour; his injuries were bad enough that he would be Medivaced stateside. I jokingly said, "Shit he wasn't even here long enough to get a tan." It was a way we all had of trying to deal with bad news about friends and squadron mates. The Major added that he wasn't the only lucky guy today, another A-4 from the same squadron had the same thing happen and the pilot had not ejected but walked out of the fire ball. He was badly burned, but was going to be ok.

DAY TWO

I had fallen asleep leaning against the left main tire on the runway side of my aircraft. The Major woke me up with a gentle kick to the bottom of my right foot. I was sleeping so soundly that I awoke with a real start. I had a quick look at my watch but could tell by the sun peeking over the horizon of the South China Sea that it was much later than I thought.

"We have to go back to Marble Mountain; the CO wants me back there this morning."

"Well, so much for the 'In Country' R&R."

"We will launch single plane and head for Marble, he's sending a replacement down and they should be here by the time we've had some breakfast and get airborne. I've told Lt Crews to assume the duties until the other section leader gets here. I've got the jeep, so let's go get something to eat."

"Yes Sir."

We were back at Marble Mountain by 1000 and after I filled out the paperwork, the ODO told me the Skipper wanted to see me.

"Spicer I'm sorry the whole thing didn't work out; heard you did some outstanding work last night. I've got to send the XO to a meeting at Wing; we may be going back aboard ship."

"Well Sir, it wasn't much like "In Country R&R.""

"I'll try and get you another good deal next time one comes up."

I looked at him, smiled and said, "Well Sir, with all the Medivac I've had recently and this good deal, I'm not sure I can stand much more of your generosity."

He chuckled, reached over, knocked the cap off my head and said, "Get the F---k out of here and enjoy the rest of your day off".

236

EPILOGUE

Twenty-six years later, almost to the day, Mel and me along with Marguerite and Mel's wife Lou were visiting the Habermacher's in Sabinal, Texas. We'd remained friends and colleagues throughout our careers. Although our paths had crossed many times while still on active duty, this was the first time we'd seen each other since retirement.

During all this time neither Dee nor I had ever spoken about or relived that night on the runway in Chu Lai, Vietnam. I'm not sure why but it just never came up.

Dee and his wife live on Dee's ancestral ranch/home there in Sabinal. Their home is on the Texas historical register so after our arrival we had to have the 25 cent tour as they called it. Carolyn, Marguerite and Lou decided to get away from the "Boys" so they could get caught up and I thought us "Boys" would just sit in the shade and do the same but Dee said, "Come on, get in the pick up, I want to take you some place."

The "Boys" all got in Dee's junky old ranch pickup truck and headed to Uvalde which is the next small town west of Sabinal. It was a good ten miles or better into town and we rode silently. I was just enjoying the scenery of west Texas. Just after entering the town Dee turned down a street and into a residential neighborhood. After a couple of turns he pulled up in front of a nice looking house.

I said, "Who lives here?"

"My Mom."

"Why'd you bring us all the way in here to meet your mother?"

Dee looked at me, smiled and said, "Cause she's always wanted to meet the sonofabitch who was crazy enough to hover a helicopter over a burning aircraft trying to save her son."

Me, Dee and Mel at Dee's ranch in Texas, 13 September 1994. 26 years after his firey night in Vietnam.

SEVEN DAYS IN OCTOBER

I had night medivac on the 1st then again on the 4th and flew for 5 hours that night. Finally on the 5th I had the day off and I really didn't want to talk to anybody. I just wanted a day that was mine. I got up late and made my way up to the officer's mess. After I got my food I was looking around for some place to sit down. The place was relatively empty since it was just before it closed for breakfast. I heard someone call my name and turned around to see a guy I knew from flight school, Bill Corley. He'd been in an H-34 squadron that had been disbanded and was now in VMO-2 flying Huey Gunships. Bill was now a section leader and I was pretty sure he was the one covering me last night during most of the 5 hours we were out.

"Hey Spice take a seat, I see you got the day off as well."

"Yeah, finally, but I'm almost too tired to enjoy it, how about you?"

"Well I've got the morning off but we are too short handed right now to get a whole day off so I'm on the schedule for this afternoon."

"Hell, how can you guys be short handed, you had a half dozen majors and I don't know how many captains when we first got down here."

"We did, but the first of September a bunch went home, then we had a few more leave the last week of the month and within the last four days we've had four pilots wounded. Nothing real bad but bad enough they are hospitalized and won't be flying for a while. In fact, I heard they are going to call for volunteers. If you're interested you could come with me after breakfast and I'll get you in to see the Skipper, you can get your bid in early.

239

You interested? I'm sure they'd love to have someone with your flight experience."

Bills nickname was Lunk. He was a very large fellow, most likely right at the limit for flight school and way too big for anything but helos. After you were around him for a while Lunk seemed like the perfect nickname.

"I just might be Lunk. My CO won't be too happy about it, especially if I don't talk to him first. What time are you scheduled to brief for your afternoon hop?"

"My brief isn't until 1400, so why don't you meet me in the VMO ready room hut an hour before and I'll get you into see the Skipper."

"Ok, but I've got to see my CO first, but no matter what he says, I'll see you in your ready room hut at 1300."

All the squadrons of MAG-16 were on the ocean side and were within walking distance of the club, mess and hooches, except HMM-362. There wasn't room for us on this side so we had some junky old spaces on the far side of the runway. You could walk, but it was a pretty good hike around the airfield perimeter road. I lucked out and caught up with our "Crew Van" making an admin run to Group Headquarters. The Skipper was holding court with a cup of coffee in what we laughingly called our ready room/operations hut. It looked like something that had been put together with items found by beachcombing. He and the operations officer were waxing eloquent on various subjects so I took a seat and waited for an opening. When the Skipper finally started to leave I made my move.

"Skipper if you have a couple of minutes I'd like a word Sir."

"Sure Spice, Whatcha got?"

"Sir, rumor has it that VMO is pretty short of pilots right now and may call for volunteers, I'd like to volunteer."

"What the hell do you want to do that for; you're liable to get your ass shot off."

"Sir I've damn near had my ass shot off here many times and quite frankly I just want a chance to shoot back, go after some of these bastards; I'm tired of taking it on the chin all the time."

"I know they are very short of pilots, that very subject came up in the squadron CO's meeting at Group this morning. LtCol Fuller will probably call for volunteers but the Group Skipper told him he has to keep it to a minimum. I can understand your feelings, and to a certain point I agree with you, but you must realize it's a totally different mindset."

"I think I understand what you're saying Sir. We spend most of our time trying to avoid a fight. Think of ways to get into and out of a fight without getting hurt. Over there I'd be going out looking for a fight."

"That's right, and most likely you'll find one every day."

"Well that's what I'd like to do."

"I'm gonna say yes, you can volunteer because I'm sure one of the things you will be doing is covering us, especially on medivac and if anybody should know the best way to do that it ought to be an experienced H-34 pilot. However, I'm gonna put some strings on this deal. You're over there on a 'Lend Lease Basis,' not permanently transferred, and I can cancel the deal anytime I want. Additionally, although you're flying over there you still have to keep up with your Aviation Safety Officer Job over here. That's my deal, take it or leave it."

"I'll take it Sir."

"I really appreciate that you came to see me first, some guys would have made a deal over there and just slid out of here. I'll call Col Fuller and tell him I'm sending you over for a 'Look See' and it's his call but my conditions stand no matter what. I'll tell him you're on your way. You know Spice, most guys would have found something a little different to do on a day off."

241

Forty-eight hours later I was on the flight schedule at VMO-2. I was to fly a full functional test hop as a co-pilot and I was flying with a Major everybody called HT. My meeting with Col Fuller had consisted of a handshake, an introduction to the operations officer, the flight equipment NCOIC, and the NATOPS Officer, who was also the same Major, HT. I was provided with an aircraft NATOPS manual, the open and closed book tests, and told I had 24 hours to get them completed. Last but not least the CO introduced me to a Lt and had him take me out for a detailed pre-flight and cockpit check out.

So far it had been a whirlwind for me but a welcome change. What I didn't like was the "LOOKS"; it was the same old deal with the guys in the squadron. All of a sudden I was on the outside looking in again, I was an FNG and not to be trusted until I earned it. This part I hated and it had been this way since I joined the Corps every time I joined a new unit. Nobody ever came up to you and said, "Hey glad to have you, welcome aboard" so on and so forth; no, they always looked at you with a jaundiced eye and waited to see what you were going to do, it was always "Wait and See". I suppose this attitude prevailed, because your lives depended on each other.

The Major was less than a personable guy but I wasn't going to let that bother me. He went through a very thorough pre-flight as he should on a test hop and gave me a lot of good information. I knew right from the start that this was a test for me. He seemed to relax a little when I told him I was a maintenance test pilot in 362.

This model aircraft was the UH-1E, Iroquois built by Bell Helicopter. The E was the Marine Corps variant of the Army UH-1B. The E had a lot of aluminum in the fuselage, a rotor brake and a hoist. The differences were because of shipboard operations by the Marine Corps. The armament was similar to the B and consisted of four forward firing M-60 Machine Guns, two door mounted M-

60 Machine Guns and two types of 2.75" rocket pods, either seven or nineteen shot. Of course it was much lighter and smaller than the old UH-34 and was powered by a 1,100 Shaft Horsepower Lycoming turbo shaft engine. For me this would be a dramatic change from the huge nine cylinder radial, gasoline powered engine in the 34. The Huey didn't look as rugged as the 34 and I wondered how much of a beating it could really take.

The aircraft didn't have wheels, it had skids. The aircraft had to be lifted into the hover and air taxied to move it around. Since all the aircraft were parked in revetments, this seemed even more difficult to do because you had to lift the aircraft into a hover in such a confined space.

I followed the Major through the engine start which was a non event compared to cranking the 34. The first thing I noticed as he engaged the rotors and got them going was the vibration. The aircraft had two very wide blades. The Rotorhead was semi-rigid. Unlike the 34, the Rotorhead was not articulated; the blades couldn't move forward or back or lead and lag. This was going to make for a much rougher ride. When he lifted the aircraft into the hover to back out of the revetment the vibration became pronounced and seemed to have a much more noticeable vertical component. I thought of the many times I had been talking to a gunship pilot and could detect a staccato shake in his voice, it was pronounced and quite noticeable; we even used to joke about it. This explained why.

With full fuel and ordnance the Major was at max power and only just above the ground. It wasn't terribly hot yet and he told me the afternoons would be the worst because of the affects of heat on density altitude and helo performance.

We lifted off the airfield and flew straight out over the ocean. The Major started putting the aircraft through the required climb and handling checks dictated by the test procedures. He seemed pleased with the handling and power. He descended the aircraft down to about 100 feet over the water and told the crew chief to throw out a smoke grenade and then climbed the aircraft back up to about 1500 feet. I could see a huge plume of yellow smoke billowing on the surface below and he rolled the aircraft into about 45 degrees angle of bank and put the nose down commencing a dive at the yellow smoke. I didn't notice the altitude he started firing the machine guns but concentrated on watching how close the tracer rounds were coming to the smoke. The coverage was impressive. The machine guns fired in this manner were not a pinpoint weapon but an area weapon and they were covering the area quite well. When he pulled off of his "Gun Run" it was the first time in a long time that I thought about "G" forces because I thought he was going to pull the damn Rotorhead off this machine. He achieved another "perched" position and made a second run only this time firing the rockets and made the same sort of pull out. As we leveled off he said, "You have control, make a couple of runs and get the feel of it."

This was a hell of a time to "Get the feel of it". I hadn't so much as touched the damn controls and now I'm supposed to make a gun and rocket run. I barely knew where the switches and triggers were. But, I'm the guy who wants to be a "Khaki Clad Killer".

"I have the aircraft."

My first impression was that this handful of aircraft bore no resemblance to that of an H-34. Just putting my boots on the rudder pedals made the balance ball go out a little to the left. Light touch and sensitivity was the name of the game. It was going to be like flying the TH-13M trainer in flight school only with guns and rockets. I flew the aircraft around in a huge circle to reposition it for an ordnance run.

The yellow smoke was still quite visible so I rolled the aircraft into about 45 degrees angle of bank, let the nose fall through and watching the airspeed and altitude, tried to duplicate the exact type of run the Major completed. I fired the machine guns and flinched with the noise as I squeezed the trigger. When I began the pull off from the run it was shallow compared to the Majors and I just couldn't bring myself to pull back on the stick and add as much power. On this type of Rotorhead there is a huge nut that holds the whole thing together; it's called the "Jesus Nut". It was called that because if it came loose or let go the next person you would meet was Jesus. It took a little longer to climb back to a perched position because of my shallow pull off but once I reached 1500 feet I rolled in on the smoke again and fired a pair of rockets. It was fascinating to watch them go, but very dangerous. I'd already heard about guys doing that and following the rockets right into the dirt so I paid very close attention to my altitude. Once again my pull off was much too shallow and this was something that would need a lot of work. I climbed the aircraft back up to 1500 feet and leveled off.

"I have the aircraft."

I relinquished the controls, raised my hands, and said, "You have the aircraft."

"Well for a heavy right footed H-34 pilot making his first gun run in a helo, that wasn't too bad Spice. I'll show you a trick or two about that and your pull off, and I'm sure you'll get on to that pretty quickly. Let's fly over in the direction of the Division's recon pad, and see if you can hover this thing. That's most likely going to be the most difficult thing for you to get used to with this aircraft."

The Division recon pad was quite large because occasionally it needed to accommodate several aircraft, especially if there were several recon teams being picked up for insertion. The Major made what I would describe as a fairly flat approach to the pad and brought the aircraft into a smooth stable hover. The Huey had a noticeable shudder when coming out of translational lift and into a hover, similar to the H-34. The Major held the aircraft in a stable three foot hover for a few seconds checking the handling as required by the test procedures. After a minute or so he seemed satisfied that all was in order and said, "You have the aircraft. Just maintain the hover for a while and when you're ready try doing a square around the perimeter of the pad. You've got plenty of room, just relax and get the feel of it. After you've done that pick a spot in the middle of the pad and set it down and pick it back up a few times."

From the instant I took the controls it was a struggle. The TH-13M came directly to mind and I started thinking about trying to keep that sensitive little thing pointed at the fence post back in flight school. I ratcheted around in the hover for a full minute and then it started to become a little easier. Just like the little 13M, thinking about moving the controls was all that was needed. If I made a conscious effort to move them it was way too much. I certainly wasn't as smooth as the Major but I was getting the damn thing around the pad and he hadn't grabbed for the controls. I translated over to the middle of the pad and sat it down for the first time. It had skids so when you sat it down you had to make sure it was coming straight down and not too firmly because if you hit too hard you would spread the skids and I'd been told that was a NO NO. The Major never said a word and I worked around the pad a couple more times and made several touchdowns, enough so that I felt comfortable, not good, but comfortable. The last time I sat it down the Major said, "Take us back to Marble."

I nodded, lifted back into the hover and then translated into forward flight. You wouldn't think cruising 35 knots faster would make a difference but it seemed different to me. The vertical vibration was distinct and after asking the

246

Major about it I was told that it was just a characteristic of the aircraft, that nothing was wrong. I made my approach to the runway at Marble Mountain and it was ok. I managed to put the aircraft in a hover and started to air taxi towards the fuel pits. I really wasn't comfortable with this because there were lots of other aircraft in close proximity. The Major let me take it all the way to the fuel pits and set it down but after refueling he taxied it back into the revetments on the flight line and I was glad he did.

Back in the ready room he said, "I think you'll do nicely. I know you're a HAC and flight leader in 362 but you'll need at least ten hours to be NATOPS qualified and we will most likely qualify you PQM very quickly."

"PQM?"

"We don't have a HAC designation in Huey's; it's Pilot Qualified in Model, PQM. The Skipper and I talked it over before and based on how you did today, we will put you on the schedule for tomorrow. Skipper wanted to start off flying you as a co-pilot with some of our experienced guys first so you understand how we do things and then we will assign you as a co-pilot to some of our least experienced guys because with your experience you should be able to keep them out of trouble. They know the aircraft real well but you've got the combat. As soon as you've built up a little time we will move you right into a flight lead position."

"Sounds good to me Major."

"Well you did just fine for a 34 guy, you got a heavy right foot but you'll get over that. You need to make sure you have the ball in the center which you will start to feel as you fly, but it's very important when you shoot the guns. If you are out of balanced flight the slip stream will throw the machine gun links into the tail rotor and those damn things will eat it up. You don't want to lose the tail rotor in one of these sonofabitches. Check the flight schedule for tomorrow before you leave."

247

"Yes Sir."

The next day I was scheduled for two hops, co-pilot on another test hop and an admin run with the Colonel. He let me do most of the flying and although we didn't get all that much flight time, just a little over an hour, I had the aircraft most of the time. The test hop only lasted about half an hour. I was a little disappointed but you have to start somewhere.

When I checked the schedule for the next day, 9 Oct, I was assigned as a co-pilot to a Lt named Ward. He was one of the more experienced pilots and I'd heard he was a good stick but a wild man. They all called him "The Savage". He'd already extended once and I heard he was going to do it again; he liked it over here.

The mission code for us today was 1T4 which meant "Armed Escort". I thought we might be escorting for medivac but was wrong; we were escorting a single CH-46 on a recon extraction. Lt Ward told me we needed to brief with the 46 crew in their ready room hut, so we went down to HMM-364, better known as the "Purple Foxes". The HAC for the 46 gave a pretty quick brief, mostly covering call signs and radio frequencies. The intelligence on the situation was that this Force Recon Team had been inserted four days ago out near the Laotian border. They were looking for possible infiltrators coming out of the hills and working their way into the Da Nang area. They had reported minimal contact or sightings and wanted out in hopes of moving to a better position on the next try. The 46 crew wanted us to hang back, let them establish communication and location of the team and only get in close if they took fire on the extraction.

When we got out to the general area of the pickup I knew that we were several miles north of Thoung Duc. The terrain was mountainous and there wouldn't be many good helicopter landing sites. I wondered if the NVA had most of them already picked out. Lt Ward had given me

248

control of the aircraft shortly after we took off so I was keeping a close eye on the 46. I heard him call the recon team on the FM radio and they answered right up, which in my experience, was unusual. The team didn't want to use smoke to identify the LZ and I didn't blame them out here. Ward spotted what he thought was the likely landing zone, called the 46 and told him to make a 180 degree turn to the right and the LZ would be at his 12 o'clock. The 46 made the turn and started a descent. We both saw a quick mirror flash coming from that location and the 46 pilot called the team and said, "Did you just give me a quick mirror flash for identification?" The team "rogered" and told him to keep it coming, that everything on the ground was quiet.

The 46 swooped into a fairly large clearing just a few hundred yards from a stream and we could see about a dozen Marines scurrying to get on board. It seemed like he was on the ground a long time and I now understood why the gunship pilots always got anxious for you to get out of the LZ. I knew at this point that the 46 was completely vulnerable, he was a sitting duck. Airborne he had a chance; the bad guys had to shoot him down. He had altitude, airspeed and could maneuver, but sitting in that zone he had nothing. I think it was the sense of total vulnerability for fellow aviators that created their anxiety. I know I felt it now.

When the 46 was up and away safely he called to us and told us he would be heading directly back to the Division Recon Pad and we could detach anytime. Lt Ward took control of the aircraft and told the 46 pilot we were detaching and switching radio frequencies. He had me switch the UHF radio to Da Nang DASCC. He didn't call the DASCC but said we would simply monitor the frequency because if someone was in trouble DASCC would be the first to try and make contact with a gunship.

As we headed east out of the mountains there were some rice paddies right up against the foot of the mountains and the transition of terrain was dramatic. I saw Ward taking a hard look at one of the nearest paddies at the foot of the mountain.

Our crew chief was a Corporal that he called Orlando. I didn't know if it was his first name or his last name. Ward said, "Hey Orlando, how many people you count in that rice paddy?"

"Six Sir."

"How many in the next one?"

"Six Sir."

"What's even numbers of men spread out just about the same distance apart mean to you?"

At first I thought he was talking to Orlando but then he said, "Captain Spicer, what's that mean to you?"

"I'd say there are a dozen farmers working in a rice paddy. What's it mean to you?"

"Infiltrators. The bastards are coming down out of the mountains, donning the black pajamas and Cooley hats, working their way across the rice paddies into the area. They probably got a rally point with weapons and supplies somewhere not far and when they all get here there will be an attack on some installation."

It was definitely a different mindset.

"I'll show you what I mean. This is probably the bottom end of the infiltration route the recon team was trying to find. Since we can't sneak up on anybody with a Huey we will by pass them and then turn around and come back on them. You'll see what I mean. Can you give me a rough idea of what grid square we are passing over now?"

It took me a couple seconds but I gave him the approximate grid along with a TACAN position of the grid as well.

"Da Nang DASCC this is Hostage 4-1."

"Hostage 4-1, DASCC go ahead."

"What is the current status of the, I shackle 7265 grid, unshackle?"

250

Shackling was something we didn't do in 34's very often but it was encoding the numbers or information just in case the bad guys were listening.

"Hostage 4-1 standby."

There was about a 2 minute delay and all the while Ward was working east from the area and letting down his altitude.

"Hostage 4-1 Da Nang DASCC, that area contains NO, repeat NO friendly's, it's a free fire zone."

"Roger DASCC, 4-1 has an eyeball on 12, repeat 12 and will be investigating and engaging if necessary."

"Roger 4-1 you're clear to fire."

Ward was now down to damn near tree top level and turned sharply to head back in the direction of the two rice paddies. He dropped down to just a few feet off the ground and pushed the nose over until we were doing max forward speed of 135 knots. He was weaving back and forth. Just as I thought we were getting pretty close he pulled up sharply. I thought the Major did it sharply but this was even more so. We popped over a small tree line that had lots of palms and a few hundred yards to our front were the two rice paddies. At first the men in the rice paddies just started to move faster towards the closest paddy dike. As Ward gained altitude and those on the ground could tell he was coming in for a closer look or more likely, to shoot, they began running. From altitude, what had looked like hoes in their hands turned out to be cleverly disguised rifles. Ward now had sufficient altitude, to start a shallow gun run right down the paddy dike. The first man to the paddy dike flipped up the lid of a "Spider Hole". (A hole prepared by the enemy that had a well camouflaged top on it to conceal them. They could fire from this concealed position and were very difficult to discover. These were used many times to ambush American troops)

251

"I didn't think these fuckers were farmers, give me guns."

I flipped the switch on the console to the gun position and Ward opened fire. He missed the first man but hit the next two and continued to strafe down the paddy dike. He turned the aircraft hard left and commenced a sharp climb coming around for another run. This time I could see some of the men on the ground shooting back. He cut loose with the guns again.

The M-60 machine guns that were mounted on the sides of the aircraft ejected the shell casings to the right. When the right hand guns were fired the shell casings went to the right and fell away to earth. However, the left hand set of guns also ejected the shell casing to the right and these had a tendency to come in the window on the co-pilots side and in the left hand cabin door. These things were hot when they ejected. When Ward opened fire the second time we were in a dive and the first several shell casings ejected came right in the window of my cockpit door that I had in the down position. A couple hit the back of my flight helmet and dropped right down on my neck inside the collar of my flight suit. I thought I was dead. The longer he fired the more casings that rained in through the window. The gunner behind me was also firing his M-60 and his shell casings were ejecting to the right which threw even more in my direction. The hot casings were flying in over my shoulder, bouncing off the console in between Ward and me, and then falling on the cockpit floor eventually rolling down into the Plexiglas chin bubble below the rudder pedals. No one seemed to think this was unusual and there was no time for any comment now. Ward continued to strafe down the paddy dike and as he did, further down the dike we could now see men coming out of more spider holes embedded in the dikes. He abruptly pulled up again making another climbing left hand turn. This time he gained even more altitude but continued to roll the aircraft back into a dive toward the target.

"Give me rockets, now!"

I selected the switch for rockets and he immediately launched a pair. We continued the dive and he continued to fire pairs of rockets, all the while, shallowing his dive angle to prolong the run. The rockets were exploding with a devastating effect on the paddy dikes and the spider holes. As some of the men tried to abandon their hidden positions they were cut down by the shrapnel from the rockets.

Near the end of the second paddy dike a man jumped out of a spider hole and started running. We could see him toss his rifle away, his hat flew off his head and he ran right out of the sandal type footwear the Viet Cong and NVA wore. We could see them fly up and land on the paddy dike behind him. He was running for a clump of trees at the end of the paddy dike and Ward was shooting pairs of rockets at him as he went. The rockets kept hitting on either side of him, blowing water and mud up from the paddies, but still he ran. Ward continued to fire until we were out of rockets and by then the man ran into the clump of trees and bushes. Ward turned the aircraft to give a clear shot for Orlando and said, "Get him Orlando, get that sonofabitch."

During our rocket run Orlando had been firing his machine gun to the side and rear of the aircraft and now suddenly he swung his gun around and started raking the clump of trees. He fired such a long burst I was surprised he didn't ruin the barrel. He emptied all the ammo he had hooked up to the gun.

"Well Sir, if that didn't kill him he's gonna wish he was!"

Ward turned the aircraft to the left again and started climbing back up to 1500 feet. We had a few rounds left for the machine guns but not many.

"We don't have enough ammo or fuel to stay in this fight but we need to see if there are anymore bad guys around here and get some help, maybe get some artillery, or better yet air, to work right down those paddy dikes, there's bound to be more of them close by."

"Any Hostage this net, any Hostage this net, this is Hostage 4-1."

"Hostage 4-1 this is Hostage 2-1and 2, what do you need Savage?"

"I need somebody to take over this fight; I'm Winchester minus (meaning he's out of ammunition) and need fuel as well. I got 8 little Indians on the ground, four more lurking in the bushes for sure."

"We think we've got you in sight, you in a left hand turn about 1500 feet?"

"For positive ID I'll reverse my turn."

"Ok, gotcha."

"Bad guys are in spider holes in the paddy dikes. I got six holes uncovered and have no idea how many more. You can clearly see them. The dikes are running east to west. We are RTB (Returning to Base) for fuel and ammo; contact Hostage base if you need us to come back, 4-1 out."

"2-1 roger out."

Ward headed the aircraft east and said, "Your aircraft, take us home for refueling and ammo."

I shot my approach to the airfield and then taxied to the fuel pits and set the aircraft down. Ward never said a word. I didn't know we rearmed and refueled at the same time. I also didn't know my duties as co-pilot were to get out and load the rocket pods while the crew chief refueled the aircraft and the gunner reloaded the machine guns. I'd never loaded 2.75" rockets before; until yesterday I'd never even fired one.

"How do I load these rockets?"

"You see those boxes over there, just get a rocket out of there and shove it back down in the tubes, make sure the back of the rocket is butted snuggly against the metal tang at the back of the pod. And don't stand directly in front of the damn thing when you're shoving it in there just in case it does go off."

"Does that happen often?"

"Not sure."

I got the pods reloaded fairly quickly and started to get back in the co-pilot's seat when Ward yelled at me.

"You're not finished. You need to reach down under the rudder pedals into the chin bubble and clean out those shell casings. If we don't they'll get so deep they start to interfere with the rudders."

It was an awkward thing to do. You had to work around the two machine guns, open the cockpit door, lean in, reaching way forward into the chin bubble, and grab handfuls of shell casings. Then you needed a place to put the damn things. You certainly didn't want to drop any out here because they could be blown up by the rotorwash and hit a rotor blade or Marine, or sucked into an engine. I was looking around and noticed the gunner pointing at a large barrel near the fueling nozzles. I finally realized it was easier to take off my helmet and fill it rather than take handfuls of casings.

When I did get back into the aircraft, Ward was on the radio talking to Hostage Base (the operations duty officer in the ready room).

"Base, 4-1 is in the pits, reloaded, the aircraft is up, standing by."

"4-1, Base, if your machine is up, don't sign it off, park it on the end of the line and go to chow. Check with the ready room when you're finished eating, we'll have more work then, Base out."

We'd been airborne a little over three hours this morning. I went up to the officers' mess with Lt Ward and after getting our food, we took a seat by ourselves. Not one word was said about the morning; as far as Ward was concerned we might as well have been on the mail run. It truly was a different mindset.

We ate in silence and walked back down to the squadron ready room. As soon as we walked in the door the ODO told us to launch and head for Liberty Bridge down in the Arizona Area, they would give us the info on the way.

There was a combined force of Marines and South Vietnamese troops making a sweep from east to west on the north side of the river leading to Liberty Bridge. From H-34's I knew that Liberty Bridge and the Arizona Area were normally hot, I'd been down there on Medivac.

Ward gave me the aircraft shortly after takeoff. He said, "Your turn, let's see how an old 34 driver does this."

At the moment we were single plane, but there had been a section (2 aircraft) from our squadron working in support of that operation. One of the aircraft had problems and had to return to base, we didn't know if it was strictly mechanical or if they'd taken some hits. We were now filling in for Hostage 6-2.

"Hostage 6-1 this is 6-2 inbound your position about 8 miles out, no joy (means I don't see you) at this time."

"6-2 welcome to the party, keep it coming, I'm at 2000 feet right hand turn talking to Night Cover Charlie 14."

"6-2 roger, looking and listening."

It took a couple minutes to close the distance a little but I saw a glint off the windscreen of the other aircraft.

"6-1 I have you in sight, deep at your four o'clock, level."

"6-2 roger in sight break, Night Cover Charlie 14 Hostage 6-1, will make my first run along the south side of the river from east to west with a right hand pull, break, 6-2 start your run as soon as I pull off target make it a guns pass right in my tracers path, right hand pull over friendly's acknowledge."

"6-2 roger, guns pass in trail, right hand pull."

I made my first gun run ever. I couldn't see the enemy like I had this morning but I could see the muzzle flashes. This was a no shit gun fight. Ward told me to time my run so that I could start shooting as soon as 6-1 pulled up, so as to keep them from shooting him while he pulled off. I made the run just like he said and it felt scary, but good. The shell casings were bouncing all over the place but I didn't notice like before, I had too much to concentrate on.

We made two runs apiece and were starting to run low on machine gun ammo. 6-1 had me switch to rockets and we each put a half a dozen down the tree line. After my last rocket run we held high and dry waiting for the FAC on the ground to tell us if we'd silenced the fire from across the river. Things were quiet for about fifteen minutes and then he reported some intermittent fire from across the river but much further up the tree line we were working.

6-1 was TACA qualified (Tactical Air Controller Airborne); he could call in an air strike and that's exactly what he did. While we were waiting on word from the ground FAC, we heard 6-1 call the DASCC on UHF and request a section of A-4 Skyhawk close air support aircraft.

Hellborne Lead and 2 checked in on the UHF frequency. I heard them tell 6-1 they were over head at 10,000 feet and had us both in sight. 6-1 called for their line up (meaning the type of ordnance they were carrying).

" 6-1 Hellborne Lead, line up as follows, Lead is wall to wall High Drag Mk-82's, with 240 rounds 20 Mike Mike, Dash 2, has wall to wall Nape, with 240 rounds of 20 Mike Mike." (The lead aircraft had 8, 500 pounds of High Drag bombs and 240 shots of twenty millimeter cannon. Dash 2 had 6, 500 pounds of napalm bombs and the same amount of twenty millimeter cannon)

This was an extremely lethal mix of ordnance; there was no messing around here. Once 6-1 dropped this mess on the tree line, whoever or whatever was in there would no longer exist.

"Roger Hellborne, target is the long tree line south of the river, friendly's are on the north side. Make your runs east to west with a right hand pull, target elevation is less than fifty feet above sea level, let me know when you're ready to observe my mark. 6-2 hold south of the tree line 1click left hand turns one five hundred feet, acknowledge."

"6-2 roger copy."

"Hellborne Lead is ready for the mark."

While I was maneuvering into position to stay out of the way of the air strike but also be able to observe its affects, 6-1 came around for a rocket run on the tree line. He was going to fire a couple of rockets to mark the target. White phosphorus rockets would have been best but I don't think either one of us had anything but High Explosive war heads on the rockets we currently had.

"Hellborne lead marks are away, I fired a pair, don't have any Willie Pete aboard."

"Hellborne lead has the mark."

"Roger lead, from my mark string your MK-82 as far as they will go down that tree line. Dash 2 from the leads first bomb drop pairs and we want to keep stringing them out to the west along the river bank."

"Hellborne lead roger and I'm in."

"Dash 2 roger."

" Lead, 6-1, have you in sight, you're clear hot when your wings are level."

I was turning the aircraft to parallel the river and we could see the lead A-4 commence his run. It looked like he was doing a "Level Lay Down" which was a good way to drop that type bomb and cover a large area. We could see the High Drag Fins open up and the bombs start to drop almost vertically to the earth. When the first bomb disappeared into the tree line we could see the shock wave long before we heard the sound. Then the noise caught up, and was tremendous. We could feel the shock waves. "BA HUNK!!! BA HUNK!!! BA HUNK!!!" They just kept coming. The bombs strung out well forward of the area we'd been shooting. There was debris several hundred feet in the air and I wondered if it would interfere with Dash 2's napalm run.

"Dash 2 is in, Lead's in sight."

"Roger 2, 6-1 has you in sight; you're cleared hot when your wings are level."

Dash 2 released two of his bombs and I could see the shiny tubes going end over end. When they hit we could feel the heat, and we were a long way away. I'm sure the Marines across the river could feel it as well. Dash 2 made two more runs and had complete coverage of the area. Whatever was down there that wasn't blown up was burned to a crisp. It was absolutely awesome.

"Hellborne Lead and 2, excellent job, your BDA (Battle Damage Assessment, their score for how well they did) is 100 over 100." (That's the best they could do).

"Roger Hostage 6-1 Hellborne copies 100 over 100. Hellborne is off switching frequencies, Dash 2 go button 9."

With that they were gone. We moved over the area for a closer look and it was complete devastation. 6-1 was talking to the ground FAC and when we heard that there was no further assistance required I headed over to join on 6-1 for our return to base. We refueled and rearmed one more time and then we were done for the day.

Since I was now a co-pilot again I had a lot of paperwork to do for the day. We'd flown for 7.5 hours today, actual flight time. It didn't count ground time for rearming and refueling. We were given credit for 8 confirmed KBA (Killed By Air) bad guys. We'd help safely extract a recon team, we'd started a fight and got some kills, which led to an even bigger fight, and Hostage 2-1 flight had run several air strikes and put a hurt on some bad guys trying to infiltrate the area. We'd covered a couple of Medivacs and finally we'd filled in on another gun fight to protect the flank of a Marine Battalion and hopefully saved lots of Marines from harm. We didn't have any confirmed kills from the air strike but the right flank of the Marines was now reported as all quiet. It took me over an hour to fill out the after action forms. Ward was long gone. I walked up to the officer's club bar and got a drink. I walked outside and sat down in the sand, lit a cigarette and wondered what tomorrow would bring. I was exhausted and elated. I felt I was "IN THE WAR", not that I wasn't before but in a different way.

The next day, October the 10th, I was assigned as Ward's co-pilot again. It was a repeat of the day before except it was the longest day I had in the war since Dai Do last May. We flew 11.2 hours, the last couple in the dark. I lost track of the number of times and places we rearmed and refueled. I made my first night gun and rocket runs and learned how difficult it was to keep your night vision when firing rockets at night. I didn't finish the paperwork until almost 2100.

On the 11th bad weather rolled in low clouds, rain and poor visibility. I was assigned as a co-pilot to the squadron XO. I couldn't pronounce his name but it was Z something. He was a little different, obviously not well liked, and from the get go, I wasn't too sure about his flying skills or his head work. We launched out for a mission near the Hill 37 area, got caught by the weather and just made it to the Hill. There was no way we were going to get in much work but we had to try. After several half ass tries he finally decided we had to quit and try to get back to Marble. The only way we could go safely would be low level, as low as we could go which was gonna be difficult because it was raining so hard visibility was crap.

The Major headed the aircraft back towards Marble but he was chugging along at about 300 feet, just underneath the overcast. This was no man's land, we were sitting ducks. If you couldn't get above 1500 you went right on the deck, weaving like a drunken butterfly; didn't matter what type helo you were flying. If you didn't, you were definitely in the small arms danger zone.

"Hey Major Z, I think we need to take it down on the deck, 300 feet isn't a good place to be."

"Oh, we are just fine. I doubt anybody's going to be out in this weather taking shots at helos, besides I don't think this area is hot anyway."

"Maybe so sir, but we're flying parallel to a very long tree line and that's never good."

"It'll be ok."

It was ok for another few minutes until the first RPG (Rocket Propelled Grenade) was fired out of the tree line and just missed to our rear. The second one went passed the nose.

"I have the aircraft!!"

Screw this guy, I'm not letting his stupidity get me and the crew killed. If he didn't like it he could get out and walk 'cause I was taking this damn aircraft down right to the deck and pulling max power to get the hell out of here.

I turned sharply away from the tree line and pushed the nose down heading for the deck. At 20 feet on the radar altimeter I turned back sharply to the left and then back to the right again continuing to open the distance from the tree line. I let the aircraft settle to about ten feet and continued to weave. I glanced over at the Major; he had his hands on his knees and was staring straight ahead. He hadn't said a word. I continued to fly until I could see the Marble Mountains and knew it was pretty safe. I pulled the aircraft up to the bottom of the overcast and leveled off.

"Your aircraft Sir."

"I have the aircraft."

He took control and brought us in for air taxiing to the fuel pits and finally to the line and the revetments. As I was filling out the paperwork, I noted that we'd only flown 3.3 hours today; after the last two days it didn't seem right but the weather was terrible. The Major didn't say a word, just signed off on the paperwork and left. I was leaving the squadron area when the crew chief, Corporal Claussen caught up with me.

"Hey Captain Spicer hold up for a second Sir."

"Corporal Claussen, what can I do for you?"

"I just wanted to thank you for taking the aircraft back there Sir; he was scaring the shit out of me and Peterson."

"You're more than welcome, see ya tomorrow Claussen."

I thought of EV back at Santa Anna, he'd said many times, "don't let some dumbass kill ya, take it, save it, and worry about the argument later." I thought of him often, he'd been good to his word; what he taught me had gone a long way towards staying alive over here.

A small Typhoon had spooled up and that was the cause of the rain. It held up operations until the 15th and I flew as Lunk's co-pilot on his TACA check. We flew for 4.2 hours and ran several flights of fixed wing prepping landing zones for recon inserts.

The Typhoon wouldn't go away fast enough and held up operations until the morning of the 18th. I flew with Lunk again and we covered a recon team insert that went off without a hitch. We flew for 2.7 hours and then returned to base to rearm, refuel, and then shut down.

When we got back to the ready room the ODO (operations duty officer) said, "Hey Spice, your Colonel wants to see you right away.

"Which Colonel do you mean, Colonel Fuller or Colonel Schlarp.?"

"Your Colonel, the Ugly Angel guy."

"Do you know what he wants?"

"No, but you're off the flight schedule this afternoon. I'm getting Fire Plug to take your place with Lunk."

Fire Plug was an FNG Lt who had joined the squadron as one of the replacement pilots in the last week. He was a strange young man. I asked him why they called him Fire Plug and he told me because dogs liked to piss on him. I didn't wait for an explanation. I wished Lunk good luck with Fire Plug and started to find a ride over to the other side to try and find Colonel Schlarp.

I was doing my best to get a ride over to 362 to see the Colonel when he found me. He pulled up alongside me on the perimeter road and said, "You looking for me by any chance."

"Yes Sir, I was just on my way to see you."

We rode in silence the rest of the way to the squadron and when he parked his jeep he told me to join him in his office. Colonel Schlarp could be a pretty gruff guy, and I think a lot of the guys feared him a little. For some reason he seemed to like me and I had always avoided his wrath, but I could tell something was wrong. I had a couple of aircraft accident investigations hanging fire but I didn't think that was it. He left me sitting in his office for a few minutes while he used the phone in the ready room. When he came back into the office he took a seat behind his field desk and just looked at me for a few pregnant seconds. Finally he broke the silence.

"Spicer, I'm pulling you back over here as of today. When we are finished here I want you to go collect your flight gear. I've just called Colonel Fuller and told him you're done. He didn't like it and was going to take it up with the Group Commander but I reminded him of my deal. I'd also cleared this deal with the Group Commander before I let you go over."

"Colonel, why are you pulling me back?"

"For a couple very good reasons. First, I need you back here. We've got a few replacements but they need to get snapped in and you can certainly help with that. Secondly, those bastards are working you like a borrowed mule. You've been over there for 10 days and you've flown 7. If it hadn't been for that small Typhoon you'd have flown all ten.

"Sir, they are trying to build up my flight time so I can be PQM and become a flight lead."

"That might be true but they are also trying to get you killed. In 7 days you've flown 30.6 hours counting this morning and if I hadn't called a halt to it you'd have flown all afternoon. They haven't flown any other pilot over there that much in the last 7 days. The only one close to you is that crazy Lt Ward and he should have been sent home months ago. Look son, I know how you feel but you can't win this war by yourself. You are a damn good pilot and one of my best officers. If you get hurt here so be it, but I'm not going to sit back and watch them let you fly yourself into the dirt. No arguments. Go get your stuff and get back here. I've told operations to put you on the schedule here for tomorrow."

I didn't know what to say or do. I'd agreed to his deal but felt sure I would be transferred permanently to VMO, but it wasn't going to happen.

"Yes Sir."

The next morning I was on the schedule with a new pilot named Anthis. He was a HAC and this was his second tour, but he hadn't been in the cockpit for quite a while. When I got to the ready room one of my favorite guys Lt Ed Crews was there and said, "Morning Captain Spicer, heard the Skipper pulled you back from VMO."

"Yeah Ed, it was a brief but meteoric career as a gunship pilot, brief but meteoric."

THE DAY WILEY GOT HIT

About the middle of October our tasking started to change a little. Instead of a steady diet of Medivac missions we were now being assigned as "Working Birds," but instead of operating in the southern area we were being sent all over the place.

According to the Stars and Stripes this morning it's Tuesday, the 22nd of October and I am scheduled to lead a flight of four up to the Dong Ha area and once there be tasked by Dong Ha DASCC (Direct Air Support Coordination Center). At least it's not Medivac. We had a six AM show for a seven AM go but since we really didn't know what we were going to do until we got there the briefing only took a few minutes and we launched early.

Our first order of business upon arrival at the Dong Ha airfield was to head directly to the fuel pits located alongside the makeshift metal runway. While we were refueling I made a radio call to the DASCC checking in for our assignments. As we suspected the DASCC wanted us to split into sections and operate as "working birds". The DASCC wanted one section (two aircraft) to work with units to the east out near Con Thien, the Cam Lo Bridge, Gio Linh, and other units scattered along the "Trace". The other section was to work the west out towards Khe Sanh, the "Rock Pile", Ca Lou, and the infamous "Razor Back". These were all in mountainous terrain and for the moment much more dangerous. The Razor Back was very close to the DMZ and was well within the artillery range of the North Vietnamese Army's' heavy artillery. I think an artillery duel between Marines and the NVA was just about a daily occurrence.

The other section leader was waiting for me to tell him where to go and I'm sure he breathed a sigh of relief when I told him I'd take the west. A cardinal rule was you never gave the other section or wingman the hardest job. If you were leading it was because you were supposed to be the most experienced.

We "rogered" our instructions with the DASCC. Our first mission was in the Khe Sanh area. I had the radio frequency for contacting the HST (Helicopter Support Team). These guys were under the supervision of the air officer or FAC (forward air controller). The FAC was a fellow aviation Marine, either a pilot or an NFO (Naval Flight Officer). Squadrons were tasked with providing aircrew to infantry units as FAC's and the normal FAC tour in Vietnam was 100 days and then the officer would return to his squadron and flying duties. It was one of the many things unique to the Marine Corps: air support for Marines, by Marines.

I dialed in the radio frequency and made the call to Dixie Diner One Four. (The One Four would be written as 14 but not read or said as Fourteen, but One Four) Dixie Diner was the collective call sign for the 2nd Battalion, 4th Marine Regiment. One Four was the code for the air officer. If the reply on the radio came back, "This is Dixie Diner One Four Actual" you were talking directly to the FAC. If the reply was just Dixie Diner One Four then you were speaking to a member of the HST. I was familiar with the Dixie Diner call sign because we'd worked a lot with 2/4 several months ago.

The radio reply was from Dixie Diner 14, the HST guys and they were ready for us which was good news. These guys were pretty well organized today and started reading off a list of things they needed accomplished this morning. I took control of the aircraft long enough for the co-pilot, 1/Lt Potts to write it all down and then told him to take control, land us in the zone and get started. The Command Post landing zone was on top of a pretty good sized hill. The Marines had blown part of the top off making a fairly level and large LZ (landing zone). Potts made a nice controlled approach and except for the last ten feet it was good.

I kept noticing a lot of CH-46 activity up to our north near the "Razor Back" so I wasn't surprised when Dong Ha DASCC called us with instructions to check in with Bright Boy 14 for some work.

Once we completed our last mission and on our way back to refuel I dialed in the frequency DASCC had given me for Bright Boy 14. I gave them a call on the FM radio.

The reply came back, "Aircraft calling Bright Boy 14 say again your call sign."

I knew the voice immediately; it was one of my best friends. We'd spent many hours studying, flying and playing golf together; I'd know this voice anywhere. It was the voice of one Lieutenant D.W. Wiley, known to most as just "Wiley" and to me and a couple other close friends as "Chuey."

Most people that knew him were unaware that he was an exceptionally talented football player and held all the passing records at Ysleta High School in El Paso. He'd attended Texas Western University and we all suspected he'd played football there but he never mentioned anything other than the name of the school. He was probably the most avid golfer I'd ever known and although he struggled as most of us did to break 90 on a regular basis, I believe he would ignore pain, hunger or thirst in pursuit of his next shot. No matter how bad his game was for the day he was always optimistic about the next round.

I was very surprised to hear his voice; I had no idea that he'd been assigned to FAC duty. I answered, "Bright Boy 14 this is Pest killer four dash one standing by for mission instruction." There couldn't be a lot of chit chat, it wasn't good radio procedure and besides more than likely the NVA was listening.

267

Wiley recognized my voice as well and without actually coming out and saying so let me know. He said he wanted us to pick up four priority passengers and take them to Dong Ha. These were most likely Marines whose tour was up and they would be on their way home, so it was a priority. I acknowledged the mission and told him we would be there for the passengers as soon as we completed our current run and refueled at Dong Ha, about 30 minutes max. He told me that would be just fine.

After refueling and enroute to Bright Boy's position I called on their FM frequency and got the 14 Actual, Wiley again. Talking in our own vernacular, Don was able to convey to me that his unit, First Battalion, Third Marine Regiment, 1/3, was moving out of their current location and being taken south for a different assignment. He also let me know that today was the last day of his 100 day FAC tour and he would be catching the last CH-46 out of their current position sometime late this afternoon.

That explained the heavy CH-46 traffic I'd been watching all morning to our north. I was surprised that hadn't attracted the attention of the NVA and brought in some artillery fire from them. I asked for the LZ brief and he told us that the passengers were in what he called the lower zone. The main lift was taking place from a landing zone on the other side of the "Razor Back". The lower zone would definitely be a safer LZ because it would be out of sight from the NVA across the river.

The "Razor Back" was an unusual terrain feature. It was a ridge that stuck up sharply right at the end of a valley. Its axis ran northeast to southwest and although there was some heavy vegetation on it, from the air it appeared to be solid rock and at its peak presented a very sharp looking edge the entire length of the ridge, hence the "Razor Back".

I hadn't been near the "Razor Back" in well over a month but I knew the lower zone wasn't just a flat LZ at the base of this rock formation; it was more like a shelf on

268

the side. It would be a good challenge for Lt Potts. He was currently flying the aircraft and I pointed to him and nodded that this was his approach and landing. He'd been doing a great job all morning and I was pleasantly surprised.

Potts made another good approach, but once again didn't handle the last ten feet very well. I was starting to pick up a trend. Once on the ground our four priority passengers came running and we were in and out of the zone in less than two minutes. This was good because sitting in a landing zone for several minutes in this neighborhood was never a good idea even if you thought the bad guys couldn't see you; they more than likely saw you coming down so they always had a good idea of where you were and never minded taking the odd pot shot at you with a mortar or artillery piece.

Once clear of the LZ and safely enroute to Dong Ha I called Bright Boy 14 to ask if they had any additional missions. I didn't talk to Wiley and assumed he was busy near the other zone with the retrograde of the Battalion.

We dropped our priority passengers at Dong Ha and after refueling again spent the rest of the afternoon working out near Khe Sanh with some of the Dixie Diner units occupying the high ground out there. On one of our trips back to Dong Ha, the gunner called me on the aircraft intercom and told me to take a look out toward the "Razor Back". He thought they had just undergone one hell of an artillery barrage. I didn't see anything at that time but did notice the Ch-46 activity had increased quite a bit.

When told by Dixie Diner 14 that we'd completed all their tasks we checked in with Dong Ha DASCC and were told we were clear to head home. My other section had finished up early and already headed south so I would see them when we got back to Marble Mountain.

Shortly after landing, and while waiting for Potts to fill out the paper work one of my hooch mates came into the ready room. As soon as he saw me he said, "Hey Spice, aren't you good buddies with a guy named Wiley?"

"Yeah, I'm real good buddies with him, why?"

"Weren't you working north today at the 'Razor Back'?"

"Yeah."

"Well we heard he got hit bad, I thought you probably knew."

"No, I don't know a damn thing, hell we were in and out of his position about 1300 (1PM) and I was talking to him before that. How bad?"

"Don't really know; just know it was supposed to be real bad and that he's been flown down here to the big Navy Hospital."

"Shit, how'd he get medivaced down here so fast?"

"I heard a bunch of them got hit and they were put on a Ch-46, taken to Dong Ha, and then put on a KC-130 and rushed down here."

I immediately caught a ride to the other side of the runway. If Wiley was at the Naval Support Activity Hospital I knew I had to get over there to see him. I got off the shuttle truck near the officers' mess and club. Transportation was hard to come by especially off the airfield. The only person in the squadron that had a jeep was the squadron CO. I entered the "O"Club and went looking for my CO, LtCol Schlarp.

The CO was seated at a table with three other squadron commanders. I never ever thought I would do something like this but I walked straight up to the table and when he recognized me I said, "Colonel I need your jeep for a while." It must have been the look on my face or the way I made my request but he didn't hesitate. He said, "It's out at the end of the club, take it and let me know when you get back."

I thanked him and left without another word. I found the jeep and got headed for the main gate very quickly. We hardly ever left the confines of the airfield by land, it was always by air and since we did not go out into any of the local villages or the city of DaNang, it felt very strange driving out the gate. I shouted, "NSA hospital" as I drove through the gate and the sentry pointed in a westerly direction.

It only took about 15 minutes to drive to the hospital. From the air, the medivac pad was easy to find, but on the ground just finding a parking place and an entrance was a totally different deal. I finally parked the damn jeep near an entrance and went inside.

Still in a flight suit and wearing a shoulder holster, I didn't get very far inside the entrance before I was intercepted by a Navy Nurse.

"Can I help you Captain?"

"Yes Lt, I'm here to see a Lieutenant Wiley, D. W. brought in today."

She walked over to a rostrum and started looking through the papers on a couple different clip boards.

"Follow me please."

The hospital was a series of Quonset huts that were put together at right angles. She led me out of the Quonset hut through a set of double doors, down a covered walk way and into another hut. The entry was in the middle of the building.

"He's in the third bed on the left, pretty doped up; I'll be in the area if you need me."

"Thanks."

The first bed to the left contained a male that was so horribly burned I could only recognize him as a male because there was a tube sticking out of his penis. His arms were in a flexed position, bandaged and bent at the elbows and his entire body was trembling. It was very sobering to say the least. I paid no attention to the occupant of the second bed but fixed my gaze on the third bed down. I was approaching on the bed's right side and from about ten feet I could recognize Don.

271

I walked straight up to the bed and as I approached couldn't help notice that Don was in bad need of a haircut and a shave and was still very dirty. As I got to the actual bed side and was able to get a full view of him the horror of what I saw hit me full force. There on the left side of the bed I could see a bloody bandaged stump where his left arm used to be. His arm had been severed in mid humerus. His abdomen area was opened up and there was further damage to his legs.

At that instant I felt things going cold, I grabbed the railing on his bed to keep from going down. I'd never passed out in my life but I was pretty sure that's what was happening. When I grabbed the railing he noticed me there and in a strained muffled voice said, "Well what the hell are you doing here my man?"

If I stayed another second or two I was going down so I heard myself saying, "Hey Don, I'll be back in just a second, hang on buddy."

Somebody grabbed me at the back of my neck and got a firm grip on my right arm. I was spun away from the bed and hustled out the double doors I'd come in and pushed down into a sitting position on the concrete walkway. From the voice and what I could see of the shoes I knew it was the nurse that had taken me into Don's bed. She roughly pushed my head down in between my knees and said, "Sit still for a minute and take some deep breaths." She never let go of the back of my neck and kept my head forced down between my knees. It took about a minute and I felt I was fine.

"Let me up."

"Not just yet, you stay right where you are and listen to me. I will let you up in about a minute and when I do I want you to get off your ass and go right back in there and talk to your friend, you hear me?"

"That's exactly what I intend to do, let me up please."

"Ok, but some guys won't and I'm not gonna put up with any of that type of crap."

"Well it won't happen with me. I don't know what happened but it won't happen again."

"It happens all the time, ok, get up and get back in there."

She turned me loose and I stood up a little shakily but managed to head directly for the double doors. This time as I approached Don's bed I knew I was ready for what I was going to see and I was trying to think of things to say or how to act.

"Hey Don, I'm back, how you doing?"

"Not too fucking good as you can see."

"What the hell happened, I was talking to you about noon."

"Shortly after you were there we got hit with some artillery fire from across the DMZ. I was up at the top of the ridge with part of the command group. You know when you get incoming there's always that split second when you decide to drop where you are or run for a bunker or hole."

His speech was somewhat muffled, I could tell he was heavily drugged and of course in tremendous pain. The whole time he was speaking he was moving both his legs alternately with little movements as if trying to get comfortable. But that wasn't going to happen.

I kept my hands firmly gripped on the steel bed rail and could not keep my eyes from wandering to the bloody stump and then down to the wounds on his abdomen. I had to force myself to make direct eye contact and keep my focus there.

"I know exactly what you mean Don."

"We had a series of holes all along the top of the ridge. Mine was about twenty yards away so I jumped down in the nearest hole with two other guys. I had one on my left and right. A round hit right on the edge of the hole, it took

273

the guy's head off that was on my left and killed the guy on my right. I think some of the shrapnel that took off that guy's head was what ripped off my arm."

Listening to this I found that I could not stand still and had to shift my weight from foot to foot and grip and re-grip the bed rail with my hands.

"Goddamn Don, what time did this happen?"

"1422 (2:22PM)."

"1422, how'd you know it was exactly 1422?"

"Cause when they were dragging me out of the hole I reached over and grabbed my arm. I wanted my watch and my ring off my left hand. For some strange reason I looked at the watch to see if it was running and it was 1422."

As horrible as this was I almost had to laugh but smiled instead; this was quintessential Wiley.

"What's gonna happen next?"

"They already fixed some of the damage down below and I think I'll be medivaced to Japan in the next 24 hours."

"Is there anything I can do or get for you now?"

"No I think I'm all in but my boot straps and feel like I'm gonna pass out."

I took his right hand and gave it a half shake and a little squeeze and said, "You hang in there damn it and I'll see you later."

I got through the double doors and out onto the concrete walkway. I was absolutely numb. I stopped and leaned against one of the walkway posts for support and stood there for several minutes. It took a while before I went to the jeep and headed back for Marble Mountain. I found my CO in exactly the same place.

"Thanks for the loan of your jeep Colonel, its back in the same spot safe and sound."

He simply waved his hand in acknowledgement, didn't ask why I needed it and I didn't feel like explaining. I walked out to the beach and sat down in the sand. There are some things that can leave you so numb the only thing that helps is solitude.

EPILOGUE

January 1972

A good amount of time passed before I was able to see Don again. When I left Vietnam in 1969 I had another overseas assignment and didn't get back to the United States until late 1971. So my first opportunity came in early February '72. My family and I had orders to the west coast and on our way from east to west I made it a point to head straight for El Paso and a reunion with Don.

At first I was apprehensive about how we would react to each other but my fears were not necessary. After a quick handshake and a half-assed hug it was simply Don and Bill again as if nothing happened. He might have been minus a limb but he was still Don, Chuey or Wiley.

I was dazzled by the things he could do, like tying a tie or simply getting dressed using only one hand. He had a prosthesis but didn't wear it often.

We were catching up over several Margaritas and he told me the rest of the story. Don had been medivaced the next day. He'd been placed on a large C-141 rigged out for medical transport and was to be flown to a naval hospital in Japan. The C-141 had beds mounted on the walls of the aircraft cabin and as he remembered they were about 5 high. He'd been placed on the bottom bunk. Sometime during the trip the bandages on his arm came loose and he started to bleed profusely. The aircraft cabin had been darkened to provide a more restful atmosphere. He'd been placed in the bed so his left side was to the isle and the nurses would have easy access if the damaged arm needed attention. However, being on the bottom bunk he wasn't so noticeable.

"Spice, I didn't know I was bleeding until I could feel my blood soaking through the sheets and starting to wet my back. It was the most pleasant sensation I have ever experienced. I was warm, comfortable and free of pain for the first time in several days, it was amazing. I don't think I ever felt better in my life."

It wasn't until one of the nurses making her way down the aisle between the bunks actually slipped in Don's blood and fell flat on her back that anyone realized what was happening to Don. He went on to explain that the medical staff immediately went into action and although he didn't remember the specifics, obviously saved his life.

He spent a couple months in the hospital in Japan and then was sent stateside to the military facility nearest his home, which for him, was Fort Bliss, right there in El Paso.

He was medically retired from the Marine Corps, with the rank of Captain. When asked what type of skills he would like to develop to prepare him for civilian life, Don said he wanted to learn how to play golf again. The military was thinking more in terms of marketable skills for getting a job, but not Don. He told them, "I don't give a shit about marketable, I just want to play golf again. I'll take care of that other stuff when the time comes". It took several tries but he finally got his point across.

He went on to tell me that before with two arms he'd struggled to break 90 and never knew why but since he'd learned to play with one arm he now routinely shoots in the upper 80's and had he known his left arm had been the problem, he would have sacrificed it long ago. Once again, Quintessential Wiley.

January 2011

I have maintained close contact with my friend ever since and am pleased to report that even after some heart valve trouble, some very annoying arthritis, and in his late 60's, he's still playing golf as many times a week as the weather in El Paso allows. In fact, only recently he shot his best round ever, a solid 77 that he said could have been even better.

Marguerite, Bill and Wiley at his home golf course in El Paso.

Wiley patiently waiting for us to catch up.

WING FRAGGER

31 October 1968, it's Halloween and the ODO (Operations Duty Officer) tells me the C.O. wants to see me. I hadn't seen him in two days. I'd had night medivac last night and never launched, which was a good thing. I checked in his office hut; he wasn't there and he wasn't flying according to the ODO. I decided to hang around the ready room and see if he would turn up shortly.

I waited an hour and he still hadn't showed up. Now the ODO tells me he's in a meeting at Group Headquarters. The latest rumor is that we are going back aboard ship to be part of an SLF (Special Landing Force) again, and that's the reason for the meeting. The last time we'd done this we'd been involved in the Battle of Dia Do and it was a big one.

While I'm waiting, the aircraft maintenance officer comes in and asks if I'd do a couple of tracking runs and maybe a test hop for him. I know how hard those guys work, busting ass 24 hours a day, so I have no problem helping out.

When I get back from my maintenance flights, the ODO tells me the Skipper is waiting for me in his office. He's a big tall man and in proportion to his field desk, it looks like he's sitting behind something that belongs to a child. He does have an extra folding chair for guests. When I walk in he offers it to me. Something is not quite right.

After we exchange greetings he says, "Spice, I've offered you up for a job on the Wing Staff."

I was stunned. I couldn't have been more so if he'd told me he was sending me FAC (Forward Air Control). The Wing Staff, I'd be at Wing Headquarters working on the Commanding Generals Staff, what kind of shit is that? He'd dragged me back from gunships, now he's sending me to the Wing Staff? I felt like I was being "Shit

Canned", what could I have possibly done to deserve this, this was "BullShit"!!!

"Colonel, I just don't understand. Have I done something wrong? If you wanted to get rid of me why didn't you leave me in VMO flying gunships? I realize I should never question and I'll do my duty, but this is just beyond surprise."

"You haven't done anything wrong Spice, it's just the opposite. You have done it all right. I wouldn't send you to the wing unless I thought you could really help and in this case you can. There's also another factor. We are going back aboard ship very shortly and "They" are stabilizing the personnel roster. You don't have enough time left on your tour over here to go with us. You would need to have at least 7 months left and you barely have four. I don't want you to go back to gunships because you would be more valuable at the wing as a "Helicopter Fragger."

"What the hell is that Sir?"

"The Wing Staff is organized just like the squadrons and all the other units. They have an Administration (G-1), Intelligence (G-2), Operations (G-3), and Supply or Logistics (G-4). Within the Operations Section (G-3) there is the G-3 himself and he is responsible to the General for the air operations of the entire wing, both fixed wing and helicopter. To make that happen there is a helicopter operations officer and a fixed wing operations officer that are responsible to the G-3 for those operations. Working under the helicopter operations officer are two "Fraggers". These are the guys that do the actual work of making assignments, they write the "Frag" order of the Wing every day based on the air requests sent in by all the ground units here in Vietnam. As you know they aren't always just American forces."

"Yes Sir, I remember being tasked with several missions in support of ARVN units."

"Most requests come from the Division, the Fraggers match up the requests with the aircraft assets that are available and then write the Frag tasking the various 'Air Groups' with the missions and the Groups in turn task the squadrons. So when Group sends down 'their frag' for us, those missions that are assigned were originated by the Wing Fraggers the night before. Does that explain what the job is?"

"Well Sir, I think I understand. It doesn't explain why in the last couple months we've been sent all over I Corps, especially all the way to northern I Corps for missions in another air group's area and it certainly doesn't explain why you're sending me."

"Oh yes it does. You just answered part of the question yourself. We've been sent all over I Corps because the wing fraggers don't know what the hell they are doing. The guys that are there now haven't been in squadrons yet. The three guys that were there all went home and because the wing was so short of helicopter pilots they didn't want to pull three pilots out of squadrons so they assigned three officers to take their places. It's not really those officer's fault; they just don't have the experience to know the job. You can't go with me to the ship, you've flown all over I Corps and you've flown two different types of aircraft and understand those missions. You've worked with ARVNS, the Korean Blue Dragon Brigade and Army Special Forces. If you could describe the qualifications of someone you'd want to be a wing fragger, you'd certainly fit the bill. You can save us all a lot of wasted flight time, and maybe even save a few lives by going there and making sure our helicopter assets are employed properly and not wasted. I offered you up because I thought you could do the most good for the effort here, not because I want to get rid of you."

"Yes Sir".

"Now you be in the G-3 at the Wing tomorrow and report to a Colonel Finlaysen's office at 0900 for an interview. He's going to select two officers and you will work for a Major Ensley if you're selected. I can't imagine that you won't be, but then I also don't know who else will be interviewed."

"Sir, if I'm not selected what happens then? Since I can't go back aboard ship with you and 362, can I go back to VMO and gunships?"

"I wouldn't worry about it, I doubt that will happen, but if it does, we will cross that bridge when we come to it. 0900 tomorrow, wing G-3, any questions?

"No Sir."

"Ok, we're done."

The next morning I caught a ride with one of our outgoing sections. The leader was a pal of mine and I had him drop me at the Wing Headquarters pad. We'd all landed here many times to pick up the mail and then went on to Marble Mountain; this morning I'm leaving Marble Mountain for the Wing Pad. I was two hours early for my 0900 meeting so I used the time to look around and see what was here. Other than the first night in country, I hadn't been back except for the mail run and then never farther than the helo pad.

I found the officers' mess and went in for some coffee. It was pretty nice considering and I could have had breakfast but I just didn't feel like eating. I wasn't nervous about this interview; I just didn't want this job. Colonel Schlarp might have had a good point but I didn't want a staff job; I came to fly. I didn't agree with Colonel Schlarp about leaving VMO but there wasn't a lot I could do, unless I didn't get picked for this job, and since I couldn't go back aboard ship with 362, then I figured there wouldn't be much to stop me from going back to gunships.

I was deep in thought when someone with a tray of food sat down at the table. I looked up and saw a buddy from

OCS. I was the first person he actually talked to in the Marine Corps. Captain Ken Boykin was putting his tray down and said, "What the hell are you doing here?"

"I might ask the same thing Captain Boykin."

"I came down last night from Quang Tri to interview for a job on the Wing Staff as a helicopter fragger."

"No Shit, that's why I'm here and I was just trying to figure a way of not getting picked for this damn job."

"You're shitting me! This is the Wing Staff, you're out of the cockpit, behind a damn desk, and odds are way in our favor that they can't kill us now. Hell, I want this job. I've survived a CH-46 breaking in half and have one Purple Heart from a slight wound to my left leg and only missed picking up two more by something less than an inch. I've flown about a hundred hours a month for the six months I've been here and know damn well it's not IF I get killed; it's just a matter of WHEN. I'm ready to let some of the other guys carry the load for a while."

"Well I know what you mean but I'd worked my way out of 34's and into gunships, I was starting to like shooting back for a change and got pulled out and back to 34's. Now the squadrons going back aboard ship, I don't have enough time to go, so I'm getting sent over here to interview for this job. I don't want it."

"You got any ideas about how many guys are here for this job?"

"I have no clue; I talked to all sorts of people just trying to find out why they call them 'Fraggers'."

"Why do they call them 'Fraggers'?"

"The term comes from 'Fragmentary Order'. You remember the 5 paragraph combat order right?"

"Yeah, SMEAC, situation, mission, execution, administration, command and communication; I remember from OCS, but remember I didn't go to The Basic School like you, I went straight to Pensacola."

"Well a full operations order has all sorts of information, stuff like topography, weather, force structure, attachments, and lots of other stuff. A 5 paragraph combat order is essentially a fragmentary order in that it only covers the essentials. For aviation, a fragmentary order or 'Frag' contains only the minimal amount of information, hence fragmentary, and is essentially a document 'Tasking' the aviation component of a combined arms force with some type of aviation support. You've seen them every day, but we refer to them as missions once we've been tasked. Usually all we get is the place where we start, a communications frequency and call sign, very fragmentary information."

"Shit, you come up talking like that in this interview and you'll get the damn job for sure. You don't want this job you better keep your mouth shut."

"I intend to do just that."

We spent the rest of the time catching up. I'd been "In Country" several months before Ken arrived. I remember being at Quang Tri the day his squadron off loaded from the carrier and came in.

We'd spent a few days showing them the ropes, and I hadn't seen Ken since. When he got his wings he'd been sent to the east coast, MCAS New River, and put into training on the CH-46 A, the Sea Knight. It's a tandem rotor helicopter; it has two Rotorheads that counter rotate. The counter rotating rotor blades have about a 6 foot overlap. It really is a marvelous machine with a lot of capability but the A models counter rotating blades had a bad habit of smashing into one another. There had been a lot of crashes before a "FIX" was discovered and the new model, the CH-46D came into being.

Ken was one of the few aircrew to survive a crash in the CH-46A and had been held at New River for assignment to the first DELTA squadron. HMM-161 came into Quang Tri and had worked exclusively in northern I Corps. His squadron had been worked hard since they'd arrived because there had been a real shortage of helicopter lift up there.

At 0845 we headed for our interview. The area the First Marine Air Wing Headquarters occupied had real buildings. I was told that the buildings were built by the French back in the colonial days and these buildings had been occupied by a unit of the French Foreign Legion. The G-3 section was housed in its own building. There were real doors, windows, although sandbagged, and it seemed strange to be entering this type of structure instead of the "South East Asian" screened-in hooch. The building actually had some form of air conditioning.

We didn't get very far inside a large room with lots of desks before we were intercepted by a Major who introduced himself as Ensley. He was the helicopter operations officer. He took our names and herded us into an office off to the side of this large room. There were six other Marine Captains sitting around on a large couch and a couple of chairs. There was a huge metal desk positioned so that the person sitting behind it could look out the door of the office and pretty much observe the entire outer room. There was no one behind the desk at the time but there was a fancy wooden name plate, the kind you could have made up here or in Thailand, that read "Finlaysen".

Four officers occupied the leather couch and two were sitting on the chairs. Ken and I assumed seats on the arms of the couch. We were all wearing our utilities which also seemed strange because normally everyone was wearing a flight suit. As I looked over the other six, I didn't recognize any one. A couple had pilot wings, a couple NFO wings and a couple wearing neither. Whether or not they didn't put them on or weren't air crew was a mystery. I hated to say this about fellow Marine officers but only one of these six looked the least bit "Squared Away", the rest looked pretty ragged, but it was obvious none of them had come out of the field, they were too white.

I heard Major Ensley call for attention on deck and we all stood up. A full Colonel walked through the door opening and went straight to the desk and took a seat. He gazed over the eight of us standing at attention and after an extended pause said, "At Ease gentlemen, please take a seat."

He started the interview with a couple of general statements about the wing and the operations section, the importance of the "Fragger" and his role coordinating things with the TACC. (Tactical Air Command Center) Then he proceeded to question each man in turn starting with the two guys sitting in the chairs. The third man interviewed was Ken. I saw the Colonel make a note when Ken told him he was from HMM-161 and a CH-46D pilot. He asked Ken why he wanted the job. The other two guys had given some bullshit answer about a staff position being good experience and would enhance their careers. Ken said, "Well sir, it's not that I want this job so much as I'm tired of getting shot at every goddamned day." The Colonel nodded and made another note.

He interviewed the four guys sitting on the couch in turn and never made a note after talking to each one. I was last. He looked at me and said, "And you must be Captain Spicer."

"Yes Sir".

"Why do you want to be a 'Wing Fragger'?"

"Sir I don't. I volunteered to get out of H-34's and go into gunships with VMO, and did for a very short while. Then was pulled back to my 34 squadron, but they are going aboard ship. I was told I don't have enough time left on this tour to go with them. So I've been sent over here for this interview, but I'd much rather go back to gunships to finish my tour."

"Yes, I know."

He picked up a piece of paper that was beside the blotter on his desk and read it over very carefully then looked back up at me and nodded. He looked over the whole group one more time, and then asked Major Ensley if he had any questions for us. The Major had been standing very quietly near the entrance to the office.

"No Sir, no questions."

"Very well then gentlemen, you are all excused. Have a look around the compound, get some lunch in the Wing Officers Mess and check back in with Major Ensley at 1300 at which time he will inform you of our decision."

There was a chorus of "Yes Sirs" and we all left the office. The other six officers scattered immediately but Ken and I were standing outside the building near an above ground bunker. Ken suggested we walk around and see where these guys lived. Our best guess was one of the other permanent type buildings. I told him I'd go along just to keep him company but hoped like hell I wouldn't be living here. We were just stepping off in the direction of what could be officer's quarters when a window on the side of the building opened and someone shouted at us.

"You two, come here!"

We did a double take and realized it was Colonel Finlaysen.

"That's right, you two get over here!"

We walked over to the open window and stood there looking at Colonel Finlaysen.

"You two sonofabitches got the job. Go get your gear, find a place to live in Officers quarters and be back here ready to go to work. You got 24 hours."

We exchanged glances and said, "Yes Sir."

Well that tore it, I had the job whether I wanted it or not.

Ken said, "I think the fix was in, especially for you and I think my CO put in a good word for me, but I'm pretty sure you had the job before you even got here."

"I got a warm fuzzy feeling you just might be right. Let's go see if we can find a place to live and then why don't you come with me to Marble to get my gear."

"Ok, I brought all my stuff with me cause I didn't want to go back to Quang Tri. You know the drill, never get separated from your stuff cause you may never see it again if you do."

Less than 24 hours later we were in the Wing G-3 at "our" desk and less than 48 hours later we'd written our first Wing Frag order and sent it out to the three Air Groups. Major Ensley had taken us by the hand and literally walked us through the procedures of our job. He was very specific that it was "our" desk because we had to share it. One of us had to be on that desk 24 hours a day. The man on the night shift was the one who actually took the information and wrote the Frag Order. Once it was published and sent out to the Groups you waited to answer the inevitable questions. After that, if everything was all quiet you could leave the desk and go to bed but if anything happened you were immediately awakened to take care of things. The other man came on an hour before the first aircraft left on their assigned missions and stayed on all day. We would change over or "Dog the Watch" every few days and Major Ensley would cover the desk during the daytime so we could accomplish the switch.

The TACC, Tactical Air Command Center, was in a room right behind us. It was fully darkened except for red lights and had lots of mission boards. It reminded me of the CIC, Combat Information Centers on the carriers. The TACC was in charge of the "Air War". The DASCC's and Air Groups reported to and informed the TACC of the status of every mission. The on duty controller could follow the progress of the "FRAG ORDER" for the day rather like following along on a program at a concert. He knew the status of each mission on the Frag and if there was a problem, he came straight to you. After a week or so I had to admit it was interesting and exciting work. It was also pretty exhausting.

The one thing Ken and I noticed was that nobody messed with us. There were lots of other officers, especially Majors and Lt Colonels that seemed to be constantly passing through asking all kinds of questions but they never stopped to bother us. If the TACC controller notified us that a helo had been shot down, or gone down with mechanical trouble, we had to order up a reaction force of grunts, or call in the Army's helicopter crane or even decide to call in a flight of fixed wing to blow up the remains of the helo. Usually it was Ken or I that made the decision, but occasionally Major Ensley would get involved. The only people we conversed with were the TACC controllers, or Major Ensley or Colonel Finlaysen. Many times if someone leaned over your shoulder it would be the Colonel. We learned quickly to keep him informed at all times if something out of the ordinary was taking place. One thing he didn't like was surprises and the General liked surprises even less.

November and December passed very quickly; the days ran together. Inside the G-3 where we worked there were no windows, so all the days seemed the same. Colonel Schlarp had been correct. Ken and I had been able to make a difference and sometimes when we were speaking to the Group operations people they even thanked us for bringing some common sense to the job. Major Ensley hardly ever said a word to us and even the Colonel seemed pleased with the way we were getting the job done. We sometimes had the impression that the Colonel had made it clear that we were to be left alone.

The Colonel did call us both in when we had a couple aircraft "Blown in Place". He wanted to know why we were so quick to order an airstrike instead of trying to recover the downed helicopter. Ken let me do the talking but we totally agreed on what we did. I told the Colonel that we'd both seen this situation before. A helo goes down from either mechanical trouble or enemy fire. We get the crew out safely and put in a reaction force. Now we got Marines on the ground. The enemy sees this as a target of improving value and engages the reaction force. We can't get the aircraft out during the middle of the fire fight and usually the damage to the aircraft increases during the fight, so it's now not worth recovering anyway. All we've done is expose more Marines to harm. However, if we get the crew out safely, the enemy will generally send in a force to look over the downed aircraft. By the time they get through with it, the aircraft won't be fixable so we try and catch them around or on the aircraft and call in an airstrike, causing as many casualties on their side as possible. When I finished our explanation the Colonel looked at us for what seemed like a long time. I kept thinking he was going to say something but he didn't; he simply nodded and told us we were dismissed.

As we approached the New Year and a TET celebration by the Vietnamese, there were rumors that the enemy was preparing for another large TET offensive but so far intelligence hadn't been able to confirm a thing. The New Year came and went without too much happening but still the rumors of a large build up of NVA forces in southern I Corps persisted. Major Ensley was called to a meeting at the Division Headquarters to discuss the feasibility of a large cordon operation but didn't have much to say when he returned.

About a week later I had the duty that night and was in the G-3 waiting on the Division's air requests so I could write the Wing Frag for the next day. It was almost eerily quiet this evening; there wasn't a single night mission, rotary or fixed wing in progress. This almost never happened. The Air Group operations duty officers had been calling wanting to know what was going on and where the Frag for tomorrow was, and I kept telling them it was unusually quiet. It was after midnight before the Division Air Requests came in via secure circuits. I looked it over and noted that it was the biggest I'd seen since I'd arrived here. We hadn't been given a heads up on anything so I simply went to work matching up available assets with the First Divisions requirements. First Division operated in southern I Corps and Third Division operated up north, in the areas Ken and I had spent so much time, right against the DMZ. The Third Division requirements for tomorrow were not unusual so I wrote the Frag for MAG-39 first and sent it out via the secure circuits. Next I started on First Divisions and quickly realized it would take every helicopter asset from MAG -16 and about half the assets from Phu Bai and all the aircraft off the LPH that was assigned to the SLF. By 0200 I'd sent the Frag to MAG-16 at Marble, MAG-36 at Phu Bai and the SLF. I sat back to wait for the questions to come in but after two hours of waiting there were none so I told Lt Hopkins, the TACC Controller, I was going to my room and hitting the rack.

I was sound asleep for a change when Lt Hopkins woke me up. He didn't send a runner, it was actually him shaking me and telling me that Captain Boykin needed me immediately. I threw my utilities on as quickly as I could and went straight to the G-3.

When I walked into the room I saw Ken at "our" desk and he had a phone in each ear. When we made eye contact he rolled his eyes and shook his head. I knew this couldn't be good but had no idea what was wrong. I looked around and didn't see Major Ensley or the Colonel. It was as eerily quiet now as it was when I left several hours ago.

"What's going on Ken? Did the NVA pull off the big attack everyone's been talking about?"

Ken didn't reply, he just gave me a glance and continued holding the phones to both ears. After a couple very long minutes he said, "Ok, Ok, I'll get back to everyone as soon as I can sort this out."

"Well, what the hell is going on, you sounded very serious."

"I was. It appears that you 'Fragged' one of the biggest operations of the war on the wrong day and when the air groups called to complain and tell me it was the wrong day, I made them do it because you had 'Fragged' it that way.

"Holy Shit!!"

"Yeah, holy shit is one way to put it. We fragged enough helos to put in a sixteen mile circle of aircraft, enough to completely encircle the suspected enemy force and cordon them off from escape on the wrong day. Both the air group's operations people called trying to tell me that it wasn't today but tomorrow and I told them if it was fragged they better get their asses in the air. So they launched to go pick up the Grunts and when they got there, the Grunts were sitting around cleaning rifles and stuff. I think they enjoyed telling the "Wing" guys that the war wasn't until tomorrow. I don't know if any of this has been brought to the attention of the "Heavies", particularly the General or the Colonel but I expect when it does we are gonna wish we were someplace else."

"We may be sent back to a squadron and given permanent night medivac."

"Why don't you go and have a nice breakfast then come back here and relieve me so I can go and at least the two condemned men will have had a hearty meal."

"Good idea."

The shit still hadn't hit the fan before I got back to relieve Ken but he wasn't gone ten minutes before the first inquiry started. Some Lt Colonel I'd never seen came up to my desk very officiously carrying a note pad and wanted to know all the details of the mistake on today's frag. I told him he'd have to speak to Major Ensley or Colonel Finlaysen. In the next thirty minutes about six more of

292

these "Horse Holders" came by all asking the same thing and I gave the same answer. Major Ensley finally came in and wanted to know if the rumors were true. I told him they were and his only reply was, "I hope you guys have a good excuse." Colonel Finlaysen came in a few minutes later and went straight to his desk and picked up the phone. While he was on the phone several of the officers that had come by me went into his office.

After going over what I did several times, it was no one's fault but mine. When the requests came in I didn't notice that the date time group on the message was for the next day. Since the requests were so late coming in I assumed they had to be for today. The only "Factor" for this fiasco was that I simply "Fucked Up". There really wasn't anything else to be said so I decided to go to the Colonel myself before he sent for me.

When all the "Fact Finders" cleared out of the Colonels office I went straight over to the door and knocked on the door frame. The Colonel was on the phone again and when he saw me standing there he hung up and waved me into the office.

"Sir, I think we need to talk."

"From what I've heard it sounds as if you are correct. You wanna tell me what happened?"

"Yes Sir, it's not complicated, I wrote the Frag for the wrong day and Boykin made them do it. It's nobody's fault but mine and all I can say is that I just "Fucked Up".

He sat behind his desk with a perplexed look on his face for several seconds.

"You just 'Fucked Up,' that's your explanation?"

"Yes Sir, that's my only explanation."

Once again the perplexed look and this time he moved his mouth in such a manner as to make a slight face and bit his bottom lip.

"So, you want me to tell the General that you just 'Fucked Up'?"

"Well Sir, I'm more than willing to tell him myself. I realize how embarrassing this is for the Wing and I could come up with all sorts of excuses but none of them would help the situation. I made a huge mistake. I feel extremely lucky that a mistake of this magnitude happened and to my knowledge nobody got hurt. I just 'Fucked Up' I don't think there's anything else to say."

The pause and the facial expression this time seemed pensive and then the expression turned to stone.

"Very well, get back to your desk and don't ever 'Fuck Up' again!"

When I left the Colonel's office, Major Ensley and Ken were waiting for me to get back to "our "desk.

Major Ensley spoke first, "Well what did you tell him and what did he say?"

"Sir, I told him I fragged the war on the wrong day and Ken made them do it. I told him I just 'Fucked Up' which is the truth and what actually happened."

Major Ensley had a startled expression on his face and Ken's normally tanned looking face turned a horrible shade of gray.

"You actually told him that? What did he say?"

"He said, 'Don't ever Fuck Up again.'"

EPILOGUE

The subject of fragging the war on the wrong day never came up again. I became a "Short Timer" with less than sixty days to go on my tour. Major Ensley went home and we got a new Major named Crowdus. He'd been shot down in a CH-46 near the DMZ and I think they sent him to the Wing Staff to recover. He took one look at what Ken and I did on a daily basis and left us alone as much as he could.

CHAPTER TEN

ORDERS HOME

When I took my seat at "our" desk in the G-3 this morning, the first thing I did was look at my "short timers" calendar. Once you had less than 90 days to do "In Country" you could call yourself a "short timer". Most guys had some method of keeping track of the days. Mine was located right on "our" desk. As of this morning I had 40 days before I could get on the big "Freedom Bird" and go home. It was going to be a long 40 days but since fragging the war on the wrong day, our work load had really increased, so it was easy to bury yourself in work or get buried by it. In any case, I really didn't want to dwell on the days I had left.

   This time at the wing had seemed strange to me and Ken had been right, it wasn't like flying in a squadron where you were very aware that any day just might be your last. You could get it on any mission or a rocket or mortar attack on your base. I guess you could define it as "The Threat Level" you experienced on a day to day basis. Since we'd been at the wing the "Threat Level" had been greatly reduced. It was a nice feeling, and yet you could never completely relax.

   We'd been told that the First Marine Aircraft Wing compound had never taken a round of hostile fire. That might have been true until Boykin and I showed up. In the three months we'd been here we'd been hit four times. The last hit was a rocket that slammed into our barracks, hitting the junction of the outside wall and an internal wall. By hitting there, most of the blast was absorbed and the damage was minimal, but the noise was spectacular.

   The only serious casualty was a Warrant Officer who had just arrived that morning. Ken and I found him standing in the large shower room with the water still running. He had several small through and through shrapnel wounds and was in complete shock. We got him out of there and took some immediate action to help stop the bleeding. We used a poncho as stretcher and carried him to the aid station. That had been the latest big excitement here except for work and made me wonder what the last 40 days would bring. I was pretty sure I'd never have a feeling of complete safety until I was crossing the coast line on my way home.

My reverie was broken by the arrival of Major Crowdus. He was a hell of a nice man but if he was in the area, you knew it.

"Good Morning Spice, how goes the war this fine morning?"

"It's pretty quiet so far Major and I hope like hell it stays that way."

"I noticed you were looking at your short timer's calendar; how many days you got left?"

"40 days as of today Sir."

"40 days, that's getting pretty short. Boykin and I are still in triple digits; it's too depressing to think about. Have you had your shopping trip yet?"

"What do you mean shopping trip? I've had one damn R&R and waited seven months for that."

"They tell me it's customary to give a guy on the wing staff a quick trip to Okinawa for a couple of days so you can buy some neat things for wife, family and yourself. The PX's (Post Exchange) have got everything you can possibly imagine for sale. Stereos, furniture, jewelry, you name it. I had a quick trip right after I got shot down and I'm hoping to get another one before I go home."

"No, I certainly haven't had a shopping trip but that would be nice."

"I'll check into it for you. By the way, your orders came in a couple days ago."

"My what?"

"Your orders, you know the ticket to go home. They are sending you to Pensacola to be a flight instructor, good deal huh?"

I couldn't believe it. Pensacola had been my first choice on the "Dream Sheet". I couldn't wait to write Marguerite and tell her the good news. I'd tried not to think about going home the whole time here. I simply wanted to get through each day in once piece. Now, knowing I actually had orders to the one place Marguerite and I hoped to go was going to be tough.

I got up early the next day and went straight to the admin section. The Flag Secretary, a Major Nelson, was the person I was told could provide me with a copy of my orders. I finally caught up with him about 0900. He handed me a copy of the message and I read it twice before I really believed it. He told me when I wrote my wife to include the copy he'd given me. He said she should have six copies made, and then, could arrange to ship our household effects to Pensacola well in advance of my getting home. That way she wouldn't have to wait on our stuff to set up her household. He also mentioned the shopping trip and said to take a copy with me and whatever I bought, I could have shipped to Pensacola as well. It would make a nice surprise for my wife. I was even more excited.

Several months ago when we were on the LPH-2, we moved off the ship and it went to Subic Bay Naval Station in the Philippines for repair. Two of my hooch mates, Ron and Tom, got to go along with the ship because we were leaving equipment, people and a couple aircraft on board until the ship got back on station in Vietnam.

I gave them a handful of money I'd been saving out of my poker stash, and told them to buy some nice things and send them to Marguerite. They'd been great shoppers and purchased some really neat stuff. Marguerite sent me a letter with pictures of her "Treasure Trove" from the Philippines; she was really thrilled. So, now if I did get a shopping trip I could send the stuff to Pensacola and give her a real surprise. I'd managed to keep all those kinds of thoughts out of my mind, but not now.

The intensity of the war had picked up ever since the big cordon operation I'd fragged on the wrong day. I had the night duty and was deep in thought trying to put tomorrow's frag together when Major Crowdus and another Major walked up to "our" desk.

"Hey Spice, do you know Major Bridgewater?"

When I looked up I knew I'd seen this officer many times before but had never worked with him or been introduced.

"Well Sir, we've never been introduced but I've seen him come and go a lot."

"This is Major Billy Bridgewater, C-130 pilot extraordinaire."

We shook hands and exchanged pleasantries. I didn't realize he was the Wing C-130 officer. The C-130 was the only large four engine cargo plane the Marine Corps had, and it also served as the airborne refueler, for our fixed wing. He was a busy guy. The good news for him was he still got to fly.

Major Crowdus said, "Look Spice, Billy says he can get you on a C-130 tomorrow for a run up to Okinawa, are you up for that?"

"Well Sir, I'm more than up for that but what about the desk; I can't leave Ken here all by himself."

"I'll fill in for you while you're gone."

"Then I'm more than ready."

Major Bridgewater said, "I'll have the flag secretary cut you orders for three days as 'Special Crew'; be ready to go about 1000 tomorrow. Meet me back in our section and we'll go down to the airfield together. The aircraft won't be on the deck long before heading back to Okinawa. We

298

don't usually allow them to spend the night here and take a chance of getting them shot up, they're too valuable and we don't have very many."

I finished business about 0200 and got back to my quarters but couldn't sleep; I was just too excited. Three days in civilization, even if it was Okinawa, was going to be heaven. No outgoing, no incoming, not many aircraft noises; 1000 would never come.

I was still awake and already packed when Ken got up to take over the desk. He was less than thrilled about my departure but I told him his turn would come. It didn't help, but it made me feel better.

Since I was "Special Crew" Major Bridgewater told me to wear a flight suit. It felt good to put one on again. I gave up and went over to the G-3 section at 0930. Major Crowdus was covering "our" desk for the moment so I went back to Major Bridgewater's section and waited.

He showed up at exactly 1000, and 45 minutes later I was sitting on the flight deck of a KC-130 crossing the coastline heading for Okinawa. The last time I did this I was lying on the ramp at the back of the aircraft and was so tired, I slept the entire way. Not today though, I was too excited to be getting out of this damn place.

We landed at MCAS Futenma, Okinawa and I thought back to the day I flew out of here to Vietnam the first time. Major Bridgewater gave me a ride over to the BOQ (Bachelor Officers Quarters) and gave me a room that actually belonged to one of the C-130 pilots but he wasn't going to be around for several days. After that it was a hot shower, a trip to the base barbershop for a real haircut and a shave. It was heaven. Next we went straight to the club for several drinks and then we went to dinner out in the town and I had a real steak. I had forgotten food could taste so good. Then we went to an Air Force club at Kadena Air Base and an Army Special Forces club and back to Futenma.   Somewhere along the way it all went very blurry.

For someone who'd tried to drink Okinawa dry I felt pretty good this morning.   I met the Major for breakfast at the Officers' Mess, and spent the rest of the morning being taken around to the various PX's to see all the goodies they had to offer.   By lunch time I'd seen most of everything there was to offer and the Major said I was on my own from here on out.   I was to meet him day after tomorrow at the flight line for a 0700 take off.

I found a phone exchange and thought about calling Marguerite but decided against that.   I didn't want to hear the sound of her voice and then get on a plane, and go back to Vietnam.   I didn't want her to get excited about me coming home, and then have something happen.   I didn't want to think about that look in her eyes when I left and I didn't want to say goodbye again.   So I just shopped.

I took taxi's called "Skoshi Cabs" from place to place and hauled all the goodies I could fit in the cabs back to the BOQ.   By the end of the day I had a pretty good pile and some stuff too big to fit in the cabs would be delivered tomorrow.   I took the Major's suggestion and got all the shopping out of the way first.

After breakfast I went back to the BOQ room to await the delivery of the last of my goodies.   By 1000 everything had been delivered so I decided to take inventory before I got in touch with the household goods people to arrange for shipment.

I had a cassette tape deck, two very large speakers, an amplifier, probably big enough to run the Los Angeles Coliseum.   I had a diamond ring that had two rows of diamonds, a princess ring with a black sapphire surrounded by diamonds, a decorative shoji screen and last but not least I got Marguerite a coffee table and two end tables made of rose wood with hand carved teak inlays that were covered with glass.   I had several large bags with cassette tapes, a

Kimono for Marguerite and some smaller stuff for Katie. It was a pretty impressive pile and I'd blown through what was a fairly full bag of money, but I knew Marguerite would love it all.

The household goods people were able to come to the BOQ room very late in the day. As fast as I'd piled it all up they emptied the room out and my load of goodies would be on its way to Pensacola in just a few days.

In my travels around the island I'd spotted a Navy facility called the Hamby Boat Docks. It was located near a very wide flat beach on the west side of the island. My guess was this had to be one of the primary landing beaches during the battle for Okinawa in World War II. I was pretty sure that years ago this was hallowed ground and lots of American blood had been spilled on this beach in taking this small island. Just the look of the place had peaked my curiosity.

I caught another Skoshi cab right outside the main gate of Futenma and had the driver take me down to the Hamby Boat Docks. It had a very long pier that extended quite a ways out into the water. Right on the beach where the pier started there was a club or snack bar. It wasn't fancy, just rough cut lumber and decorated in a very nautical theme. They served both American and Japanese food and the smell from the kitchen was wonderful. When I sat down at the bar I was the only one there. The bartender was an Okinawan but he spoke perfect English. I told him I wanted a "Big" beer and he produced an ice cold Orion in a huge bottle. At first taste, I knew I'd found the right place.

A few more Americans drifted in, but the place never got crowded. I left my bar stool long enough to purchase another pack of smokes and as I walked back to my stool I looked down the pier and realized that the sun would be setting over the Pacific very shortly. I got a fresh ice cold Orion and walked all the way down to the end of the pier. I sat down and leaned up against one of the large pilings. I watched the sun set until it was completely out of sight. It was the most peaceful moment I could remember in a long time. I thought about being a young Marine watching the sunset over the Pacific in California and wondering what the world was like where the water touched the other shore. I thought about all the things I'd seen in the last year, the horrible things, and I thought about the men who would never see another sun set and realized how lucky I had been.

I met the Major for breakfast at the Officers' Mess; I wanted one last good meal before going back. After this three day trip, the remainder of my time was going to be hard to take. I didn't know how these C-130 guys did it bouncing in and out of Vietnam. It was too much culture shock.

The flight back was a non-event. The Major was the aircraft commander on this flight and actually gave me a chance to fly this huge thing. He said if I could fly an H-34 I could fly anything. He'd tried to fly one once and couldn't even taxi the damn thing. I had a good chuckle and took his seat for about twenty minutes. It was like flying a greenhouse with six or seven of your best friends. I don't think I'd have made a very good C-130 pilot.

As I got off the aircraft in DaNang I saw Major Nelson in a jeep parked damn near under the wing. As soon as he saw me he motioned vigorously for me to come to the jeep. He seemed to be in a real hurry.

I jogged over to the jeep and said, "Gee thanks Major, I didn't expect to be picked up."

"I don't normally provide airport pick up service but in your case, I have to make an exception. I'm glad you were on that aircraft because you have to be on another aircraft heading home in a little less than 5 hours."

My heart jumped, my first thought was that something had happened to Marguerite or Katie.

"I have some really good news. Your orders have changed. You have to be out of here today and on your way. We are working on your orders right now. You have enough time to pack a bag and get anything else ready you would like to ship. You will only be authorized travel; you don't have time for any leave. The Marine you are replacing has to be back in the states in ten days to start Amphibious Warfare School."

"Major, what the hell are you talking about? I thought I was going to Pensacola, home to the states."

"We didn't want to tell you that you were being considered for this position in case you weren't selected. But you were, and headquarters sent a message that came in late last evening announcing your selection and changing your orders. Congratulations, it a real dream job."

"Major what the hell have I been selected for?"

"You'll only be in the states long enough to pick up your family because you and your family are going to England. You are going to be an exchange officer with the Royal Marines and the Royal Navy."

EPILOGUE

The Sea Stories in this book as in the first book "Stripes to Bars" have been related as I remember them happening. During this period in the Vietnam War, I firmly believe you could substitute any of my squadron mates names for my name and the stories wouldn't change much at all. The same would be true for just about any Marine or Army Helicopter Pilot, Crew Chief, Door Gunner, Corpsman or Medic.

In most of the stories I'm the co-pilot and what I wanted to portray was the essence of the other guys, pilots or aircrew, the "ROTORHEADS". The Robbie's, Vinnie's, Biff's, et al. I certainly wasn't a hero, I would have said my experiences were average and I'd bet the other guys would say the same thing. I've tried not to embellish the stories but tell them with the emotion that was felt by all but never expressed.

Ron, Tom, John, Dave, Biff, Max, Vinnie, Mel, Wiley, Rod, Bob, Larry, Pete, Lunk, Tygart, Wilson, Johns, Nose, Villarreal and "Doc" Jones are all real people. They aren't characters invented for a novel; they are the quintessential "ROTORHEADS".

From the Latin: Saepius Exertus, Semper Fidelis, Frater Infinitas.

English Translation: Often Tested, Always Faithful, Brothers Forever.

Max on the far left, P.S. Makowka behind him, Biff in the foreground, Buzz Knight in tan flight suit and Robbie on the far right. Max, Biff and Buzz are all deceased.